"Interpreting the Bible is the task of every Christian, but most of us get lost somewhere between what it meant *then* and what it means *now*. Both are necessary if our understanding of and living out the text is to have any integrity. Paul Louis Metzger's highly recommended Resonate volume on the Gospel of John helps us bridge this divide, taking us back to John's original meaning—and walking us forward to today so that we might live and be the light this dark world so desperately needs."

BRETT C. BLAIR, www.Sermons.com and www.Seminary.com

"This combination of pop culture, social critique and serious evangelical theology would probably become a discordant mess in less skilled hands. But Paul Louis Metzger blends them into a highly readable harmony in this thought- and heart-provoking book."

TOM KRATTENMAKER, *USA Today* board of contributors, and author of *Onward Christian Athletes*

"Here is a lively, modern mind colliding with a divine, ancient text. We know what a commentary is, and this book is not one (though it does explain and expound the text of John like conventional commentaries). We know what a sermon is, and this book is not one (though it does apply the word of God to our lives and our culture like good sermons do). Nor is it a commentary with sermons spliced in. Give up trying to fit it into existing categories. Metzger's take on John, as the initial offering in the Resonate series, is a genre-defying performance that provokes, interrogates and ponders, and invites the reader to join in the process."

FRED SANDERS, associate professor of theology, Torrey Honors Institute, Biola University

"Paul Louis Metzger is that rare breed: a theologian who feels the pulse of culture ar　　　　　　　　　　　ht. He's brought that co　　　　　　　　　　**EUR**lt is a delight for those ν 226.5　　Metzger, Paul Louis.ave."

STEVE METZGER The gospel of　　rsquare Church
　　　　　　John

"Than　　　　　　　　　　gically informed, and sp　　　23.00 ; TARM　　n John's Gospel is for the　　　　　　　　　　the text but who want to encounter afresh the triune God to which it bears witness. Metzger draws the readers in and opens up the text but not so that we see only the text but *through* the text to God—so that God speaks through the text to us. Theology for the church to the glory of God!"

ROBIN PARRY, author of *Worshipping Trinity* and *Lamentations* (Two Horizons Old Testament Commentary)

"Paul Louis Metzger asks the questions that biblical scholars and contemporary readers pose concerning the Gospel of John and provides fresh, vivid explanation of the Gospel that is substantive in biblical insight and illuminating in contemporary application. Whether you're perplexed by John's Gospel or struggling to apply it to your life, this book deftly addresses both with a friendly, conversational style."

ED CYZEWSKI, author of *Coffeehouse Theology*

"Dr. Metzger is a master weaver intertwining the love story of the Scriptures with the stories of life, past and present, so that we might 'see God' and be inspired to follow him with all our heart, soul, strength and mind. He brings salient and succulent pieces of yarn from the Gospel of John, John Steinbeck, John Perkins and others, and invites us to clothe ourselves in the beauty of God's tapestry that we in turn might beckon and clothe others."

MICHAEL TSO, M.D., director of training, His Mansion Ministries

RESONATE SERIES

THE GOSPEL OF JOHN

When Love Comes to Town

PAUL LOUIS METZGER

Foreword by Leonard Sweet

Afterword by Rick McKinley

IVP Books

An imprint of InterVarsity Press
Downers Grove, Illinois

InterVarsity Press
P.O. Box 1400, Downers Grove, IL 60515-1426
World Wide Web: www.ivpress.com
E-mail: email@ivpress.com

InterVarsity Press® is the book-publishing division of InterVarsity Christian Fellowship/USA®, a movement of students and faculty active on campus at hundreds of universities, colleges and schools of nursing in the United States of America, and a member movement of the International Fellowship of Evangelical Students. For information about local and regional activities, write Public Relations Dept., InterVarsity Christian Fellowship/USA, 6400 Schroeder Rd., P.O. Box 7895, Madison, WI 53707-7895, or visit the IVCF website at <www.intervarsity.org>.

Design: Cindy Kiple

Images: painting of Christ: Ecce homo by Georges Rouault. Photo by Philippe Migeat at Musee National d'Art Moderne, Centre Georges Pompidou, Paris, France. CNAC/MNAM/Dist. Réunion des Musées Nationaux / Art Resource, NY

ISBN 978-0-8308-3641-3

Printed in Canada ∞

Library of Congress Cataloging-in-Publication Data

Metzger, Paul Louis.
    The gospel of John : when love comes to town / Paul Louis Metzger.
      p. cm.—(Resonate series)
    Includes bibliographical references.
    ISBN 978-0-8308-3641-3 (pbk.: alk. paper)
    1. Bible. N.T. John—Commentaries.   I. Title.
    BS2615.53.M345 2010-06-29
    226.5'07—dc22

                                                                              201024970

| P | 18 | 17 | 16 | 15 | 14 | 13 | 12 | 11 | 10 | 9 | 8 | 7 | 6 | 5 | 4 | 3 | 2 | 1 |
| Y | 25 | 24 | 23 | 22 | 21 | 20 | 19 | 18 | 17 | 16 | 15 | 14 | 13 | 12 | 11 | 10 |

To my parents,

who introduced me to Jesus

through the Scriptures

and through their lives

CONTENTS

FOREWORD

It is not easy for someone trained in a scientific mindset with Enlightenment notions of truth to understand how apparently opposite things can happen at the same time and both be true. But they can both be true, as the biblical world and our post-Enlightenment culture testify.

The most important book of the Bible we can read for the twenty-first century is the Gospel of John. While the apostle John has been called a "dialectical theologian" by biblical scholars as diverse as C. K. Barrett, Rudolf Bultmann and Paul Anderson, I prefer to think of John's Gospel as a paradox icon, or a p*aradoxicon*. The iconic image of John's Gospel is the eagle. No bird flies higher than the eagle. But "eagle eyes" are the strongest in the animal kingdom. Soaring high in the heavens, an eagle's eye can pick out the tiniest detail on the ground.

This same paradoxical curving of "opposites" into connection and conversation is one of the most distinctive features of John's Gospel. There is no higher understanding of Jesus' divinity as the "Son of God" than in John's Gospel. There is no fuller understanding of Jesus' humanity as the "Son of Adam" or "the Human Being" than in John's Gospel. John is the "I AM" Gospel because Jesus appears in his mysterious "I AM-ness" as part of the triune life of the Godhead, while Jesus is also present in his concreteness, as "I am the door," "I am the true vine," "I am the good shepherd," and so on. John stands with his head in eternity and his feet in Eden.

I was reminded of the paradoxical nature of John's Gospel when reading the amazing "commentary" you are holding in your hand. With this book, *The Gospel of John: When Love Comes to Town*, Paul Louis Metzger has invented a whole new genre of literature, a hybrid commentary where the best in biblical scholarship is coupled with theological reflection on the text that is accessible to the layperson. What a novel and glorious experience to be reading a meditation which becomes an exegesis which becomes a devotional which becomes a homily—all in the space of a few pages. I fully expect this new form of "commentary" to become a standard form in the future.

Metzger, like all the Gospel-centric writers (not just John), portrays Jesus as the One who comes in surround sound. If you hear only one thing, you aren't hearing Jesus.

Come and live. Come and die.
Be as wise as serpents, innocent as doves.
Lord I believe. Help my unbelief.
You want to be first? Be last.
You want to find yourself? Lose yourself.
You want to be exalted? Be humble.
The Prince of Peace came to bring a sword.
Give to Caesar what's Caesar's, and to God what's God's.
Good morning, saints. Good morning, sinners.

But what brings the "opposites" together and connects them is the sign of the cross. John's Gospel was once known as the "Book of Signs." But the "sign" above all signs is the cross, which brings together the vertical and the horizontal. Jesus' love is *agape* love, made up of two dimensions: love of God and love of neighbor. The horizontal and the vertical go hand in hand. How do you show love of God? Love your neighbor. And vice versa.

The Gospel of John: When Love Comes to Town reveals how the Spirit of God forms in us cross-shaped minds, bodies and spirits. Christians live a *cruciform life*—a connective (well-connected?) life that brings the polarities together: the ebb and flow of love and hate, belief and unbelief, joy and suffering, trust and uncertainty. The cross is what bridges the banks, binds the ends and marries the extremes of being.

Leonard Sweet, Ph.D.
E. Stanley Jones Professor of Evangelism at Drew University and Visiting Distinguished Professor at George Fox University

SERIES
INTRODUCTION

We live in an increasingly biblically illiterate culture—not simply in knowing what the Bible says but also in knowing how God wants to use his Word to draw us closer to him. The contemporary situation has drawn greater attention to the need for biblical and theological reflection that is culturally engaging. Yet the need isn't somehow new.

In every age and in every region around the world, the church needs to be concerned for the biblical sense (what does this particular book of the Bible mean?) and its cultural significance (what does it have to say to us in our particular setting?), never confusing the two but *always* relating the two. Only then can our reflections resonate well both with Scripture *and* with people's life situations. As you can imagine, it's a daunting challenge.

This is the challenge I face daily in my work as a professor at Multnomah Biblical Seminary in Portland, Oregon, and as director of its Institute for the Theology of Culture: New Wine, New Wineskins (www .new-wineskins.org). Many of my students do not come from Christian homes and have never been exposed to Scripture in a meaningful way, but they often come well equipped at engaging pop culture. Other students have been long entrenched in the Christian subculture and struggle to engage meaningfully in a pluralistic context that does not recognize the Bible as truthful and authoritative for life. Thankfully, Portland is a wonderful living laboratory in which to prepare for ministry within an increasingly diverse setting—ministry that brings the Bible to bear on that context in a theologically sound and grace-filled manner.

The aim of the Resonate series is to provide spiritual nourishment that is biblically and theologically orthodox and culturally significant. The form each volume in the series will take is that of an extended essay—each author writing about the biblical book under consideration in an interactive, reflective and culturally engaging manner.

Why this approach? There are scores of commentaries on the market from biblical scholars who go verse by verse through the biblical text. While extremely important, there also is an increasingly urgent need for pastors who feel right at home within the biblical text to bring that text home to today's Christ followers by interacting with the text expositionally, by placing it within the context of contemporary daily life, and by viewing their personal stories in light of the original context and unfolding drama of ancient Scripture. There also is an increasingly urgent need for people who feel right at home within contemporary culture but who are foreigners when it comes to Scripture to inhabit the world of the Bible without abandoning their own context. God would have us live in both worlds.

Speaking of context, it is worth noting how this series emerged. I was participating at a consultation on the future of theological inquiry at the Center of Theological Inquiry in Princeton, New Jersey, when David Sanford contacted me to ask if I would serve as executive editor for Resonate. His timing could not have been better. During the consultation in Princeton, we discussed the need for academics to be more intentional on writing to popular culture and not focus exclusively on writing to our peers in the scholarly guild. We also discussed how greater efforts needed to be made to bridge the academy and the church.

In addition to dialoguing with David Sanford and sketching out what I would envision for such a series (as outlined in this introduction), I spoke with several biblical scholars at the consultation. One of them went so far as to tell me there was no need for another commentary series, for there was an overabundance of them on the market. When they heard the vision for Resonate, they encouraged me to move forward with it. Like them, I believe a series of this kind could go a long way toward encouraging and equipping today's pastors and teachers to engage each book of the Bible in a thoughtful and rigorous manner.

That said, I have been told that this series is very ambitious—bringing practitioners and academics together, and especially in this unique manner. Some volumes are written by thoughtful practitioners and others by practically oriented academics. Whether practitioner or academic, the authors do not approach the subject matter from the standpoint of detached observers but rather as fully engaged participants in the text—always working with the community of editors I have assembled along with managing editor David Sanford and general editor Dave Zimmerman at InterVarsity Press.

Instead of going verse by verse, the author of each Resonate volume draws insights from the featured biblical book's major themes, all the while attentive to the context in which these themes are developed, for the purposes of guiding, guarding and growing readers as they move forward in their own spiritual journeys. In addition to focusing on the major themes of the biblical book under consideration, the author of each volume also will locate that particular biblical book within the context of the triune God's overarching narrative of holy love for Israel, church and world.

Our aim with this distinctive new genre or approach is to have one finger in the ancient Scriptures, another in the daily newspaper, and another finger touching the heart, all the while pointing to Jesus Christ. This is no easy task, of course, but when accomplished it is extremely rewarding.

Each contributor to Resonate seeks to bear witness to Jesus Christ, the living Word of God, through the written Word in and through their own life story and the broader cultural context. So often we go around Scripture to Jesus or stop short at Scripture, not penetrating it to get to Jesus' heart—which is the Father's heart too. Instead, each of us needs to depend on God's Spirit to discern how our culturally situated words and stories are included in the biblical metanarrative, and to learn how to bring God's Word home to our hearts and lives in a truthful and meaningful manner.

We trust that you will find this and other Resonate volumes beneficial as you exegete Scripture and culture in service to Jesus Christ, church and world, and as God exegetes your heart through his Word and Spirit. With this in mind, we dedicate this series as a whole to you as you embark on this arduous and incredible journey.

Paul Louis Metzger, Ph.D.
Executive Editor, Resonate
Easter Sunday, 2010

ACKNOWLEDGMENTS

I wish to thank the staff of InterVarsity Press, especially Dave Zimmerman, Andrew Bronson and Bob Fryling, for their enthusiastic partnership and support for this volume and this series. I also wish to thank my fellow editor for this series, David Sanford, for his shared vision and passion and, along with Dave Zimmerman, for his significant investment of time in this manuscript. I wish to thank my present and former Multnomah Biblical Seminary colleagues Drs. Albert Baylis and Ron Frost for their keen editorial insights concerning the biblical text, theological themes and spiritual values in John's Gospel, and my seminary colleague and Johannine scholar Dr. Stephen Kim for his gracious interaction on this Gospel. My assistant Beyth Hogue has provided invaluable support, as have my editorial assistants for this volume, William Thompson and Braxton Alsop. As ever, I want to thank my wife, Mariko, and our children, Christopher and Julianne, for daily walking with me, for bearing with me and for pursuing Jesus with me. Last but certainly not least, I want to thank my parents, William and Audrey Metzger, to whom I have dedicated this volume.

THE RESONATE
EDITORIAL TEAM

Executive Editor
Paul Louis Metzger, Ph.D., professor of Christian theology and theology of culture, and director, The Institute for the Theology of Culture: New Wine, New Wineskins, Multnomah Biblical Seminary/Multnomah University

Managing Editor
David Sanford, Credo Communications, and advisor, The Institute for the Theology of Culture: New Wine, New Wineskins, Multnomah Biblical Seminary/Multnomah University

Old Testament Consulting Editor
Karl Kutz, Ph.D., professor of Bible and biblical languages, Multnomah University

New Testament Consulting Editor
Albert H. Baylis, Ph.D., professor of Bible and theology, Multnomah Biblical Seminary/Multnomah University

Gospel of John Consulting Editor
Ron Frost, Ph.D., educational and pastoral care consultant, Barnabas International

Editorial Assistant
Beyth Hogue, administrative coordinator, The Institute for the Theology of Culture: New Wine, New Wineskins, Multnomah Biblical Seminary/Multnomah University

INTRODUCTION

The rock group U2 recorded the song "When Love Comes to Town" with blues legend B. B. King on their *Rattle & Hum* tour of America. I love to listen to that song, with its talk of shipwrecks, shipwrecked romances and lives. I especially love the verse in which King bellows that he participated in crucifying Jesus and witnessed Jesus' victory of love.

What does this have to do with a book on John's Gospel? John—a fisherman and the beloved disciple—writes about God's victorious love revealed in Jesus that delivers us from shipwrecked lives. This book is a tour through John's Gospel involving cultural reflections and my spiritual journey. Everything is different since love came to town. Following the contours of the song, some of us were sailors lost at sea; others of us made love under red sunsets, only to abandon our lovers later; still others of us were dirt, living on the street.

Yet all of this changed when love rescued us—when the divine Lover came to town, since God's love revealed in Jesus came to town and since Jesus conquered the great divide. That tune and that verse will be playing in the background as you read the pages that follow, which echo the beat of God's unconditional, relational, sacrificial and holy love disclosed in John's Gospel. Like me, you were that sailor, the lover who jilts and the jilted lover. Like me, you were the dirt at others' feet. And like me, you were the blind or lame man on the street, the woman at the well and the woman caught in adultery, the fisherman, Israel's teacher, Rome's governor and the soldier at the cross. But no matter who you and I were then, everything is different now that Jesus conquered the great divide that separated us from God and opened the way for us to respond to his loving call. And what if you have not yet responded to God's call on your life? Toss aside the spear that you and I used to pierce Jesus' side, and drop the dice that you and I threw to divide his clothes. Now you can be the disciple whom Jesus loves. This is your story—the day love comes to your heart's doorstep, the day love comes to town in grace and truth.

John 3:16, perhaps the most famous verse in the Bible, reveals God's motivation in sending his Son: to love the world and to draw people into communion with himself in and through his Son (and as we shall see through other texts, through the Spirit). John 1:14 indicates the manner in which God's Son—the divine Word enfleshed—reveals God's love: in grace and truth (Jn 1:14). God as revealed in Jesus does not treat us as our sins deserve, but he doesn't let us live the lie either. God's love revealed in Jesus is not the casual, fleeting love so often present in our culture today. Rather, it is pure and good and constant and holy. His glorious love is manifest as a perfect marriage of grace and truth; it is steadfast and true.[1] Have you experienced it? Will you experience it now?

◆ ◆ ◆

In keeping with the discussion above, I believe the apostle John wrote this love story of grace and truth.[2] I also believe that he wrote it between A.D. 85–95, and likely from Ephesus.[3] Moreover, I maintain that John's purpose was to evangelize people, especially Jews and Jewish proselytes, and to edify second- and third-generation Christ-followers who had not seen Jesus, strengthening them in their faith and their love relationship with Jesus as revealed in this Gospel. Near the close of the book, John (the beloved disciple) speaks to this twofold purpose when he tells Thomas that those who have not seen and yet believe are blessed (Jn 20:29), adding that "Jesus did many other miraculous signs in the presence of his disciples, which are not recorded in this book. But these are written that you may believe that Jesus is the Christ, the Son of God, and that by believing you may have life in his name" (Jn 20:30-31). I believe this passage contains a twofold purpose: calling people to faith and confirming believers in faith.[4]

John's words recorded as John 20:30-31 specify the nature of "Gospel" literature. What is a Gospel? A biography? A history? A theology or catechism? A Gospel includes elements of each, but cannot be identified with any one of them. A Gospel is a category unto itself; it is God's good news written to help people come to faith and grow in their faith in Jesus, their Messiah.[5]

John wrote his Gospel because his life was coming to a close; he was burdened to pass along a testimony of Jesus' teachings and deeds and person to John's spiritual children throughout history. All kinds of counterfeit teachings were surfacing about Jesus, and his followers were having debates about various matters of faith. As one of Jesus' apostles, John wanted to set matters straight so as to reveal Jesus as the fullness of grace and truth, fulfilling and surpassing the revelation that had come before him through Israel. John desired that people would come to faith and grow in their love relationship with the triune God in and through Jesus—the Christ, the Son of God in the flesh.[6]

God in the flesh is divine love enfleshed. God does not simply talk the talk; he walks it too. God's Word, God's Son comes to earth, moves into our neighborhood, moves in with us and takes up residence in our hearts. We are talking here of his incarnation and our reception. There are challenges along the way, as he makes connections with us. People often react and reject him. I have often reacted and rejected him too. We even humiliate, betray and deny him, but he is exalted in his humiliation at our hands through his cross and resurrection. In the midst of everything we do to him and in spite of us, he invites us into relationship.

I have set forth an outline of the book, for the sake of flow of thought and plot development, that reflects the movement noted here. I will explain this approach after briefly engaging a predominant outline. Many outlines for the Gospel of John have been proposed, including "Prologue" (Jn 1:1-18), "Book of Signs" (Jn 1:19–12:50), "Book of Glory" or "Book of the Passion" (Jn 13:1–20:31) and "Epilogue" (Jn 21:1-15). Although I resonate with John 1:1-18 serving as the prologue of the whole Gospel and see that John 21:1-25 basically concludes the book, I struggle with dividing the majority of the book into "Book of Signs" and "Book of

Glory" or "Book of the Passion." What is to be made of the fact that the actual passion narrative does not begin until chapter 18? And is there not a sense in which the whole book is about signs used by God to reveal and conceal? Moreover, the whole of the Gospel is leading to the passion of Christ.[7] In place of this famous outline, I propose the following (alluded to briefly above): "Incarnation and Reception" (Jn 1:1-18); "Initial Connections" (Jn 1:19–4:54); "Reactions and Rejection" (Jn 5:1–12:50); "Preparations" (Jn 13:1–17:26); "Humiliation/Glorification" (Jn 18:1–20:23); and "Invitation" (Jn 20:24–21:25).

The rationale for the outline is as follows. John 1:1-18 gives an overview of the book in the sense that many of the themes that appear in the Gospel are foreshadowed here. I have titled this section "Incarnation and Reception" because it focuses on the incarnation of God's Word, the Son of God, and how people respond to him in various ways—many rejecting him, others believing in him.

John 1:19–4:54 presents Jesus engaging many individuals and groups in unique ways in various contexts: from John the Baptist and his disciples, including Andrew and later Simon Peter (Jn 1:19-42), to Philip and Nathanael (Jn 1:43-51); from the wedding party and guests including his family and disciples at the wedding in Cana in Galilee (Jn 2:1-12), to his disciples and the religious establishment in the temple in Jerusalem (Jn 2:13-25); from Nicodemus and John the Baptist again (Jn 3), to the Samaritan woman and a royal official (Jn 4). As the living Word made flesh rather than an abstract concept reserved for a textbook on a shelf, Jesus connects with people, addressing and engaging them in their life situations with profound awareness and sensitivity. The confrontation at the temple cleansing in John 2 foreshadows the outright rejection of Jesus to come, as the authorities challenge him to provide his basis of authority for cleansing the temple. The pronounced and sustained reactions (and eventual rejection of him) do not begin until chapter 5. Although there are positive connections made in John 5–12, as in the case with the man healed of blindness in John 9, the growing opposition and attacks on Jesus are predominant in the section. Thus, I have titled John 1:19–4:54 "Initial Connections" and John 5:1–12:50 "Reactions and Rejection."

In John 5, we find Jesus healing a man on the Sabbath and claiming that he does only what his Father does, making himself out to be God's Son and equal with God. As a result of the healing on the Sabbath and the claim to deity, the religious power brokers try to stone him (Jn 5:18). Not only does the Jewish establishment react and reject Jesus because of his claim to be God's Son, but scores of Jesus' own disciples disown him because of his claim that he is the bread of life, whose body they must eat and whose blood they must drink to receive eternal life (Jn 6:25-71). Jesus' own brothers react to him, mocking and challenging him to reveal himself to all Israel at a festival in Jerusalem if he truly is the Messiah (Jn 7:1-5). In chapter 8, we find those John ironically refers to as "the Jews"[8] wanting to kill Jesus again because of his claim to exist before Abraham—more specifically, to be the God revealed to Moses as the great I AM (Jn 8:58-59). This section sets forth other rejections of Jesus, including the determination of the Jewish ruling council to destroy him—based on his raising of Lazarus from the dead (Jn 11:45-57)—and to kill Lazarus too (Jn 12:9-10). Later, in John 12, we find Jesus speaking about the hour of glory arriving—the hour of his passion and death (Jn 12:23-29).[9] This leads into the next section: "Preparations."

I have titled John 13:1–17:26 "Preparations" because Jesus is preparing his followers for his passion, death and resurrection, whereby he will prepare a place for them in his Father's house through his saving work (Jn 14:1-4). Along with this and other things, Jesus prepares them for the descent and activity of the Spirit (Jn 14:15-17, 25-26; 15:26; 16:5-15), life together that requires love and sacrificial service (Jn 13:12-17; 15:9-17) and persecution (Jn 15:18-27; 16:1-4). He promises to take them to be with him, to be with them and that the Spirit will come (Jn 14:1-4, 15-21; 16:7). He warns them (Jn 15:18-27; 16:1-4) and prays for them (Jn 17:6-26), even while praying for himself in preparation for what lies ahead (Jn 17:1-5). John 13 involves the foot washing that takes place at the Last Supper. Chapters 14–16 are known as the farewell discourse, and chapter 17 is often referred to as Jesus' high priestly prayer. The events and teachings set forth here, along with the arrest and trial before the Sanhedrin and Peter's three denials in chapter 18, take place on one night. The inclusion of such a great amount of material from one night shows this material's importance to John, not only in terms of understanding Jesus' life and ministry and preparation for his immediate followers but also for John's audience (including us), who are included in the latter portion of the high priestly prayer (Jn 17:20-26).

John 18:1–20:23 presents Jesus' passion, death and resurrection. Together, they present the hour of glory. I have referred to this section as "Humiliation/Glorification" rather than "Humiliation *and* Glorification" because the humiliation itself is part of his glory. So the occasion of glory is a paradoxical reality with different dimensions and also phases, disclosing his death as glorious and revealing his death and resurrection as one reality. Jesus' humiliation/glorification is foreshadowed in Jesus' humble act of service in washing his disciples' feet (Jn 13:1-17). After Jesus' farewell discourse and high priestly prayer in the garden (Jn 14-17), the passion begins with Jesus' arrest when Judas betrays him into the hands of his enemies (Jn 18:1-11) and his trials before the Sanhedrin and Pilate (Jn 18:19–19:16), including the disgraceful treatment of him by the Roman soldiers (Jn 19:1-3). Perhaps even more cruel to Jesus than the soldiers' treatment of him is Peter's denial of him during his trial before the Sanhedrin (Jn 18:12-26). The passion climaxes in his crucifixion, death and burial (Jn 19:16-42), and culminates in his resurrection and first glorious appearances—to Mary Magdalene and then to his disciples (Jn 20:1-23).

Lastly we come to the section titled "Invitation" (Jn 20:24–21:25). John lets us know in John 20:30-31 that he has not written his book as a mere history lesson or theological treatise. Rather, it is a letter of invitation, wherein John calls on his readers to respond to Jesus' claim on their lives as the Son of God who entered the world to save the world through his miraculous signs, especially the chief signs of the death and resurrection. John's book allows no place for abstract reflection, for it is a Gospel; as such, it is an invitation to believe and grow in faith in Jesus Christ as Savior and Lord. There is no opportunity for taking it or leaving it, or for taking Jesus lightly. Jesus' claim on John's readers' lives is a matter of eternal life and death. John would have us know that Jesus' claim is also on our lives. There can be no response of "No comment" or "Try again later (as in: the next life)." There can only be a yes or no to Jesus here and now. Either Jesus becomes our Savior and Lord and we enter into eternal life, or we retain lordship over our own lives and remain in death. What will it be? We may have doubted Jesus' resurrection, like Thomas did (Jn 20:24-25). Indeed, this section opens with Jesus addressing Thomas's doubt and transitions to John's audience as Jesus tells his listeners that those who believe in him without seeing him are truly blessed (Jn 20:29). Yet Jesus leads Thomas to deep devotion (Jn 20:26-28). We may have denied him, as Peter did (Jn 18:15-27). Yet Jesus leads Peter into the riches of restoration (Jn 21:15-22). We may have always devoutly believed in him, as John did. Still, Jesus overwhelms John again and again (Jn 21:24-25). John wants us to know that Jesus will draw us to himself, leading us from doubt into deep faith. Jesus will restore and renew us, embracing us in his love and forgiving us for having denied him. And Jesus will engulf us in our devotion time and time again as we drink from him through our reading of John's Gospel, filling us and blowing us away. In each case, John would have us finish our reading in awe and wonder, with the thrilling sense that we have met Jesus anew and that he is worthy of our worship. For he is love and life and grace and truth, and through faith in him we enter into the fullness of life.

◆   ◆   ◆

Imagine what the world would have been like if love—Jesus as the Lord of love—had not come to town. What would John's life—and yours and mine—have been like? Could Bono have been the songwriter he has become without John as a lyrical mentor? Even better than asking the "what ifs" is imagining what the world—your world—can be like as you meet Jesus again and again through your reading of John's Gospel, just as I have engaged Jesus through my meditations on the Gospel of John recounted here. As you meet the incarnate Son of God for the first time or the millionth time, how will you respond?

INCARNATION
AND RECEPTION

John 1:1-18

As stated in the introduction to this volume, John 1:1-18 serves as the prologue for John's Gospel as a whole, as it sets forth many themes that will appear throughout the book. The following essay, "That Sense of Touch," will highlight many of these themes. At the core of the prologue is the attention given to Jesus' incarnation and how people respond to him as the Word made flesh. The sections that follow ("Initial Connections," "Reactions and Rejection," "Preparations," "Humiliation/ Glorification," and "Invitation") include content that unpack what is set forth in "That Sense of Touch."

"That Sense of Touch" constitutes the first major section of this volume. This opening section is unique in that it foreshadows much of what follows as Jesus comes close and touches us as the incarnate Word and Son of God. The other major sections are longer and self-contained, and so I will introduce those sections with summary or overview essays. There will also be transitional essays preceding them, which both bridge sections and focus on themes that span the entire Gospel as well as this volume.

THAT SENSE OF TOUCH
John 1:1-18

Deep down in our souls, we all long for a sense of touch. Whether we are talking about infants in Romanian orphanages hitting their heads against walls because they have no one to hold them, or drivers in Los Angeles crashing into one another because they miss that sense of connection to others, as in the movie *Crash*, we all long for that sense of touch.

Crash chronicles the collisions of people from different ethnic backgrounds in L.A., showing how racism is alive and well in our contemporary cultural context. At the outset of the movie, Detective Graham Ward reflects upon a car collision that he (an African American) and his partner (a Latino) just had with a Korean American. Ward makes the following claim: "It's the sense of touch. Any real city, you walk, you know? You brush past people. People bump into you. In L.A., nobody touches you. We're always behind this metal and glass. I think we miss that touch so much that we crash into each other just so we can feel something."[1]

We do long for the sense of touch. We do often crash into one another racially. But there are other reasons that we crash into one another. Those of us who are Christ-followers often crash into nonbelievers when witnessing to them, engaging in drive-by evangelism. No matter our faith commitments, we are all prone to crash into others in a variety of ways. We are often hasty, rushed, abrasive and insensitive, approaching one another from intolerance or indifference. We are often driven by hate or the love of wanting to prove ourselves right and righteous over against others. Fortunately for all of us, Jesus does not crash into us. He approaches us in love and grace as the Word of God and as the living truth (Jn 1:14; 14:6). John's Gospel reveals that as the Word made flesh, Jesus comes alongside us and touches us with the gracious truth of his holy love (Jn 1:14; 3:16).

What is the significance of John's use of "the Word"? Often, scholars go to the Greeks or Hellenized Jews such as Philo for the background. John was likely aware of Philo and, before him, Plato and his doctrine of the *logos*. Yet even though there may be validity in tracing the usage of this term to these roots, we should give prime consideration to the Old

Testament background. In the Old Testament, the Word is connected with *creation* (Gen 1:3—2:3; Ps 33:6), *revelation* (Jer 1:4; Is 9:8), and *deliverance/salvation* (Ps 107:20; Is 55:11). Also, the Word is personified as Wisdom in Proverbs 8.[2] In keeping with what I noted about the prologue foreshadowing the rest of the Gospel, Jesus as God's personal Word creates, heals and gives life (Jn 1:3; 4:43-54; 5:1-9; 9:1-12; 11:1-44), makes known (Jn 14:5-14) and comes to save (Jn 3:1-21). We will take up each of these aspects of the Word's activity in this essay, beginning with his creative work.

John tells us that God creates all things through his eternal Word: "In the beginning was the Word, and the Word was with God, and the Word was God. Through him all things were made. Without him nothing was made that has been made" (Jn 1:1, 3). God's very own eternal self-expression—his Word—brings into being the whole universe, all the way down to you and me. The relational language that John uses flows from interpersonal communion with the divine life revealed through the Word. God's communal being, which involves his personal Word, provides the basis for God's loving initiative and relational engagement with his creation.

No doubt you've seen pictures of the Sistine Chapel in Rome. In Michelangelo's painting, God has just created Adam and is reaching out to touch him. In the painting, Adam looks as if he's still getting his bearings, as if God is just waking him from a very long, deep sleep. God is the one who first makes contact. In fact, Adam wouldn't even be in the picture—or Michelangelo for that matter—if God had chosen not to create. We do not first touch God. God first touches us. God does so through his eternal and personal Word of creation, revelation, salvation and incarnation.

God speaks the universe into being through his eternal and personal Word. What God says he does. In fact, when God says it, it is done. So often we hear words like "Talk is cheap." We often witness the divorce between word and action. A husband tells his wife that he loves her and then sleeps all over town. A father tells his son that he loves him but never shows up for his baseball games or band concerts. A mother tells her daughter that she will never leave her and yet hands her over to grandparents so that she can pursue the nightlife when her husband bails on her. Grown children tell their elderly parents how much they miss them, but never bother to visit. There aren't too many people whose words are as good as actions being performed. But God's speech is active, and it produces results. God does what he claims he will do. In fact, his creative word is life-giving, bringing all things to life.

In addition to God's Word being creative and life-giving, God's Word is also revealing: "In him was life, and that life was the light of men" (Jn 1:4). Perhaps John is reflecting back on Genesis 1 in which God says, "'Let there be light,' and there was light" (Gen 1:3). Perhaps John also has Psalm 119 in mind. There the psalmist says, "Your word is a lamp to my feet and a light for my path" (Ps 119:105). God's Word reveals God to us, and his Word reveals our own lives to us too. As God's very self-expression and light of illumination, God's Word tells us what God is really like. God's Word also tells us the most important things about ourselves. Such truth telling is in itself life-giving, even when the truth stings and hurts. It functions as a cleansing balm applied to an infected, open wound. By addressing not only the symptoms but also the source of our broken, diseased condition, we can find healing—lasting healing.

But all too often, we'd rather not hear the truth and enter into the light of God's presence. It's too painful. While we all long for the sense of touch, God's touch makes us vulnerable, perhaps even makes us feel as if we are losing control. All too often, we cannot handle the gracious truth of God's love, and so we cover it with lies and ideology. Václav Havel writes,

> Ideology is a specious way of relating to the world. It offers human beings the illusions of an identity, or dignity, and of morality while making it easier for them to part with them. As the repository of something suprapersonal and objective, it enables people to deceive their conscience and conceal their true position and their inglorious *modus vivendi*, both from the world and from themselves. It is a very pragmatic but, at the same time, an apparently dignified way of legitimizing what is above, below, and on either side. It is directed toward people and toward God. It is a veil behind which

human beings can hide their own fallen existence, their trivialization, and their adaptation to the status quo.[3]

We try to hide behind such things as lies and ideologies rather than deal with the truth, especially when *the* Truth is staring us right in the face as God incarnate (Jn 1:14). We would rather lie about the Truth, resort to ideology or simply ignore the Truth, if at all possible. It is hard enough when witnesses like John the Baptist tell us about the Word who gives light to the world. John comes as a witness so that the world might believe in the Word of life and light (Jn 1:6-8, 15; see also the sections involving John the Baptist in Jn 1:19-34 and 3:22-36). The Word does not leave himself without witnesses. We have no excuse, especially given that the Word has taken the time to make his dwelling in our midst, coming up close and getting personal (Jn 1:9-10, 14).

The light and darkness themes appear throughout John's Gospel (see the transitional essay titled "The Dark Side of the Force"). A master of metaphor, John often uses physical day and night to convey spiritual and moral light and darkness. For example, Nicodemus comes to Jesus at night (Jn 3:2) and is in the darkness (Jn 3:19-21). Later he comes into the light of life, even when everything else around him is shrouded in darkness (Jn 7:45-52; 19:38-42). Judas goes out at night into the darkness to betray Jesus (Jn 13:27, 30). Jesus is the light of the world (Jn 8:12). There is a strong polarity between light and darkness in John's Gospel. The light shines in the darkness, but the darkness does not understand it and cannot overcome the light (Jn 1:5).[4]

The moral aspect to the light and darkness polarity is borne out by the fact that the personal Word comes to the world and to his own people but is not recognized or accepted. "He was in the world, and though the world was made through him, the world did not recognize him. He came to that which was his own, but his own did not receive him" (Jn 1:10-11). Jesus makes contact with us (see "Initial Connections"), but we often react and reject him (see "Reactions and Rejection"). Why do we often reject the Word when he makes contact with us? Connected to our fear of vulnerability and losing control is love of the darkness. As Jesus says, "Light has come into the world, but men loved darkness instead of light because their deeds were evil" (Jn 3:19).

We live in the spiritual darkness of self-delusion. As a result, we cannot tolerate real love when it touches our hearts. We can settle for love as a commodity. We can even make a compartment for love. But God as love revealed in the person of Jesus will not allow us to commodify or compartmentalize him. And so we kill him.

No one likes to hear bad news—especially about themselves. How can we listen to an indictment that reveals to us our need and spiritual bankruptcy and hardness of heart, especially when we so often justify ourselves and make ourselves out to be in the right? This is especially true of us who grew up thinking of ourselves as God's chosen people—not just good Jews, as in the case of John's Gospel, but also true-blue Baptists and Lutherans and other steadfast religious or even emerging spiritual types. We often think that others are broken, that others have baggage and that others are standing before God's judgment seat. Not us; we've arrived. We may even be so blind as to think that we reached out and touched God before he ever thought of reaching out to touch us.

Why do insiders so often reject the message and receive the guilty verdict? God comes to his own chosen people, and they reject him (not the other way round). Throughout John's Gospel, we find that insiders often reject God's message centered in Jesus. God does not reject them, but they reject God. While the world at large does not recognize him either, many outsiders do get it. Yet the insiders—the few, the good, God's kind of people—often don't want it. Maybe many outsiders in John's Gospel get it because they know they're outside, because they're tired of living the lie and because they want God's life-giving truth, no matter how painful it is. And yet even the awareness of their brokenness comes from God. (For more on this theme of insiders and outsiders, see "Non-Members Only.")

Now for the rest of us. While we long for that sense of touch from God as those created by God and wired for intimacy with God, we often pull back. The very thing we want we reject. The very thing we want most we find most difficult to give. In John's Gospel, God's people are crying out for their Messiah, but many do not recognize him in their midst; if they do, many do not want what he offers them. He doesn't come to give us what we want but what we need: intimacy with God. But intimacy, especially intimacy with God, is difficult to embrace, especially when our hearts have so often been burned by others. We sometimes spurn God's love out of fear of being burned by someone who gets close.

The movie *Good Will Hunting* chronicles the story of a brilliant young man (played by Matt Damon) who protects himself from being hurt by others until love finally breaks through to him. It takes the forceful, loving embrace of Will's counselor (Robin Williams) to tear down Will's walls of self-defense, which have kept people from hurting him ever since his stepfather badly beat him when he was a child. Will's counselor becomes his real father, not some biological-or-legal-by-marriage-father-figure impostor. Will's counselor does not simply tolerate Will. He does not begrudge his existence and beat him, or allow Will's tough-guy exterior or brilliance to repel him. He touches Will. He embraces him. Although Will fights it at first, he finally breaks down and weeps in his counselor's arms, and then travels across the country in pursuit of the young woman he loves but has kept at arm's length for so long.

When we are used to being beaten or—perhaps worse—ignored, it is very difficult for us to accept God's acceptance of us and his embrace. God does not tolerate us, as many of our parents do, treating us like "accidents." God loves us. Sometimes God has to embrace us forcefully (though not violently) so that we cannot break away to hide and so that our hearts' walls will break so his love can flow through.

Will's counselor speaks truth into Will's life, telling him while he embraces him that the beatings he received as a child from his stepfather were not his fault. There is a difference as well as a parallel between Will's life and our own. Although we were at fault, God forgives us and removes our sins and heals the wounds of our broken condition. God does not hold our sins over our heads or beat us with them. God removes them and welcomes us into his family. God's Word receives us into God's family as we respond to the good news and believe in him.

God's Word is creative and life-giving, and it reveals God to us as well as our need for God. As such life-giving truth comes home to us and saves us, we are born anew and enter God's family. Those who receive God's Word are welcomed into God's family, a family not of natural but of supernatural origins: "Yet to all who received him, to those who believed in his name, he gave the right to become children of God—children born not of natural descent, nor of human decision or a husband's will, but born of God" (Jn 1:12-13). John's Gospel is aimed at inviting people to know and grow in vital communion with God through his Word, Jesus (see "Invitation").

Any birth is miraculous—so mysterious, so beautiful and so amazing. If natural birth is miraculous, just think how miraculous a birth is that is not the result of natural descent or a husband's decision. We are talking about divine decision here. God is no fickle deity who willy-nilly does things without planning, like many parents do when their hormones take over. When God plans a supernatural birth, he uses ultimate foresight. God doesn't make mistakes or accidents, and God doesn't abort or reject us if we have defects. All that is required of us is to trust in and accept his acceptance of us. And even our acceptance of God is a gift from God that comes to us at birth based on God's love and calling, not our merit. It's part of our inheritance as his children whom he loves.

Giving birth is a painful process, and raising children takes a lot of humble love and patience. You can't speak to your child about the complexities of life or of deep theology as you would to your best friend or your professor. You have to speak in a way with which little children can connect. I couldn't talk to my kids when they were little the way that I talk to my students in advanced courses in theology. That's the way it is with God's Word. That's why he becomes flesh and blood: "The Word became flesh and made his dwelling among us" (Jn 1:14).

When God's Word comes to us, the Word doesn't speak to us at the level of rocket science technology or even at the level of auto mechanics. The Word simplifies his message for us as spiritual babes. He gets down on his hands and knees and speaks baby talk to us. "Baby talk" is a simple description of what we theologians call "accommodation." Here's what the great John Calvin says about the matter:

> For who even of slight intelligence does not understand that, as nurses commonly do with infants, God is wont in a measure to "lisp" in speaking to us? Thus such forms of speaking do not so much express clearly what God is like as accommodate the knowl-

edge of him to our slight capacity. To do this he must descend far beneath his loftiness.[5]

The Word gets down on all fours, descending "far beneath his loftiness," lisping and speaking baby talk so that we little children can understand. And the Word doesn't just speak with lisping words but with deeds. In fact, the Word is deed. The Word doesn't do drive-by evangelism. He stops, stoops and stays with us, showing us that his love for us is not just talk. As Eugene Peterson puts it, "The Word became flesh and blood, and moved into the neighborhood."[6] In fact, as God in the flesh, he allows us to climb up into his lap or lean against him, just as John does (Jn 13:23) and as Jesus does with his Father (Jn 1:18).

As God's saving knowledge comes home to us, we long for intimacy with God. We long to get close because we realize that what we see in Jesus is what we get with God. As those to whom the Word has revealed himself, we have come to realize that his glory is full of grace and truth, and full of humility and self-sacrifice, as John's Gospel makes clear. (See "Preparations," the transitional essay "Fifteen Minutes of Fame and the Hour of Glory," and "Humiliation/Glorification.") "We have seen his glory, the glory of the One and Only, who came from the Father, full of grace and truth" (Jn 1:14).

Our sense of Jesus' all-surpassing and glorious grace and truth is confirmed by the witness of John the Baptist and by Moses as well. As great as they are, they realize that the incarnate Word of God is superior to them (Jn 5:31-47). "John testifies concerning him. He cries out, saying, 'This was he of whom I said, "He who comes after me has surpassed me because he was before me."' From the fullness of his grace we have all received one blessing after another.[7] For the law was given through Moses; grace and truth came through Jesus Christ" (Jn 1:15-17). As great as the law (Jn 1:17) and Bethel (see "Stairway to Heaven") and the temple (see "Trinket Shop") and the Sabbath (see "Missing the Forest, Missing the Trees") and the manna from heaven (see "Happy Meals") are, Jesus is the fulfillment of all Old Testament types and realities. He alone is the fullness of salvation as the ultimate grace and truth, and he alone can truly satisfy us—not Moses or some Old Testament institution or individual saint (see "False Redemption"). For Jesus comes to us as God in the flesh, revealing God's *shekinah* glory in the tabernacle of his body, full of grace and truth.[8]

As Jesus comes close, he touches us in a way that no one else can, transforming us from the inside out for all eternity. It is not that Moses' law does not contain grace or that it is lacking in truth. But the grace and truth of the Word enfleshed is far superior to what comes through Moses.[9] How can it be otherwise? For only the enfleshed Word comes to us from the bosom or side of the Father. He alone comes from above and is the one and only Son of God. The rest of us are from below (Jn 3:31-36 and 8:23-24). We only enter into God's family through union with the Word enfleshed (Jn 8:23-24), as we are born again (or born from above) as we believe in the one who is lifted up on the cross (Jn 3:1-21). The Word, Jesus, exists in eternal communion with God, and we only enter into communion with God through faith in God and Jesus, whom God has sent (Jn 17:1-5).

At the close of the prologue, John tells us that Jesus is in the bosom of the Father: "No one has ever seen God, but God the One and Only, who is at the Father's side [in the bosom of the Father], has made him known" (Jn 1:18). Jesus' intimacy with his Father is profound. Given their vital relationship from all eternity, Jesus truly makes God known, for he is God *in the flesh*. No one had ever seen God face to face in the past, but now we find him revealed in the face of Jesus. Jesus is the fullest manifestation of God, and so is *full* of grace and truth (Jn 1:14).

And so we have received Jesus' all-surpassing grace and can minister God's gracious touch to others—Christian and non-Christian alike, just as he has touched us. As John says in 1 John 1:

> That which was from the beginning, which we have heard, which we have seen with our eyes, which we have looked at and our hands have touched—this we proclaim concerning the Word of life. The life appeared; we have seen it and testify to it, and we proclaim to you the eternal life, which was with the Father and has appeared to us. We proclaim to you what we have seen and heard, so that you also may have fellowship with us. And our fellowship is with the Father and with his Son, Jesus Christ. We write this to make our joy complete. (1 Jn 1:1-4)

Jesus climbs into our skin, assuring us that God understands us. It's almost as if Jesus has read Atticus Finch's words in *To Kill a Mockingbird*: "If you can learn a simple trick, . . . you'll get along a lot better with all kinds of folks. You never really understand a person until you consider things from his point of view . . . until you climb into his skin and walk around in it."[10]

Communication requires that one understand someone else and make oneself understood. As Jesus climbs into our skin to assure us that he understands us, he also gets into our hearts to make himself known and to invite us to know him. Even though Jesus says many things that are difficult to understand, love communicates well in any language, no matter one's proficiency level. I know people full of grace, and I know others full of truth. But I have never come across anyone like Jesus, who is full of both grace and truth in equal measure.

Grace and truth go hand in hand and bring healing as God reaches out to touch us with his love: just as he touches Adam all by himself in the garden, just as he touches John, just as he reaches out to embrace babies locked away in Romanian orphanages and just as he makes a sudden impact on isolated drivers in L.A. It's all about touching and being touched, or banging one's head, crashing and being burned.

TRANSITION
The Egg-Headed God and the Gospel of Jesus

AS WE HAVE NOTED, THE WORD EXISTS for all eternity with God in vital communion (Jn 1:18). John 1:1 tells us that the Word was in the beginning with God and is God. One could easily get lost in deep theological and trinitarian reflection on the divine Word of John 1, and how the Word is with God and is God from all eternity. And while deep theological reflection on the divine Word has a vital place, there is never room for esoteric, egg-headed abstractions when dealing with the God disclosed in John's Gospel. John does not want us to know the triune God in the abstract but to know the Father and Son in the Spirit experientially, participating in the divine life (Jn 17:3). If the Word were simply a logical ideal, one could simply reflect logically. But God calls on us to reflect experientially, for the Word is personal and becomes incarnate as Jesus Christ, and the Father invites us to enter into interpersonal communion through Jesus in the Spirit. The best trinitarian reflection throughout the ages has always involved focused consideration on union and communion and participation.[1]

With this interpersonal and communal framework in mind, consider the many well-intentioned explanations of the doctrine of the Trinity that seemingly make God out to be a mathematical formula or a giant egg. You know: "Just as 1 x 1 x 1 = 1, so too God is three persons yet one"; or "Just like an egg shell, egg white and egg yolk make up an egg, the three persons of the Trinity make up the one God." No wonder people look a bit puzzled when I passionately say John's Gospel is so trinitarian—as if that should make them want to read it![2]

The Trinity is not some mathematical puzzle to solve or a recipe calling for egg whites and egg yolks, and it cannot be reduced to some creedal statement, no matter how well (or badly) formulated. God is personal truth, and as such, undergirds our truth claims. Where do I find support for *this* claim? In John's Gospel, of course. Jesus is God's ultimate Word, who was in the beginning with God: "In the beginning was the Word, and the Word was with God, and the Word was God" (Jn 1:1). He is "the way and *the truth* and the life" (Jn 14:6; italics added). Eternal life does not equal knowing statements *about* him, but *knowing* him: "Now this is eternal life, that they may know you, the only true God, and Jesus Christ, whom you have sent" (Jn 17:3). In the Bible, true knowledge is personal and participatory. Adam knew Eve, and they had a child (Gen 4:1-2). While there is a difference between physical and spiritual knowing, they are both profoundly personal and participatory. Such experiential knowledge undergirds those truth claims we rightly make about God in Christ through the Spirit. For those who worship God must worship him in spirit and in truth (Jn 4:24), and the Spirit is the one who leads us into the truth of Jesus: "But when he, the Spirit of truth, comes, he will guide you into all truth. He will not speak on his own; he will speak only what he hears, and he will tell you what is yet to come. He will bring glory to me by taking from what is mine and making it known to you" (Jn 16:13-14).[3]

Such knowledge of God starts with Jesus' knowledge of the Father. "No one has ever seen God, but God the One and Only, who is at the Father's side, has made him known" (Jn 1:18). Later, this Gospel will tell us that John, the beloved disciple, reclines next to Jesus at the Last Supper, leaning back against Jesus' side (Jn 13:23-25). Knowledge is personal, communal and participatory.

Knowing Jesus entails knowing God, as in the case of John and the other disciples, but rejecting Jesus entails a failure to know God. How can it be otherwise, when God is Jesus' Father? "'You do not know me or my Father,' Jesus replied. 'If you knew me, you would know my Father also.' He spoke these words while teaching in the temple area near the place where the offerings were put. Yet no one seized him, because his time had not yet come" (Jn 8:19-20). Since Jesus and God are one (Jn 10:30), how could it *not* be the case that rejecting Jesus is rejecting the Father?

You can't put this God on a shelf. The Word becomes flesh and blood in our midst, living among us, encountering us where we live (Jn 1:14). He comes looking for you—*you* the religious scholar, *you* the well woman, *you* the lame man and *you* the fisherman: Nicodemus, the Samaritan woman at the well, the paralytic by the pool and Peter on the shore.

Each person, in his or her own way, would have preferred to deal with the egg-headed God. It's so much easier to deal with God in abstractions and formulas and recipes. But when God destroys your theories and abstractions and you come face to face with God in Jesus, you can't avoid the unavoidable. To Nicodemus he says, "You must be born again" (Jn 3:7). To the woman he says, "Go, call your husband and come back" (Jn 4:16). To the paralytic: "Do you want to get well? . . . Get up! Pick up your mat and walk" (Jn 5:6, 8). And to Peter: "Do you love me? . . . Feed my sheep" (Jn 21:17). None of this he says to condemn; he speaks a distinctive word to each one of them to get beyond the façade and the pretense. Then he can touch each one of them in a special way so that they might come to worship God in spirit and in truth.

The only one mentioned above about whom we remain uncertain is the paralytic. When the authorities question him, he tells on Jesus for healing him. I am like that man: do I want to be made well? I'm not sure at times, just like I'm not sure he knew what he really wanted. Did he really want to get well? I like my pretense and façade. I like leaning on crutches, and so I don't like it when Jesus kicks them out from under me. I also don't like it when Jesus comes to me and says, "Do you love me?" At least I don't have to worry about Jesus telling me to go call my husband! I can handle that story. And I like the woman's delay tactics, as she raises theological abstractions about different places for worship: Samaritans worship on this mountain and Jews on that mountain . . . (Jn 4:20). But Jesus says to you and me what he says to her: each of us must worship in spirit and in truth (Jn 4:23-24).

So which will it be? In spirit and in truth, or in abstractions? In flesh and in blood, or in old books filled with formulas and recipes that collect dust on their shelves? Will we truly believe in Jesus or simply believe certain things about him?[4] Which will it be? It all depends on who it will be—the egg-headed God, or God in Jesus reconciling to himself you and me.

◆ ◆ ◆

I knew an egg-headed guy who worshiped the egg-headed God. He would use the gospel to validate himself, including his mathematically formulated doctrine of the Trinity. He could rationalize everything and disprove all his adversaries in apologetics debates, making no apologies to his wounded and dying converts. This continued on for some time, until the Trinity became more than something to understand and became someone whose love he experienced. He came to realize that all his proofs didn't prove anything because he didn't really believe them himself. They left him hollow, even though he got a high from proving others wrong. Perhaps what cracked him was that those in his midst who knew God's love did not validate him based on his factual prowess about God but based on the fact that God really loved them—and him too. Such nurture changed his nature. The Trinity went from being the grand egg white, yolk and shell to being the God who is lover (the Father), beloved (the Son) and the one who binds the Godhead in love (the Spirit).[5]

This man will tell you today that insecurities led him to seek to validate himself using Christianity—insecurities that were based on people's cruelty to him as a youth. All his attempts to overcome such victimization lasted until God validated him. God's Spirit cracked his invincible shell with God's vulnerable love—the very love that led the Father to give his Son to the world so that we might receive and believe.

The man of whom I speak is one of my best students. He used to challenge a lot of what I said in class, which was fine in and of itself. His reason for doing so was the problem. He was turning seminary into a cemetery with his attempts to justify and save himself. He just didn't get it. But now he gets it. And now he helps me get it as he challenges me in a different way, encouraging me to move from reflecting on this God of triune love to experiencing God's love myself. He has gone from simply being one of my best students to being one of my best teachers, helping me experience the truth that the God of triune love truly loves me.

What about you? You don't need to be a theological Einstein, like the Swiss Karl Barth, to understand this truth, even though it was through Barth's theological tomes on trinitarian theology—including his discussion of formulas—that I came to know more fully the depths of God's love disclosed in Jesus. Interestingly enough, Barth is often quoted as saying, "Jesus does not give recipes that show the way to God as other teachers of religion do. He is Himself the way."[6] Jesus doesn't give us recipes and formulas; he is the truth and life. Barth's theological instincts were profoundly Christocentric and relational, as reflected in this statement and the one that follows. In an interview session during Barth's sole trip to the States toward the end of his life, a reporter supposedly asked Barth to sum up the gospel in simple terms. Barth's supposed response? The same response my Sunday School teacher led me to give as a child: "Jesus loves me this I know, for the Bible tells me so." That computes far better than $E=MC^2$ or any mathematical formula any day, don't you *think*? Now, won't you *experience*?

John would have us experience the Word made flesh—not simply understand him and theologize over him but receive him and experience his love. As John 1:12 indicates, "Yet to all who received him, to those who believed in his name, he gave the right to become children of God." As Jesus connects with people, many will reject him—even from his own community. Yet the call to respond is an open invitation that runs throughout this Gospel. It remains an open invitation, even to those who have not yet believed in him or so far have rejected him. As Jesus connects with individuals and groups of people throughout John's Gospel, notice their responses and reactions. Take note as well that Jesus as the Word of God is by no means egg-headed but soft-hearted. Jesus is no mathematical puzzle but a living person longing for loving communion with his creation, making us children of God.

INITIAL CONNECTIONS

John 1:19–4:54

In this section of John's Gospel, we find Jesus making initial connections with various individuals and communities: John the Baptist; John's disciples, including Andrew who also introduces his brother Simon Peter to Jesus (Jn 1:19-42); Philip and Nathanael (Jn 1:43-51); his mother Mary, his own disciples and the group at the wedding in Cana (Jn 2:1-12); the religious leaders, merchants and other people gathered at the temple in Jerusalem (Jn 2:13-25); Nicodemus (Jn 3:1-21); John the Baptist once again (Jn 3:22-36); the Samaritan woman at the well and her Samaritan village community (Jn 4:1-42); and the royal official who comes to Jesus in Galilee (Jn 4:43-54).

One of the most striking features of this section is that Jesus never engages individuals and communities in a rote manner. While you should expect "rote" if you are dealing with an abstract ideal, it would be unwise to expect sameness and predictability when preparing to meet God in the flesh. If you presume that Jesus encounters people—including you—in a predictable and methodical manner, you are in for a rude awakening.

Who knows how often John the Baptist interacted with Jesus growing up? The text does not tell us, but the text does tell us that John the Baptist knows that Jesus is the Messiah—the one who would baptize with the Holy Spirit—based on the Spirit's descent on him (Jn 1:32-34). John will later say that he is not worthy to untie the thongs of Jesus' sandals (Jn 1:27). No doubt, John (rightly) feels inadequate in relation to Jesus, because Jesus is uniquely marked by the Spirit's presence and he is the Lamb of God who will take away the sin of the world (Jn 1:29-34). The Spirit's descent and Jesus' ongoing work of taking away the world's sin are both indications that Jesus is the Messiah. Instead of placing stock in his celebrity status among the people, John acts in a saintly manner, serving as a witness to the only one who can take away his sin and the sins of the entire world.

John does not hide the revelation of Jesus that he has received but confesses it freely to others, including his own disciples (Jn 1:29-36). As a result, some of John's own followers leave John to follow Jesus (Jn 1:37). When they ask Jesus where he is staying, Jesus tells John's disciples to come and see (Jn 1:38-39). Just as the Spirit remains on Jesus, Jesus allows them to remain with him (Jn 1:32-42). Whereas the Spirit's clear descent in the form of a dove leads John to declare that Jesus is the Messiah (Jn 1:32-34), it is spending the day with Jesus that leads John's disciple Andrew to say to his brother Peter that Jesus may be the long-awaited one (Jn 1:39-42). Jesus finds Philip, and not the other way round. What would you expect from a God who is alive and loving? He doesn't wait for us to seek him; he seeks us out! It is Jesus' declaration to Nathanael, followed by Jesus' promise to him that Nathanael would meet God, that moves Nathanael beyond cynicism about Jesus *of Nazareth* to belief in him as the Messiah. Instead of rejecting Jesus because he views Nazareth as a godforsaken place, Nathanael now looks at Jesus himself as the place where God meets us (Jn 1:43-51). God connects us to the incarnate Word in various ways. The same is true of what happens in chapters 2–4.

In John 2, we find Jesus connecting with people and revealing his glory in completely different ways. First he turns water into wine at a wedding in Cana of Galilee, thereby saving the day and shielding the master of the banquet from humiliation (Jn 2:1-10). Then he turns over the tables and disrupts the business of the moneychangers and merchants in the temple in Jerusalem, thereby cleansing God's house of dishonor (Jn 2:13-17). Following Jesus' cleansing of the temple, "the Jews" (members of the religious-political establishment) demand from Jesus a sign to demonstrate his authority to disrupt daily operations in the temple. Jesus predicts his bodily death and resurrection, speaking figuratively in temple language (Jn 2:18-21). Each of these initial connections or encounters with Jesus is instrumental in cultivating his disciples' faith in him (Jn 2:11, 22; the latter response of faith is bound up with the sign of his resurrection from the dead). When in Jerusalem, Jesus' miraculous signs lead many people to believe in him (Jn 2:23). Jesus does not perform miraculous signs and mighty deeds to wow people but to create relational faith and to turn flawed faith into vital, living faith, as we will soon see with Nicodemus. While many people come to believe in Jesus because of his miraculous signs, Jesus does not entrust himself to them because he knows what is in their hearts. He does not need their testimony about him (Jn 2:24-25), just like he doesn't need Nicodemus's testimony, as John 3 discloses.

Jesus connects with the Pharisee Nicodemus in just the right way, as we would expect from Jesus. Given that Nicodemus is a teacher of the law and leader among the Jewish people, Jesus appeals to the Scriptures. Yet Nicodemus does not expect Jesus to tell him he needs to be born again as an old man and by the Spirit rather than the flesh. Given that he is a distinguished religious teacher, we might not expect this message either and may instead presume that Nicodemus has insider status with God. But Jesus does not need Nicodemus's testimony or the affirmation of the ruling class. He knows what is in their hearts, and he knows that Nicodemus has flawed or distorted faith. Instead of entrusting himself to Nicodemus, Jesus calls on him to repent and believe. Jesus does not engage Nicodemus in order to wax eloquent on finer points of theology or biblical exegesis; instead, he challenges Nicodemus to read the ancient Scriptures anew and respond with a new heart of living faith in him (Jn 3:1-21).

Those who truly connect with Jesus—like John the Baptist—are able to rest securely in their position and place before Jesus. John the Baptist has no trouble confessing that Jesus is the Christ/Messiah, and that John must become less while Jesus becomes greater (Jn 3:27-30). The same is true of the apostle John. He testifies to the truthfulness of

Jesus' message, aligning himself with it and calling on us to accept God's good news as well (Jn 3:31-36). The only way we can find meaning and purpose in life is to accept Jesus as God's grace and truth in all their fullness.

At first, the Samaritan woman tries to hide from the truth. The truth of her life is painful to her, and Jesus' conversation only further exposes her shameful condition. But the revelation of Jesus' glorious love moves her beyond shame to the recognition that this Jesus who stands before her desires to quench her thirst for love, to redeem her life and to make her whole (Jn 4:1-26). By this point in the Gospel, we find that Jesus connects with all types, religious leaders and lowly women being but a few examples. In each situation, he seeks to draw them out from half-truths and lies and flawed faith so that they might find a living faith in his truth-filled and grace-filled embrace. Sometimes people—even his disciples—stand in the way of effective witness, missing opportunities to connect with those (like the Samaritan woman) who are outside their comfort zones; yet Jesus is patient with them and prepares them to make the most of opportunities that God will give them down the road (Jn 4:27-38). Sometimes Jesus uses people like the Samaritan woman to make the initial connection with their people groups, leading people to believe in him through such individuals' witness. But at some point, Jesus reveals himself directly to people, as he does to the Samaritan woman's village, when he spends an extended period of time with them (Jn 4:39-42). Sometimes Jesus even leads people into faith by sending them on their way accompanied only by a word of promise. This is how he connects with the royal official in John 4, in which he tells the man that he should depart for home, where he will find that his son is made whole (Jn 4:43-54).

Jesus connects with each person or group uniquely and distinctively. In each instance, Jesus is revealed as larger than life. How can it be otherwise when we are dealing with God in the flesh? The very Word through whom all things exist cannot be exhaustively fathomed, although we can engage him as the revealed mystery of God. As he connects with us, we should realize, along with John and Nathanael and the woman at the well, that this Jesus is God's Messiah and our salvation and life. Moreover, we should realize that our lives must be redirected so that we become true and authentic witnesses to others.

CELEBRITIES AND SAINTS
John 1:19-42

We all need heroes. Heroes call us to rise above mediocrity and live life to the full with courage and conviction. In our search for heroes as Christ-followers, though, we need to go in search of saints in a culture overcrowded with celebrities.

John the Baptist is a saint, although he could be a celebrity if he wanted to be. John is on a nationwide tour with his fire-and-brimstone message, and his debut album/book/movie *Highway to Hell (Original Version)* is at the top of the music and movie charts and book rankings. Leaders of the people all around him are asking him explicit or implicit questions like, "Are you the Christ?" "Are you Elijah?" "Are you the Prophet?" (Jn 1:20-22). Such questions show that John's star is rising, that he is awakening people's long-dormant hopes in the messianic fulfillment of the ages.[1]

But John "confessed freely, 'I am not the Christ'" (Jn 1:20). I don't know how free I would be to deny I'm the Messiah, even though it would be blatantly dishonest and ridiculously wrong to claim that I was. But I believe that on our bad hair days we all want to be God; most of us would be tempted to fudge the truth to get us at least halfway there.

Just think. If John would only claim—even for a few weeks— that he is the Messiah, he could make a killing branding and marketing his camel-hair clothing line with leather accessories and doing TV ads for the locust and wild honey food-product industry. Given a chance to score so big, John confesses more freely than many of us would.

Why does John confess so freely about Jesus, and why wouldn't many of us? One big reason is that John's parents raised him to believe that he is best suited to be number two, a forerunner to someone more important. Our culture, on the other hand, encourages us to believe that each one of us is number one.

Perhaps John's father Zechariah also told him the story of when he failed to believe the angel's word that he and his wife were to have a son;

as a result he had not been able to speak until he had put it in writing that his son's name would not be Zechariah, but John, just as the angel instructed. Only then was his father's tongue loosened, and he was free to speak (see Luke 1). John probably learned early on that if you want to speak freely, speak rightly what God tells you to say.

John speaks freely as a forerunner, pointing to Jesus with his forefinger and every fiber of his being. Above the Swiss theologian Karl Barth's writing desk hung Matthias Grünewald's (c.1475–1528) painting of the crucifixion. What struck Barth so deeply was the figure of John the Baptist who stands to one side, pointing at the crucified Jesus with a gnarly finger. Barth wanted his whole theology, including his *Church Dogmatics* (which is over six million words), to serve as a pointing forefinger—to Jesus. Are all of the six-million-plus words from our mouths serving as pointing forefingers to Jesus? What of our lives? Who are we pointing to—Jesus or ourselves?

A celebrity—cultural icon—is someone who points to himself or herself, not to Jesus. A saint is someone who points to Jesus through his or her life. This is true of John the Baptist: "I am the voice of one calling in the desert, 'Make straight the way for the Lord'" (Jn 1:23). John is but a voice, but what a voice! He is but a voice crying out in the Judean wilderness to prepare people for the Lord. Many within the religious and political establishment in Jerusalem—the center of power—will eventually do everything possible to oppose Jesus, pursuing their own dead-end destinies by seeking to destroy him.[2] How often do you and I do the same thing as these power brokers? May we listen to John—this voice crying out in the wilderness—and prepare the way not for ourselves, but for the Lord.

John's life and language are iconic. He points beyond himself and this world to the divine. Cultural icons are those who represent a distinctive cultural ethos and era. Given that our current era is defined by self-absorption, it is fitting that this age's cultural icons are so self-absorbed. Just look at the tabloids next time you are waiting in line at the grocery store. They're meant to absorb you as you stand there. I wonder what many shoppers are thinking (*If only that were me on the cover with . . .*)

The iconic representatives of ancient Christianity hardly resonate with the current cultural iconography of self-absorption. For one, many of the ancient iconic representatives such as Polycarp, or John the Baptist for that matter, reflect lives absorbed by redemptive suffering. Take Polycarp, for example. Polycarp was the apostle John's disciple and a great leader in the early church. His icon hangs above my desk in my office. Polycarp was martyred as an elderly man. Tradition tells us that when Polycarp stood before the Roman imperial magistrate, the ruler, out of sympathy for Polycarp's aged condition, pleaded with him to recant of his faith in Jesus. Polycarp's response haunts me: "Eighty and six years have I served him, and he hath done me no wrong; how then can I blaspheme my king who saved me?"[3] Today, by contrast, we often ask: "What has Jesus done for me lately (as in now)?"

Back to John. John the Baptist will later be executed because of his faithful witness to God. Herodius's daughter receives the imprisoned John's head on a platter for winning Herod's favor by dancing so beautifully before his dinner guests (Mt 14:1-12). What a way for a prophet to end his life—at a dinner party. But that's just how many other witnesses to Jesus would end their lives: literally serving as the lights of Emperor Nero's dinner parties as they were torched to death.

Such iconic witnesses represent well the Lord, whom the apostle John portrays as suffering horrific pain and shame during his passion and public execution. Those of us in the Western church who gain iconic status must ask ourselves which cultural era we represent: the "Christian" era of self-absorption or the Christian era absorbed by redemptive suffering? Whereas many emergent church leaders, like their boomer church counterparts before them, are treated as Christian celebrities in the States, their brothers and sisters across the globe face daily the threat of being treated like first-century saints.

So there is a crimson hue to the lives of iconic witnesses of the ancient church. So, too, there is a translucent quality to the ancient Christian version of the icon. When you look at icons of the Eastern church, it's as if you can see right through the figures to the kingdom that lies beyond. This is another reason they are called icons—they are windows into the divine. Today, by contrast, many icons or cultural celebrities have an opaque quality about them. They are self-referential; they are trying to gather as much attention as possible, through fame or even infamy in some cases.

The translucent, see-through quality noted above does not mean that we all look the same. John the Baptist and Jesus, though cousins, are very different from one another. While translucence does not suggest sameness, it does suggest that we are at our best when we are pointing beyond ourselves—in all our diversity and in all our differences—to Jesus.

This translucent quality to the iconic also suggests that icons are relational. To point beyond oneself to another is to be relational. Our greatest heroes in the church point beyond themselves to Jesus. At the same time, their regard for Jesus and the people far outweighs their own self-concern.

My greatest living hero is Dr. John M. Perkins, an African American evangelical Christian and civil rights leader nearly beaten to death in Mississippi in 1970 for his work defending the rights of poor blacks. He is the author of numerous books and an advisor to several U.S. presidents on matters of poverty and race.[4] From all accounts, Dr. Perkins is a celebrity. But he does not fit that label if we are thinking of self-absorption. As a living icon in the best Christian sense of that term, Dr. Perkins serves as an effective window to Jesus. It is worth noting that like John the Baptist before him, Dr. Perkins has lived outside centers of power and yet has shaped centers of power through his prophetic witness to the Lord. Along these lines, his regard for Jesus and Jesus' concern for the poor far outweighs his own sense of self-importance. I find that he points me in Jesus' direction and in the direction of those most in need.

This point was brought home to me one evening in 2007 in Portland, Oregon, when I was driving the now-elderly Dr. Perkins to a benefit dinner. He was to serve as the keynote speaker at the dinner, which was raising money for an inner-city community development ministry that brought jobs and housing to ex-offenders and youth. As we drove along—fittingly on a street called "Martin Luther King Jr. Boulevard"—I asked Dr. Perkins what it was like for him now in Mississippi. Dr. Perkins replied matter-of-factly, "I'm kind of a hero now in Mississippi. It seems that every time the state newspapers write something about reconciliation, they quote me. It's as if I created the word," he said with a laugh. There was a pause in the conversation. And then as he was looking out the window of the car, he went on to say something that will always stay with me: "But when I think about how many homes my fame has built for the poor in Mississippi, I realize that my fame hasn't built any homes for the poor. So I don't put no stock in my fame." There were no television or newspaper reporters in the car—just Dr. Perkins, his daughter Elizabeth and his young chauffeur (me). That young chauffeur almost lost control of the car. I rarely come across such a value system—in others or in my own heart.

The Christian celebrity leverages the gospel for her or his own benefit. The saint asks God to leverage his or her own life and "fame" for the gospel and for people. The celebrity wants to be famous. The saint wants to be influential so that others might meet Jesus. The celebrity will sacrifice others for his or her own ascension. The saint will sacrifice herself or himself for the benefit of Jesus' elevation and others' union with him—preparing the way for the Lord in their barren wilderness, especially among the least of these on the streets of Portland, Oregon; Jerusalem in Judea; and West Jackson, Mississippi.

Who is the greatest of all? Who is the Messiah? It's not John the Baptist. That's what makes John great. That's in part what makes him worthy of the term *icon*, traditionally conceived. He confesses freely that he is not the Christ—the Messiah—"the Man."[5] "'I baptize with water,' John replied, 'but among you stands one you do not know. He is the one who comes after me, the thongs of whose sandals I am not worthy to untie'" (Jn 1:26-27). John knows that Jesus is greater, for he remarks that Jesus is before him. (See Jn 1:30 where John says that "a man who comes after me has surpassed me because he was before me." I take this to be a claim to Jesus' pre-existence—see Jn 1:1, for John is slightly older than Jesus in terms of Jesus' earthly existence.) John also knows that Jesus is greater because the Spirit descends on Jesus, signifying that Jesus will baptize with the Spirit (whereas John only baptizes with water; see Jn 1:32-34). Moreover, John knows that Jesus is greater because Jesus alone takes away the sin of the world. Right after claiming that he is not worthy to untie the thongs of Jesus' sandals, the text tells us that John exclaims two days in a row that Jesus is the Lamb of God. He is the Lamb of God, who takes away the sins of the world: "The next day John saw Jesus coming toward him and said, 'Look, the Lamb of God, who takes away the sin of the world!'" (Jn 1:29). "The next day John was there again with two of his disciples. When he saw Jesus passing by, he said, 'Look, the Lamb of God!'" (Jn 1:35-36). As a result of John's witness, two of his own disciples follow Jesus. One of them is Andrew; Andrew in turn finds Simon (Peter) and brings him to Jesus (Jn 1:35-42). John knows that he runs ahead and prepares the way so that others will follow Jesus. He understands that he is number two, and that number one far surpasses him in importance and value. That's what makes John the Baptist so valuable to the kingdom.

Those who prepare the way are exceedingly rare. Unfortunately, what's not so rare today is the cult of celebrity inside and outside the church. We don't need any more dime-a-dozen celebrities. What we do need are saints who bow low to Jesus and prepare his way like John did. Will you also prepare the way?

STAIRWAY TO HEAVEN
John 1:43-51

I remember all the commotion about back-masking when I was a kid. People kept playing rock and roll albums backward, trying to find subliminal messages. It was rather startling and crazy. Two examples come to mind. "Turn me on, dead man" was supposedly back-masked into the Beatles' "Revolution #9," giving rise to the "Paul is dead" myth, and "My Sweet Satan" was supposedly back-masked into Led Zeppelin's "Stairway to Heaven."

Jesus alludes to the Genesis version of the stairway to heaven tune in this early episode in John's Gospel. In Genesis, Jacob has a dream of a ladder reaching to heaven with angels ascending and descending on it (Gen 28:10-22). John is preparing his readers for all that follows in his Gospel tale by including Jesus' allusion to this Old Testament text in his conversation with Nathanael.

Nathanael is amazed that Jesus is able to see him from a great distance—even before his friend Philip calls him. Jesus knows the kind of person he is, even before meeting Nathanael. Before introducing Nathanael to Jesus, Philip wonders out loud to his friend if Jesus of Nazareth might be the long-expected Messiah. Nathanael is deeply suspicious given Nazareth's bad reputation: "Nazareth! Can anything good come from there?" (Jn 1:46). But he soon learns not to judge a book by its cover —or a song by its title.

After Jesus tells him where Nathanael was, and the kind of person he is, Nathanael changes his tune about who Jesus is: "Rabbi, you are the Son of God; you are the King of Israel" (Jn 1:49).

Jesus responds: "'You believe because I told you I saw you under the fig tree. You shall see greater things than that.' He then added, 'I tell you the truth [a point of emphasis; when would Jesus ever tell a lie?], you shall see heaven open, and the angels of God ascending and descending on the Son of Man'" (Jn 1:50-51).

There's no back-masking going on here. Jesus is clearly claiming to be the ultimate Bethel—the place where we meet God. Angels will descend on him and ascend from him, just as they did while Jacob dreamed at Bethel. Jesus is the stairway to heaven. He is greater than Jacob and his ladder.

The same type of thing happens throughout John's Gospel. Some scholars call themes such as the stairway to heaven or bread of life or light of the world or good shepherd *replacement* or *fulfillment themes.* For example, just as Jesus is the ultimate Bethel, Jesus is the living water, greater than Jacob or his well (Jn 4:1-26). Jesus is the ultimate temple, greater than the temple in Jerusalem (Jn 2:18-22). Jesus is the true bread of heaven, greater than Moses or the bread he gave the people (Jn 6:1-59). Jesus is the true light, greater than the light of the feast of tabernacles (Jn 7:2; 8:12). Jesus is the good shepherd, so unlike the poor shepherds of Israel (Jn 10:1-30). Jesus is the true vine, unlike the bad vine of Israel (Jn 15:1-17).[6] Jesus sums up the Hebrew Scriptures in his person and work. His story encloses all of Israel's history—and all of human history for that matter, as the narrative of the eternal Word and Creator made human flesh. It is a microcosm of the whole. The entire Scriptures point to him and bear witness to Jesus taking up and transforming all of Israel's history. With the allusion to Jacob's ladder, John sends you this less-than-subliminal message right from the start of his Gospel.

While a suggestive writer, John never sends subliminal messages.

Subliminal messages pass below the radar of perception and consciousness, as in the case of back-masking. Sometimes they do so deceptively, operating contrary to the literal meaning conveyed to the listener or reader on the surface level. While John may reframe such themes as glory in view of the cross, he makes this point very clear. He doesn't hide his claims from you or place the most important items in small print. He doesn't send you cryptic messages covered by department store background music, trying to trick you into buying something that you didn't want. No. Although John commandeers such words as *glory*, undermining their ordinary meanings, his new meanings become clear to all in due course. The contrast is displayed in the light of day for all to see, not hidden below the surface in dark shadows.

John's use of metaphor is multifaceted and suggestive, and it brings to mind an almost infinite host of biblical allusions wrapped up in Jesus of Nazareth. Another writer named John made profound use of biblical imagery in his novels, such as *East of Eden* and *Cannery Row*. Like John the apostle, John Steinbeck had no use for subliminal messages and was a master at conjuring up the powers of suggestion. Just as the apostle sees the whole of Israel's history—indeed the world's history—through the story of Jesus, Steinbeck sees his stories set in Salinas and Monterey, California, as microcosmic displays of the cosmic drama.

I've been to Salinas. There's nothing really special about it. In fact, Salinas comes to mind whenever I think of Nathanael's words: "Can anything good come from . . . ?" Salinas has seen better days. My family and I lodged there a few summers ago when we visited the region. All the reasonably priced places in or near Monterey were booked, so we had to stay in Salinas. The one bright spot for me was the Steinbeck museum. As we viewed the displays in the museum, Steinbeck's stories came to life. And his stories brought life to Salinas. His tales gave us a taste of the transcendent as we climbed the stairway of Steinbeck's imagination.

Can anything good come from Salinas? Yes: Steinbeck and his cosmic dramas that take place in that seemingly godforsaken town. "Can anything good come from Nazareth"—another seemingly godforsaken town? Certainly: Jesus of Nazareth, the lead character in God's epic story. Jesus transcends Nazareth. He transcends Jacob and Adam in

Genesis, and he transcends Adam Trask in *East of Eden*: "You shall see heaven open, and the angels of God ascending and descending on the Son of Man" (Jn 1:51).

There is nothing subliminal in John's message, but everything about it is filled with the power of suggestion. In Steinbeck's works, Salinas is a major player on the world stage. Because of Jesus, Nazareth, Bethlehem, Bethany and Cana of Galilee are world-class towns in John's Gospel, outclassing and rivaling the greatest cities. And when your story becomes a part of his story, when you see yourself as one of the characters who appear in the script of his grand production, your faded-glory hometown and even your jaded personal history there—like my hometown of Elgin, Illinois, and my life growing up there—take on cosmic and epic proportions, with a touch of the transcendent.

There's nothing subliminal about this Gospel. But there is so much here that is suggestive of something greater than you have ever experienced. Don't judge the Gospel of John by its simple prose. Don't judge "Stairway to Heaven" by its title, and don't judge Jesus by his home town of Nazareth. Judge everything in terms of its relation to him. To those of you who are present-day Nathanaels, there is more here than meets the eye as you climb the ladder of John's imagination and as you meet Jesus, who is the place where we meet God—Bethel, the true stairway to heaven.

SAVING THE BEST FOR LAST
John 2:1-12

Not every day with Jesus is like a party, as the temple scene that follows this account in John 2 makes clear. But Jesus does know how to have a good time. He can really party. Here, in this text, we find Jesus with his mother and his followers at a wedding in Cana in Galilee. They're having a good time—that is, until the wine runs out. The caterers thought they had planned for everything, but they miscalculated how much people would drink (there was nothing holding the guests back, since there were no laws on drinking while riding donkeys). Running out of wine at their wedding? Not a good symbolic start to the new couple's lifetime of marriage: that is, the best is already past.

Mary knows how bad things can go in planning and performing a wedding. While there may not have been any first-century bridezillas, and while Mary's society didn't spend forty to seventy billion dollars a year on the wedding industry, people could still lose their cool and their honor and their fortunes on wedding day. No matter how hard Mary and others try, there's no guarantee that wedding planners can avoid unexpected dilemmas and disasters.

No matter how hard Mary had tried, there was no way she could cover her bulging midsection on her own wedding day many years earlier. Maybe that's why Mary sympathizes with the bride and groom in their present dilemma and comes to their rescue: she calls on Jesus.

Jesus doesn't seem so concerned at first about the bride and groom's little problem. In fact, he seems to regret his mother asking him to intervene and help them out of this crisis. While I believe there is affection in their exchange, I also believe Jesus mildly rebukes his mother. I believe Jesus seeks to create some space between his mother and himself: he wants Mary to understand that his mission in life is much larger than responding to her request to perform a miracle. (Even with this in mind, I would not recommend giving a Mother's Day sermon based on this passage.) So Jesus says: "Dear woman, why do you involve me? . . . My time has not yet come" (Jn 2:4).[7]

In my desire to be "biblical" in all my responses, I've used this line in responding to my wife when she has asked me to take out the garbage. I wish my wife were as "biblical" as me. She usually misquotes Mary's response of "Do whatever he tells you" (Jn 2:5) to "Do whatever *I* tell you"!

Even though Jesus' statement does not work for me, and even though Jesus rebukes his mother, Mary still has confidence that Jesus will help the wedding party get out of this embarrassing situation. For whatever reason and regardless of how he responds to his mother, Jesus moves into action. He tells the caterers to fill six large jars with water. They do exactly what he says, just as Mary instructs them. Seemingly out of context, John introduces the reader to a few facts about the jars; to some this information might appear to have no other value than as potential answers to Trivial Pursuit questions. These six stone water jars were "the kind used by the Jews for ceremonial washing, each holding from twenty to thirty gallons" (Jn 2:6). We will see soon enough that this information is likely far from trivial—and not just because these jugs were far bigger than most kegs!

Some of the catering team may be getting nervous that Jesus is going to get spiritual on them and perform some religious rituals with these ceremonial cleansing jars instead of dealing with their problem. They have no time for such nonsense. Yet they follow Jesus' instructions anyway. What choice do they have? They have no other options. But they really have nothing to fear. Jesus does more than meet their expectations on this occasion; not only does he turn the water into wine, but he also makes the best wine imaginable. Jesus tells the servants to have the master of ceremonies drink from one of the jars, which he does. Here's his response:

> The master of the banquet tasted the water that had been turned into wine. He did not realize where it had come from, though the servants who had drawn the water knew. Then he called the bridegroom aside and said, "Everyone brings out the choice wine first and then the cheaper wine after the guests have had too much to drink; but you have saved the best till now." (Jn 2:9-10)

Saving the best for last. And here the bride and groom were thinking the best is already past. Not only does Jesus save the day; he also saves their marriage!

Sometimes you may doubt that Jesus has your best saved up for last. Certainly, John himself would have given up on life before writing his Gospel if he thought that the life he was living was as good as it would ever get. But John knows that just as Jesus saved the best wine for last at the wedding in Cana in Galilee, Jesus will save the best wine for last for John and the rest of us; so, save the date for the marriage supper of the Lamb. With this in mind, the six ceremonial jars filled to the brim with water (Jn 2:6-7) and turned into wine that is far better than what had run out in Cana may very well foreshadow the marriage supper of the Lamb, of which John writes in his last book—Revelation.[8] If true to John's intent, this wine serves as a glorious foretaste of what's to come.

Regardless of what is to be made of the marriage supper of the Lamb, we do get a glimpse of Jesus' glory in this account, even though his hour of glory has not yet come (look ahead to "Fifteen Minutes of Fame and the Hour of Glory" for a discussion of this theme). But Jesus is not some glory-monger. He's not some miracle worker out to impress people. He performs miracles in our midst so that we come to believe in him, not so that we sign him up for *American Idol* or enthrone him in centers of power here below. With this in mind, I love what Andreas Köstenberger says about this text: "It surely is significant that this revelation of God's glory in Jesus consists not in a spectacular display of power, but in a quiet, behind-the-scenes work that remained largely unnoticed and impacted only a select few . . . It is in Jesus' humanity that God's glory is revealed."[9] Again, Jesus performs the first of his miraculous signs so that people might believe in him and not to gain fame or centers of power: "This, the first of his miraculous signs, Jesus performed in Cana of Galilee. He thus revealed his glory, and his disciples put their faith in him" (Jn 2:11).[10]

This verse gets at the heart of John's Gospel—which is to get to your heart. As John says near the end of the book, "Jesus did many other miraculous signs in the presence of his disciples, which are not recorded in this book. But these are written that you may believe that Jesus is the Christ, the Son of God, and that by believing you may have life in his name" (Jn 20:30-31). John carefully picks and chooses from among Jesus' miraculous deeds.[11] He's not trying to put on a show but to show you who Jesus is so that you might believe and have life in him—just like John and the other disciples who put their faith in Jesus at the wedding in Cana so long ago.

As we look back to this event and as we look forward, we see that this wedding in Cana is not to be relegated to the pages of remote history. For one, there's no aftertaste to the best wine that they drink there. Rather, as already noted, this wedding likely serves as a foretaste of the approaching marriage supper of the Lamb. Life as we know it—where we drink cheap wine and it always runs out—is not as good as it will get. Jesus always saves the best wine for last. I'll drink to that. Will you join me?

TRINKET SHOP
John 2:13-25

Jesus makes connections with people in different ways. For one, he doesn't always affirm our cultural practices. Although he protects the ceremonial integrity of the wedding in Cana of Galilee and safeguards the master of the banquet and wedding party from a humiliating scene (Jn 2:1-12), in the temple in Jerusalem he makes a scene and confronts what has become accepted ceremonial practice in the commerce surrounding temple worship. Here we find the religious establishment creating space for merchants to sell their ceremonial goods in the temple area, trivializing the temple. Jesus won't put up with it.[12] So we find Jesus going from being the life of the party at the wedding in Cana of Galilee to being the one who crashes the party in the temple in Jerusalem—and all within the space of a few verses!

The notion of Jesus overturning tables at the temple is hard to categorize, and it challenges our domesticating agenda for Jesus. We often forget that we cannot commodify Jesus, even though we unwittingly tend to trivialize and "trinket-ize" him in our minds and practices, turning him into our very own genie in a bottle, good luck charm or bobble-headed doll that we can purchase at the local Christian bookstore. We fall prey to this way of thinking and behaving because we become complacent in our spirituality, consuming and commodifying everything religious for our convenience.

We make Jesus fit our expectations and prepackage him so that we can consume him whenever we like. If we had been with Jesus in the temple courts (Jn 2), we would never have allowed him to act in such an uncivil, uncultured, unpredictable and inconvenient manner, messing with our messianic plans for him—and us. But like his disciples, we really have no choice in the matter. You *can't* commodify and prepackage Jesus. In fact, you can never package him.

The disciples have no way of knowing that the temple cleansing recorded in John 2 is coming. But it wouldn't matter if they do. The same Jesus who doesn't celebrate Mother's Day to our liking (Jn 2:4: "'Dear woman, why do you involve me?' Jesus replied, 'My time has not yet come'") messes with our religious rituals and customs.

When it was almost time for the Jewish Passover, Jesus went up to Jerusalem. In the temple courts he found men selling cattle, sheep and doves, and others sitting at tables exchanging money. So he made a whip out of cords, and drove all from the temple area, both sheep and cattle; he scattered the coins of the money changers and overturned their tables. To those who sold doves he said, "Get these out of here! How dare you turn my Father's house into a market!" (Jn 2:13-16)

From everything that we have seen so far of Jesus in John's Gospel, we would never have known that he could act in such a manner. In the case of the wedding in Cana, at least he honors his mother's request and changes the water into wine. But here there's no compromise. He doesn't ask the money changers to lower their prices. He doesn't ask them to move their tables to the back. According to Mark's Gospel, he won't even let people carry merchandise through the temple courts (Mk 11:16). While John's Gospel tells us that Jesus is angry because they have turned his Father's house into a market (Jn 2:16), Mark's Gospel comments that Jesus is also angry because they have turned God's house of prayer for the nations into a den of robbers: "And as he taught them, he said, 'Is it not written: "My house will be called a house of prayer for all nations'? But you have made it 'a den of robbers'" (Mk 11:17).

I wonder what Jesus would do if he were to walk through our church doors some Sunday morning and see our coffee bars with the sweetly flavored lattes, the merchandise we sell in our church stands and the clothes we wear there. And what would we do to him if he were to start "moving furniture" around and cracking the whip? In John 2, the religious leaders question Jesus, wanting to know what gives him the right to mess with their church growth strategies (Jn 2:18). Mark tells us that they go so far as to begin plotting Jesus' death because they fear him (Mk 11:18). Already in John's Gospel, even in chapter 2, we sense indications of the conflict that will ensue and the reactions and rejection that will follow later.

Jesus' followers make the connection between Jesus' actions and the psalmist's words: "Zeal for your house will consume me" (Jn 2:17, quoting Ps 69:9). Jesus can put up with a lot, but he won't tolerate us making light of his Father's house of prayer for the nations. His zeal for his Father's house literally consumes—physically kills—him.

There are various ways in which we hinder worship of God today among "the nations." It kills me when the designer jeans and party dresses we wear to church keep people without those things from stepping inside our church doors and worshiping God. This reminds me of a story a friend of mine once told me. He invited a woman from the neighborhood in which he lived to visit his neighborhood church with him. After several attempts, she finally agreed to go. It's important to note that the church building was in an inner-city neighborhood; other than my friend, the people who attended the church did not live in the community. Many of them used to live in the community, but they moved out when the neighborhood became run-down. Still, the members made the trip every Sunday morning to worship there. These churchgoers had no vital connection with the community surrounding their church building, and their Sunday morning dress demonstrated that they were of a different class. As a result, it made it nearly impossible for my friend to bring anyone from the neighborhood with him to church. Case in point: when my friend went to pick up the woman who lived in his neighborhood to go to church with him, he had to wait for some time as she desperately tried to make herself presentable. She finally appeared in a dress, but it didn't fit her. My friend could tell that she was filled with extreme apprehension, anxiously trying to meet the church's unspoken dress code and social expectations. She never attended the church with him again.

Have we turned what are supposed to be houses of prayer for the nations into dens of robbers and markets? Maybe it's not our dress codes or our coffee bars or our trinket shops. Maybe the real robbery goes on deep inside our hearts: zeal for Jesus' Father's house often gives way to other things consuming or killing us spiritually, such as spiritual complacency. I rob God—and the church—and myself—every time I go to church to go through the religious motions rather than to meet God.

My guilt along these lines became painfully obvious to me not long ago when I stood near the communion table and could barely concentrate on the song being sung up front. Distractions over little things rather than delightful desperation in the presence of an all-consuming, holy, loving God was the problem with me. The man two rows in front of me to the right—directly by the communion table—was disheveled in body, clothes and spirit. Though he didn't appear to have much to offer at the table or in the offering plate, his widow's mite of merit far outweighed my value on the scales of spirituality. He knew something of God's severe mercy and grace. God's holy love undid him, while I stood back—detached—in my formality and complacency. His experience of God was a beautiful thing to experience. This disheveled man's spiritual state of being led me to evaluate my spiritual estate then and there and every week since then.

I may not buy indulgences, and I may not indulge myself on a free-market consumer spirituality in which I carry Jesus around as a genie in a bottle or put him around my neck like a good luck charm. But do I put my whole body and soul into worship and in the offering plate when it comes around? What will I do when Jesus comes around next time?

Unlike the temple, Jesus comes around. While it is stationary, he is constantly moving. No matter how hard we try, we cannot control him. He is the ultimate temple, the place where we ultimately meet to worship God. The Jewish leaders ("the Jews") miss this point, and so they question Jesus:

> Then the Jews demanded of him, "What miraculous sign can you show us to prove your authority to do all this?"
>
> Jesus answered them, "Destroy this temple, and I will raise it again in three days."
>
> The Jews replied, "It has taken forty-six years to build this temple, and you are going to raise it in three days?" But the temple he had spoken of was his body. After he was raised from the dead, his disciples recalled what he had said. Then they believed the Scripture and the words that Jesus had spoken. (Jn 2:18-22)

In contrast to these authorities, Jesus' disciples go deeper into faith through recounting this incident and Jesus' words after Jesus is raised from the dead. In the meantime, at this first Passover feast recounted in John's Gospel, many people believe in Jesus' name. I don't think the people here comprehend that Jesus is the ultimate temple where we worship God or that he will be the ultimate Passover Lamb who will take away our sins. But they do know he is special because of all his miraculous signs, and so they believe in his name: "Now while he was in Jerusalem at the Passover Feast, many people saw the miraculous signs he was doing and believed in his name" (Jn 2:23).[13]

Who knows how deep or sure their faith is? Only Jesus knows. He knows how flawed human faith is, and so he does not entrust himself to them: "But Jesus would not entrust himself to them, for he knew all men. He did not need man's testimony about man, for he knew what was in a man" (Jn 2:24-25). Jesus doesn't need their testimony; he knows them—and us—inside out (Jn 2:24-25). Unlike the religious leaders who question him because of their customs and the people in the crowds who believe in him because of his external signs, Jesus sees inside. He seeks people after God's own heart and, as the law's fulfillment, is concerned for the spirit of the law rather than the trappings of the law.

As the ultimate temple of God enfleshed and as the Passover Lamb raised from the dead, Jesus cannot be commodified. I'm counting on it—not in some accounting way, where I make a profit from Jesus or buy him at the cheapest price. But I'm counting on him in his severe mercy and grace to change my heart. This is the most costly exchange of all. I'm counting on him to overturn the tables of my soul and consume me with his holy love. What about you?

MY OWN PERSONAL JESUS
John 3:1-21

You may know the song "Personal Jesus." There are three famous versions of it—one by Depeche Mode, another by Marilyn Manson and the third by Johnny Cash. I'm not quite sure what the intent of the first two versions of the song are—perhaps mockery of Jesus and the church. Depeche Mode may have been after a secular ethic, which would entail putting the sacred to death. It is quite possible that Marilyn Manson, in person and in song, has sought to provide a cultural critique of "churchianity" for presenting an artificial Jesus who exists to give us whatever we want, and I mean *whatever*. Where did that idea of personal Jesus come from?

Neo, one of the characters in a recent book, says that the definition of "saved" has been "shrunken and freeze-dried by modernity," and reduced to "personal savior" talk. Neo calls for

> a postmodern consideration of what salvation means, something beyond an individualized and consumeristic version. I may have a personal home, personal car, personal computer, personal identification number, personal digital assistant, personal hot-tub—all I need now is personal salvation from my own personal savior . . . this all strikes me as Christianity diced through the modern Veg-o-matic.[14]

Whether or not a postmodern consideration will help us get beyond this problem, we do need to move beyond the individualized and consumeristic version of faith so prevalent today. But that does not mean we need to move beyond a personal Jesus—just a plastic one. Let's not throw out the baby with the bathwater.

This leads us to John 3—the ultimate passage from the Bible on the need to have a personal relationship with God through Jesus Christ. Here Jesus tells Nicodemus, a religious leader and member of the Jewish ruling council (Jn 3:1), that he needs to be born again—to become a spiritual newborn baby: "I tell you the truth, no one can see the kingdom of God unless he is born again" (Jn 3:3).

Jesus gets personal with Nicodemus—very personal. Jesus knows what's in Nicodemus's heart, just like he knows what's in everyone's heart, and so does not need human testimony about people (Jn 2:24-25). Jesus knows that Nicodemus has been playing the religion game way too long and that he has flawed faith based on the traditions and testimonies of his old boys' club (the Jewish ruling council) rather than true faith based on God's Word and the Spirit. That's why Jesus responds to Nicodemus in the way he does—up front and directly. As Jesus connects with Nicodemus, he is not scorning him, but he is seeking to crack his hard heart bound up with the pride of his position and the praises of his peers.[15] There's no time to waste; Nicodemus is experiencing hardening of the arteries.

Although it's a good thing to develop thick skin, it's bad when it leads to a hard heart. Years of religion can do that to you, you know? I know. I teach this stuff for a living. And when you make your living off of religion like I do, you can easily move from being a Christ-follower who happens to have a religious profession to being a religious professional who happens to be a Christ-follower. (I like my personal Jesus, but not when he gets too personal. It's then that I wish he were plastic.) You start objectifying and sterilizing spirituality, turning its "I-Thou" questioning of you into third-person description intended for someone else and rhetorical questions that no one need answer. Instead of seeing yourself as being read by the Bible, you stand over the Bible as judge, jury and hang man. Instead of being mastered by divinity daily in the trenches, gutters and dark alleys of life, you put master of divinity (M.Div.) and pile-it-high-and-deep (Ph.D.) degrees on off-white walls in sterile offices. I face this danger daily in my heart. We're talking about degrees all right—third-degree burns that destroy our relational nerve endings, making it impossible for us to feel God's touch. We need new flesh, a new heart, a new birth.

The new birth entails being born of water and the Spirit, not simply having a facelift or making New Year resolutions to be a better person. Flesh only gives birth to flesh, not spiritual realities. Jesus is talking about a total makeover involving dying and being born again from above. Jesus challenges Nicodemus for not understanding these things, for Jesus is drawing from the Hebrew Scriptures, in particular Ezekiel 36, which speaks of being cleansed by water and the Spirit (Jn 3:5-12; see Ezek 36:25-27).

Nicodemus clings to his peer group's assessment of all things spiritual, and he invites Jesus to become a member of his old boys' club, but Jesus will have nothing to do with it. It's as if Jesus is saying to Nicodemus, "No thank you. I don't need your affirmation, or the affirmation of your old boys' network. I know what's in your hearts (Jn 2:24-25). Besides, you don't know what you are talking about. Search the Scriptures and you will see that you must start over, being born from above and from the inside out. The only affirmation I need is that of my Father." As a result of Nicodemus's appeal to the affirmation of the Jewish ruling council in the dark secrecy of the night (Jn 3:2), Jesus calls for the truth he has received from his Father to be proclaimed in broad daylight: "I tell you the truth, we speak of what we know, and we testify to what we have seen, but still you people do not accept our testimony" (Jn 3:11). They only accept the testimony of one another, signifying their flawed faith and need for new birth.

A new birth is not like a new car or new home or new personal digital assistant or initiation into an elite society made up of one's noblest peers. It means death to self—like Jesus hanging from a tree. It signifies new life with God—moving from flawed to vital faith that comes from above as the Spirit descends upon us. John 3 involves life in the Spirit and death to our autonomous ways as we cling by faith to the crucified Jesus. We often fail to connect Jesus' call to Nicodemus in John 3 about the need to be born from above with Jesus hanging from a tree above our heads later in the same text. But it's there: "Just as Moses lifted up the snake in the desert, so the Son of Man must be lifted up, that everyone who believes in him may have eternal life" (Jn 3:14-15). We have to abandon our autonomous ways and dependence on our peers for approval. Instead, we must throw ourselves completely on Jesus, just as the Israelites threw themselves on the mercies of God when bitten by poisonous snakes; only by looking to the bronze serpent hanging on the pole God had Moses make would they be saved.

In order for you and me to be reborn, Jesus has to die—to be lifted up on the tree, the cross of wood. Moreover, we all have to die with him to be reborn. Someone may say at this point, "I thought we were talking about newborn babies. What does that have to do with death and dying?" Everything. Life and death always go together. It's part of the circle of life. And besides, I even have the old lullaby "Rock-a-Bye-Baby" on my side—with babies, the danger of death and trees and wind blowing, just like in John 3. The only thing missing is an old man:

> Rock-a-bye baby, in the treetop,
> When the wind blows, the cradle will rock,
> When the bough breaks, the cradle will fall,
> And down will come baby, cradle and all.

Death has everything to do with the new birth, since new birth is not like repackaging. The new birth is a totally new start, a complete transformation. Through death with Jesus and through life in the Spirit, we are born again.

Maybe the song "Personal Jesus" functioned like a lullaby for Johnny Cash. Cash remade that song. Perhaps it had something to do with Cash being reborn, when he felt God gave him a new lease on life after he nearly died from drugs, booze and broken relationships. Unlike the "churchian" Jesus that Marilyn Manson may be critiquing, this version of "Personal Jesus" sounds very personal and life-giving. Unlike the consumerized, sterilized and artificial Jesus of "churchianity," Cash's Jesus isn't plastic, for he knew what it meant to desperately depend on this personal Jesus to get him out of the mess he had made of his personal life. Someone I know well who met Cash said that he appeared very fragile, though in a good way. Perhaps he was even like a little child or baby when it comes to faith. Despite his tough-guy exterior, Cash knew the depths of his brokenness and how dependent he was on God to save him. Maybe that's why he places such emphasis on the final words to "Personal Jesus": "Reach out and touch faith." Cash knew the depths of his redemption.[16]

Don't throw out the newborn-baby or personal-relationship Jesus with the bathwater. Cash didn't. Nor did my wife, who is a native of Japan. I remember talking to her at length about how seldom we think of cosmic redemption—the fact that redemption is more than personal. Although she's all for talk about Jesus redeeming structures and the cosmos, she told me that I shouldn't throw out the baby with the bathwater. While redemption is more than personal, it's not less than personal. You see, my wife is the only Christ-follower in her clan. When she heard the good news in Tokyo many years ago—that there is a personal God who loves her and wants to have a relationship with her, not an impersonal force—it made all the difference in the world to her. It makes all the difference to her now. What about you?

Just as Jesus told Nicodemus that night that he needed to be born again, today he is saying the same thing to all of us. You don't need to be an old man to struggle with this idea that we have to be born again and become like little children to enter the kingdom of God. You can be young and feel really old. I was talking about this theme in class one day at the seminary where I teach. A very precious and genuinely transparent young man said in front of the whole class, "I don't know how to become a little child. I don't know what that's like because I was never allowed to be one." This is a common occurrence among young people. But why?

Many kids today find out about adult sex way too early in life because they've been molested by a parent, foster parent or another adult. They have to learn how to survive emotionally and in so many other ways, because they've never really had a father or a mother to carry and hold them. Some parents push their kids so hard to become sports superstars or concert violinists or rocket scientists that their kids don't have the opportunity to just be kids. And here's the paradox: people who were never allowed to be children are never able to grow up. They have a hard time committing to things and always feel stressed out and tempted to quit, because they've seen their parents or other caregivers quit on them throughout their lives when the going gets tough. They're forced to parent themselves and so find it difficult to relate to others in a mature fashion. Because they have not understood the sacred significance of entering into and staying in meaningful relationships, they have a hard time with boundaries and stepping inside and outside relational safety zones. MySpace is your space, and your space is my space, and we wander from chat room to chat room, chattering away but rarely getting deep.

Jesus enters our space. He sits down to talk with us face to face, never as a pop psychotherapist or as the town gossip. He's never chatty. Maybe he lived in a chatty culture, however, just like ours. Maybe that's why he always said for emphasis, "I tell you the truth," making sure people knew he meant what he said. Jesus enjoys hanging out, but he's not one for surface talk: "*I tell you the truth,* no one can see the kingdom of God unless he is born again" (Jn 3:3; italics added). Jesus is the soul's physician. He's got a great bedside manner for a doctor, but he won't beat around the bush and avoid telling you the hard truths—"You're going to die. You need to be born again."

The great thing about this doctor is that he doesn't leave the room as soon as he drops the bomb. He stays with you. In fact, he begins open heart surgery right then and there—if you let him. In fact, he gives you his heart. In fact, he gives you his Father, and his Father gives his one and only son for you. Jesus knows what it's like to be a kid, to be a son. He didn't have to grow up too soon, so he can help you become a child. He knows what that's like. Would you like to know what that's like?

Jesus tells us that we need to be born again, to become like little children, to enter the kingdom of God through faith in Jesus by the Spirit. Little children trust. They reach out and touch faith when they know that they are loved. When I grow up, I want to become a little child. I can become a little child because there is a heavenly Father who loves me so much that he gave his one and only Son for me. It's not as if God's Son goes grudgingly to death to give me life. He and the Father give sacrificially of themselves together: the Father gives himself by giving up his one and only Son, and the Son gives himself. They act in this way freely, willingly and communally. They do this for you and me, and for everyone else. As God's Son, Jesus, says to Nicodemus, so he says to us today: "For God so loved the world that he gave his one and only Son, that whoever believes in him shall not perish but have eternal life" (Jn 3:16). Such interpersonal truth is so affirming and securing for all of us whose hearts have been penetrated by this love. My student who opened up his personal life in that seminary class is on his way to knowing Cash's version of the personal Jesus, because he's coming to grips with being gripped by this same Father's and this same Son's love—a love that will never let him go. He's on his way to becoming a little child as he goes on his way to a Master of Divinity degree and to becoming a spiritual leader. He is being mastered by the divine Father's love and by God's firstborn Son's love. Sometimes we need to be told it's okay to be a little child: to laugh and cry, and to want to be held and to die to our adult selves and be born again. Reach out like a little child and touch faith.

ROCK STAR
John 3:22-36

Have you ever wanted to be a rock star, perhaps even bigger than the king of rock-and-roll?

I remember watching the *Elvis* movie in which Kurt Douglas plays Elvis. The king of rock-and-roll had been out of commission and was now returning to the big stage. He was hearing reports, however, that the

Beatles' fame was eclipsing his own. The king of rock-and-roll couldn't bear the news—after all, he was the king. Elvis could have taken comfort from the fact that, according to John Lennon, the Beatles had also become more popular than *the* King—Jesus—by 1966. So Elvis was in good company. Roll back to Jesus' heyday—back around A.D. 30. Jesus' star is rising, whereas John the Baptist's star is setting fast. Before Jesus appears on the scene, John is the hottest ticket in town, but not anymore. Put yourself in John's shoes—or sandals. Here you are—the king of dunk-and-up baptisms—and your followers bring you reports that everyone is turning to Jesus. Jesus' disciples are actually baptizing more people than you are (Jn 3:26; 4:2). No doubt, John's own followers are entertaining thoughts about joining Jesus' bandwagon. John and his group are no longer the main attraction; they are the backup band.

What do you think John the Baptist's response would be? Anger? Envy and jealousy? Think again. Here it is:

> To this John replied, "A man can receive only what is given him from heaven. You yourselves can testify that I said, 'I am not the Christ but am sent ahead of him.' The bride belongs to the bridegroom. The friend who attends the bridegroom waits and listens for him, and is full of joy when he hears the bridegroom's voice. That joy is mine, and it is now complete. He must become greater; I must become less." (Jn 3:27-30)

As he looks across the universe, John the Baptist knows his place in the big scheme of things. His feet are firmly planted on the ground: "A man can receive only what is given him from heaven" (Jn 3:27). Talk about perspective. John does not try to climb to the stars, seize heaven's throne or take matters into his own hands; he receives everything he has, including his station in life, from God. John does not have a Messiah complex. He reiterates to his followers what he has already told them: he is a forerunner for the Christ, not the king himself. He is the friend of the bridegroom, not the bridegroom himself.

Could you imagine the best man at a wedding standing in the center of the aisle, winking and waving to those gathered for the wedding and not allowing the bridegroom to take his place up front where he belongs?

Could you imagine a forerunner refusing to relay the message that the king is coming, proclaiming instead that the king has arrived and that he is it?

In subtle and not-so-subtle ways, we all struggle to be satisfied with being forerunners and friends of the bridegroom. Each of us in our own way wants to be the Messiah, the king, the bridegroom. We want to be number one. We want to be God. We may not want praise choruses sung to us; that would feel too strange. But each of us has a hard time putting Jesus' will ahead of our own. That's what makes John the Baptist's response so special. The response is all the more special because John actually delights in these roles; it's not that he has just resigned himself to the fact that he is a forerunner and friend. "The friend who attends the bridegroom waits and listens for him, and is full of joy when he hears the bridegroom's voice. That joy is mine, and it is now complete" (Jn 3:29).

John may not have always felt this way. Maybe when he and Jesus played together as boys, John wanted to be number one. As the older cousin, John was probably a bit stronger and faster. John likely got the upper hand in all their contests and won all the races (maybe that's why he was well-suited for being a forerunner—he always got there first). It's harder for the older one to give pride of place to the younger in most families; it may have been hard for John growing up. But John had parents—Zechariah and Elizabeth—who did not teach him that he was number one. As stated in "Celebrities and Saints" (Jn 1:19-42), John's parents taught him that he was number two. (What a marked difference from many parents today!)

Each of us is number two—at best. We need to think like John: "He must become greater; I must become less" (Jn 3:30). John's joy is made complete when the news reaches him that Jesus has taken center stage at the main event. But how do we get there? How do we find our joy in becoming less so that Jesus becomes more?

There is no easy answer. It's a daily question requiring a daily dying; but it's a daily dying whose answer is a daily living. Each of us has a part to play. Each of us is a forerunner. Each of us is the bridegroom's friend. Each of us is on stage with Jesus, playing in the band. We participate in his story, and I would rather add to it than detract from it. In my best moments, I would rather play my part in harmony than distort the sound.

I would rather shine the spotlight on Jesus than on myself, because he sings and plays so much better than I do. On my best days, I find my joy in playing backup for him, for he makes my joy complete. He truly is the main attraction. Jesus must become greater and I must become less. That's reality. But what is not necessarily reality is that I will perform my backup part well on stage today or tomorrow. Will I try to take over lead vocals or play the guitar solo? Will I be a thick and ordinary disciple, or an extraordinary one who becomes less so that Jesus can become more?

On March 4, 1966, John Lennon said in an interview with reporter Maureen Cleave in the *London Evening Standard*:

Christianity will go. . . . It will vanish and shrink. I needn't argue about that; I'm right and I will be proved right. We're more popular than Jesus now; I don't know which will go first—rock 'n' roll or Christianity. Jesus was all right but his disciples were thick and ordinary. It's them twisting it that ruins it for me.[17]

Many Christians took shots at Lennon after this interview was published. But many of them missed the point. Lennon was simply speaking of what he observed to be true: the Beatles were exceptionally popular (whether they should have been or not), and many of Jesus' disciples were thick and ordinary and had "ruined it" for people. While Jesus is doing just fine today—more than all right and bigger than the Beatles— something also needs to be said in defense of Lennon. As disciples, we are often thick and ordinary. Ordinary Jesus-followers try to make themselves greater and Jesus less. Now how thick is that, given that we're but forerunners and the bridegroom's friends? Thick and ordinary disciples cloud people's perceptions of Jesus when they refuse to "vanish and shrink," ruining it for people who would want to know Jesus. Extraordinary followers and forerunners like John the Baptist make the Christian faith reappear and grow. The latter bear clear witness to Jesus, magnifying him so that others can truly come to know him.

People like John the Baptist realize that Jesus must become greater and they must become less, for Jesus is from above and speaks the word of God through the Spirit without limitation and has received everything from God (Jn 3:30-36). In contrast, John the Baptist, John Lennon and I are from below. John 3 closes with words along these lines:

> The one who comes from above is above all; the one who is from the earth belongs to the earth, and speaks as one from the earth. The one who comes from heaven is above all. He testifies to what he has seen and heard, but no one accepts his testimony. The man who has accepted it has certified that God is truthful. For the one whom God has sent speaks the words of God, for God gives the Spirit without limit. The Father loves the Son and has placed everything in his hands. Whoever believes in the Son has eternal life, but whoever rejects the Son will not see life, for God's wrath remains on him. (Jn 3:31-36)

I want to accept Jesus' testimony, for he is from above and is above all, rather than accept the testimony of those from below who speak from below (Jn 3:31). I want to accept Jesus' word inspired by the Spirit (Jn 3:34), rather than accept the words of those who speak from the spirit of the age. I want to accept everything that Jesus says because he receives everything from the Father (Jn 3:35), rather than accept what the father of lies says (Jn 8:44). I want to certify with my words and life that God is truthful (Jn 3:32-33), and to vanish and shrink so that Jesus can become greater in my life (Jn 3:30).

I want to make it my life's ambition to prove John Lennon wrong, but in part by proving him right. To prove Lennon wrong, I—and Christians across the world—must become less, so that Jesus might become more. To use Lennon's words, we must "vanish and shrink." I know that Jesus will outlast the Beatles, Elvis, and rock-and-roll. But will he outlast our egos? We must delight in playing backup like John the Baptist rather than posing as rock stars. Staying in tune and sticking to the beat, we must resist the urge to take over as lead singer or to interrupt the chorus line to play guitar solo in Jesus' band.

UNQUENCHABLE THIRST
John 4:1-42

We obey our thirst. No one has to tell us to do so. We all do it. But some of us give the appearance of obeying it more than others do—like the Samaritan woman in John 4. Perhaps that is why she is so refreshing.

Jesus has been making such good connections with the people in Judea that his disciples are baptizing more disciples than John. The religious leaders are taking note of it. As a result, Jesus leaves Judea for Galilee and has to pass through Samaria on his way (Jn 4:1-4; see also Jn 3:26-30). Jesus comes to Sychar in Samaria, where Jacob's well is located. He's dog-tired and thirsty, having walked such a long way, and so he sits down by the well at about the sixth hour in the heat of the day (Jn 4:4-6). Perhaps he's waiting for someone to come by and dip a bucket into the well so that he can ask for a drink.

An unnamed Samaritan woman comes to draw water. She's no ordinary woman. Otherwise, she would not be drawing water in the heat of the day. All the other women from her village had come to the well several hours earlier to draw water for their families. But she's not like the other women. She has too many secrets, even though her secret life is well-known to all.

Jesus asks her to give him a drink of water: "Will you give me a drink?" (Jn 4:7). None of his followers would have ever asked this woman for a drink. They are too moral for that. No wonder Jesus had sent them to town to buy some food (Jn 4:8)! If his disciples had been there and had heard his request, they may have rebuked Jesus for his lack of social etiquette and moral scruples. (Later, when they do appear, they take note of him being with the woman yet remain silent [Jn 4:27].) The woman is also shocked. "You are a Jew and I am a Samaritan woman. How can you ask me for a drink?" (Jn 4:9). John adds a note for the reader that Jews do not associate with Samaritans (Jn 4:9); this is true even years later when John writes the Gospel. Not only does Jesus associate with her; he asks to drink from her water jar. Jews weren't supposed to touch what Samaritans touched. To add insult to injury, Jesus is a Jewish man, and she is an outcast among her people. But Jesus gets beyond all that, breaking through all the social taboos to reach out and touch her with God's holy love.[18]

The woman probably wants the water that would take away her thirst (Jn 4:15) for several reasons. Going to the well is the only way to get water. For a woman or a child, it isn't easy to get water from the well. It is especially difficult for her, given the shame she bears in addition to the jar. She bears an especially heavy burden, for as we find out, she has had five husbands and the man with whom she now lives is not her husband (Jn 4:16-18). The woman has an unquenchable thirst for love, but like Johnny Lee's country song "Looking for Love" says, she has looked for it in all the wrong places.

A lot of men have made promises to her in exchange for something. No doubt she is a little jaded. But all Jesus wants is a cup of water—and a conduit into her heart so as to pour God's love into her life. He doesn't want anything else. Jesus even tells his followers later that his food is to do the will of his Father, which is to lead people like this woman back to God (Jn 4:31-38). The payoff in return for giving him a cup of water is huge—receiving the living water of eternal life (Jn 4:10; 13-14). This unnamed woman begins to hope again.

In Africa, many people are beginning to hope again—as a result of the work of Living Water International, Advent Conspiracy and other ministry efforts aimed at providing clean well water for drinking.[19] One African pastor told a member of the Living Water International staff that many white people from the States had promised to provide clean drinking water but that until now, the promises had remained unfulfilled. Things are changing, and the people are beginning to hope again.

The Samaritan woman is beginning to hope again, and it all starts with Jesus asking her for a drink of water from her bucket. She realizes he's no ordinary Jewish man, just as he realizes she's no ordinary Samaritan woman. Jesus knows her story but does not condemn her. He still asks her for a drink. But this is no ploy: Jesus really is thirsty and in need of her help. As the woman ministers to Jesus by giving him water for his parched lips and mouth, he moves closer to minister to her by offering water for her thirsty soul and redeeming her story.

The Samaritan woman is beginning to hope again. Yet she has a difficult time coping with Jesus' penetrating points about her life, and so she resorts to theologizing in the attempt to change the conversation. Even though she is drawn to Jesus, she tries to hide her story behind folklore and hearsay. Just as many among Jesus' own people would reduce spirituality to a bunch of religious rules taught by humans instead of God, so the woman tries to reduce true worship to a matter of worshiping at some place: "'Sir,' the woman said, 'I can see that you are a prophet. Our fathers worshiped on this mountain, but you Jews claim that the place where we must worship is in Jerusalem'" (Jn 4:19-20). Jesus tells the woman that God seeks worshipers who worship in spirit and in truth—not in folklore:

> Jesus declared, "Believe me, woman, a time is coming when you will worship the Father neither on this mountain nor in Jerusalem. You Samaritans worship what you do not know; we worship what we do know, for salvation is from the Jews. Yet a time is coming and has now come when the true worshipers will worship the Father in spirit and truth, for they are the kind of worshipers the Father seeks. God is spirit, and his worshipers must worship in spirit and in truth." (Jn 4:21-23)

Perhaps the woman hides behind folklore because, although she has an unquenchable thirst for love, she can barely stand before the overwhelming sensation of Jesus' probing care and attention that hits her like a mighty river flowing down through a mountain range. It would be so much easier for her and for us if religion could be reduced to worshiping on this or that mountain. It is so upsetting when worshiping on mountains gives way to sharing personal space with the Messiah, connecting person to person and heart to heart. Jesus looks her in the eye and treats her like a human being. Jesus' probing gaze is the most difficult, frustrating, powerful, heart-gripping and beautiful thing she has ever experienced. She doesn't know how to respond.

The best option available to her is to hide—until she can hide no more. The woman moves from hiding behind some mountain to hiding behind her hope in some distant Messiah figure: "The woman said, 'I know that Messiah' (called Christ) 'is coming. When he comes, he will explain everything to us'" (Jn 4:25). But just as Jesus removes the mountain that stands between him and her heart, so too he brings the distant future into the present: "I who speak to you am he" (Jn 4:26).

The woman cannot stand it any longer, so she leaves her bucket at Jesus' feet and runs as fast as her feet will take her back to her village to tell others—to tell everyone (Jn 4:28-29). She no longer cares what *they think of her* because she knows that the Messiah is near and that *he cares for her.* Jesus redeems her story. She is no longer ashamed of it. She tells the village that Jesus tells her all that she had done—"Could this be the Christ?" (Jn 4:29).

Jesus loves her—even though he knows her story. She can now face her village with this inextinguishable, fiery love and this living water that satisfies her unquenchable thirst. It flows within her heart from Jesus and overflows to others. This Samaritan woman is so compelled by Jesus' love that she becomes one of the first evangelists. Jesus takes away her shame. He redeems her story and redeems many others in her village through her (Jn 4:39-42). That's connection. That's salvation.

Just as Jesus comes close to the woman at the well, Jesus comes close to us. Jesus has an unquenchable thirst to love us that extinguishes our shame and guilt. Obey your thirst and respond to his love.

LAST RESORT
John 4:43-54

He has tried everything—doctors, medications, perhaps even the local medicine man and TV evangelist faith healer. Nothing has worked. This royal official's power and wealth are of no use to him. What good is all his power and wealth when it can't heal his boy? Desperation sets in. His son is close to death in Capernaum (Jn 4:46-47).

He has one last resort: Jesus is back in Cana of Galilee. He has heard of Jesus turning water into wine. Maybe Jesus could heal his son too. So this royal official casts aside his pride and begs, which is not easy for any of us to do, especially someone accustomed to others begging him for things. This time it's his turn to beg, however, and so he begs the local wonder-worker to come and heal his boy.

Jesus responds with a lesson on faith: "'Unless you people see miraculous signs and wonders,' Jesus told him, 'you will never believe'" (Jn 4:48). What good is theology and faith? They can't heal his boy—he needs action. Every minute counts. So, he presses Jesus further: "Sir, come down before my child dies" (Jn 4:49).

Jesus also presses him further. Jesus won't come with him. If you or I were in Jesus' sandals with his wonder-working magic, we would probably go. It is such a great career move opportunity for him. Who knows how the man might repay Jesus if Jesus were to go with him and heal his son? But Jesus is not taken with the man's position or with making it on the big stage. Whereas Jesus has recently gone and stayed with the lowly Samaritans for two days, he won't go with this royal official.

Jesus won't take this royal official's money or play to his power or fame, but the royal official must take Jesus at his word: "You may go. Your son will live" (Jn 4:50). What other choice does he have? The man must go without Jesus; all he takes with him is Jesus' word. But that will gain for him far more than all his own power and money could win him.

Jesus' word is all he needs. By this very Word—Jesus—God created the heavens and the earth. "Through him all things were made" (Jn 1:3). God said it, and it happened. Now that's power. Jesus' word is power. At the moment Jesus says the boy will live, the boy is healed.

The Samaritan woman and her whole village took Jesus at his word. But he wasn't from there; as John reminds us, a prophet is not without honor except in his own country (Jn 4:44). Maybe that's why Jesus has to push the royal official—Jesus' own people demand to see signs in order to believe (whereas the Samaritans believe based on Jesus' word alone; see Jn 4:39-42). In any event, Jesus wants the man to believe in his word without having to see miraculous signs (Jn 4:48). In the end, the royal official takes Jesus at his word and goes. In fact, the text makes no further mention of the man pleading with Jesus; he simply accepts Jesus' declaration that the boy will live and departs (Jn 4:50).

On his way home, the official's servants meet him with the news that his boy lives (Jn 4:51). He wants to know when (Jn 4:52), and realizes that the boy recovered at the exact time that Jesus had told him, "Your son will live" (Jn 4:53). Not only does the royal official believe that Jesus can heal his son at his word, but also he and his household believe in Jesus because of his miraculous sign: "So he and all his household believed" (Jn 4:53).

John tells us that this is the second sign that Jesus performs in Cana of Galilee (Jn 4:54). John later tells us that the goal of Jesus' miraculous signs and wonders is to drive us to faith in him: "Jesus did many other signs and wonders that are not recorded in this book, but these are written that you might believe that Jesus is the Christ, and that by believing you might have life in his name" (Jn 20:30-31). Jesus leads the royal official to the point of complete dependence—taking Jesus at his word apart from visible presence and, once doing so, believing in him. (See also Jn 20:29, where the resurrected Jesus appears to Thomas and claims: "Because you have seen me, you have believed; blessed are those who have not seen and yet have believed.") Jesus and John challenge their audience to take Jesus at his word and believe in the testimony regarding the signs that reveal Jesus' glory.

Just like the royal official, Jesus pushes us to take him at his word and believe. Sometimes all we've got is Jesus' word. Sometimes Jesus refuses to perform signs for us in person. He's not in the business of jumping through our religious hoops and performing magic tricks for us so that we'll think he's cool. Even when he does perform signs, he presses us to move past the glorious signs themselves to personal faith in him.

Do you look at Jesus simply as a miracle worker? Will you only believe in him if you see his miraculous signs? What happens if he doesn't perform signs when you ask him, pushing you to take him at his word— even if fulfillment of his word is way off in the distant future? But Jesus is in his word. He will give himself to you, just as he gave himself to the Samaritans, just as he gave himself to Nicodemus. Move past the sign to Jesus himself and to his word. But you will only do this when you truly see Jesus as your last resort (just like the royal official), when you see Jesus as all you've got, when you see him as what you need more than anything else.

Before becoming a Christ-follower, Anne Lamott writes, "Mine was a patchwork God, sewn together from bits of rag and ribbon, Eastern and Western, pagan and Hebrew, everything but the kitchen sink and Jesus."[20] Some of us may have even taken hold of the kitchen sink. Sometimes even that seems better than holding onto Jesus, holding only onto him.

Many of us don't really want to be associated with Jesus. We may appeal to him to perform a miracle or two, but nothing more. Moreover, we don't want to be identified with Samaritans or television evangelists or little old ladies who use Christianity as a crutch to help them get by. We want to be strong—like the royal official—before he met Jesus. So we pick and choose and mix and match. We might even ask Jesus to perform a miracle or two, but we dare not believe in him or depend on him and his word until he forces the issue—until our "son" is at the point of death, and until we find that everything we ever counted on doesn't count at all. When desperation sets in, faith sets in. It's all we've got. He's all we've got. Last resort.

TRANSITION
Monkey Fist

WE NOW TRANSITION FROM CONSIDERING the initial connections Jesus makes to reflecting upon the sustained reactions to Jesus and the rejection of him. While there are numerous instances of people responding positively to Jesus in the "Reactions and Rejection" section (such as the man healed of blindness in John 9 and Mary who anointed Jesus with perfume in John 12), the emphasis in the following section is largely on the growing opposition that he experiences. No doubt much of the opposition is bound up with the leaders of the people clutching desperately to things in order to maintain control in life and not wanting to submit to Jesus and his word. They are like monkeys with their hands caught in a jar—trapped by their own desires to get what they want, including control. Yet they will not let go.

◆　◆　◆

How do you catch a monkey? Put peanuts in a jar with an opening that is a bit smaller than a monkey fist, and then wait for the monkey to show. Once the monkey places its paw in the jar to get a fistful of peanuts, you've got him. He would rather hold on to the peanuts than let go and be free. I'm like that monkey. Way too often I take matters into my own hands and clench my fists, wanting to be in control of my destiny instead of entrusting all things to God with open hands and an open heart. This is the missing link to life.

We often clench our fists and close our hearts rather than respond to God with open hands and open hearts. We often approach God in this way because we like to be in control, even mistakenly thinking that we control God. Throughout John's Gospel, people's negative reactions and rejection of Jesus are bound up with people wanting to be in control of their destinies. Like us, they like to turn spirituality into sin management, reducing salvation to behavior modification rather than viewing it as a loving relationship with God through faith in Jesus.

As noted in the discussion of John 2:13-25, the religious leaders take issue with Jesus for overturning tables in the temple and for claiming that he will destroy the temple (his body) and raise it again in three days. While the imagery of Jesus' body is lost on them at this point, the point is not: he claims to have control over the temple, which implies that they don't. The religious elite try to control access to God and are threatened when God tabernacles in their midst, turning the tables on their idolatrous ambitions. The power brokers' consternation increases in John 5 when Jesus, who is our ultimate Sabbath rest, heals a man on the Sabbath. The living Word who breathed the Torah into existence as his written Word is Lord of the Sabbath and the Scriptures as a whole, challenging the rulers' attempts to function as masters of God's written Word. Jesus says to those who react to his lordship over the Scriptures, "You diligently study the Scriptures because you think that by them you possess eternal life. These are the Scriptures that testify about me, yet you refuse to come to me to have life" (Jn 5:39-40). In John 6, Jesus calls on the masses to move beyond looking to him for free handouts of food, but to look for food that will last forever—himself as the bread of life. They like Jesus as a vendor of food, even religious food. But they don't want to engage Jesus as their food—their life sustenance. The masses like to pick and choose from the spiritual smorgasbord; they want to be in control, including most of his disciples (Jn 6:25-71). In John 8, Jesus challenges those who confess faith in him that they must submit to his teachings, which alone can free them. In reaction to his claim, these supposedly new converts assert that they are free because they are Abraham's descendants and therefore have God on their side. Jesus confronts their seeming ancestor worship and nationalistic piety by saying that they are children of the devil. Jesus reveals to them that only those who believe in him are truly related to Abraham and free (Jn 8:31-47). Whether we are talking of the temple or Scripture or bread or national identity or anything else, we must understand that Jesus is Lord and that we are not in control. He is. If we want to be free, we must surrender control of our lives to him. We must let go of the peanuts in the jar.

Being a Christian is a very vulnerable call. As with any meaningful relationship, we can only have vital communion with God if we give our whole selves. We have to let go of ourselves, letting go of the "peanuts" of selfish ambition and letting go of seeking to control destiny. God in his mercy forces us to quit clenching our fists and closing our hearts. He frees us, opening our hearts in faith by his Word of holy love. We must come to the end of ourselves, dying to ourselves and living in union with Jesus. No wonder Jesus dies for our sins on a cross with outstretched arms and open hands, crying out to God with a broken heart. Only in this way can we be saved—with open hands and arms and hearts. Although severe, God is supremely gracious and merciful in his judgment. Through faith in Jesus, who surrendered his destiny to the Father and had confidence in his Father's love for him, and through his love for us, we can be free from the trap of the peanut jar.

Jesus must be allergic to peanuts. He never seems to get his hand caught in the peanut jar. So his would-be captors cannot catch him until he gives himself up to them: "Yet no one seized him, because his time had not yet come" (Jn 8:20). "Again they tried to seize him, but he escaped their grasp" (Jn 10:39). Only later, in the garden, do they seize him, for his time has finally come: "Then the detachment of soldiers with its commander and the Jewish officials arrested Jesus. They bound him" (Jn 18:12). And yet, even here, Jesus is in control; he has them eating from his hand:

> Jesus, knowing all that was going to happen to him, went out and asked them, "Who is it you want?" "Jesus of Nazareth," they replied. "I am he," Jesus said. (And Judas the traitor was standing there with them.) When Jesus said, "I am he," they drew back and fell to the ground. Again he asked them, "Who is it you want?" And they said, "Jesus of Nazareth." "I told you that I am he," Jesus answered. "If you are looking for me, then let these men go." This happened so that the words he had spoken would be fulfilled: "I have not lost one of those you gave me." (Jn 18:4-9)

Jesus is in control because he knows his life is in his Father's hands. His followers can trust him because the Father has entrusted all of them into Jesus' hands. Not one of them is lost.

Although he's not lost, Jesus' disciple Peter is a handful. I can connect with Peter when he cuts off the high priest's servant's ear (Jn 18:10). He's sensing spiritual vertigo as he realizes the mob accompanied by Judas is going to take his hopes and aspirations—in Jesus—away from him. And so Peter seeks to dish out a little vertigo himself. It's too much for Peter when Jesus rebukes him for defending him against those who have come to seize Jesus and take him away: "Jesus commanded Peter, 'Put your sword away! Shall I not drink the cup the Father has given me?'" (Jn 18:11).

Then there's the episode after Jesus rises from the dead and predicts how Peter will die: "'I tell you the truth, when you were younger you dressed yourself and went where you wanted; but when you are old you will stretch out your hands, and someone else will dress you and lead you where you do not want to go.' Jesus said this to indicate the kind of death by which Peter would glorify God. Then he said to him, 'Follow me!'" (Jn 21:18-19). Peter doesn't like what he hears, so he wants to know what will happen to another disciple, John, who is close by: "Lord, what about him?" (Jn 21:21). Jesus' response is classic: "If I want him to remain alive until I return, what is that to you? You must follow me" (Jn 21:22). In other words: let go of the peanuts, Peter.

Just like the monkey with a fistful of peanuts—or dollars—we tend to seize everything rather than receive it. We treat the most important things, including life and death, like those peanuts and dollar bills, commodifying time and relationships and turning salvation into a transaction. But we cannot commodify the life God gives us, no matter how hard we try, for it ever remains God's gift. As John says in the prologue to the Gospel, "Yet to all who received him, to those who believed in his name, he *gave* the right to become children of God—children born not of natural descent, nor of human decision or a husband's will, but born of God" (Jn 1:12-13; italics added). And then in John 3, Jesus is recorded as saying, "For God so loved the world that he *gave* his one and only Son, that whoever believes in him shall not perish but have eternal life" (Jn 3:16; italics added).

Even though we cannot commodify the life God gives us, still we often try to seize it. Why do we do it? Certainly a lack of trust has something to do with it. But why don't we trust? Why do we try to take matters into our own hands—including the peanuts—rather than entrust all things to God? Why do I live life with a clenched fist rather than with an open hand? That's so contrary to the life of faith, for faith itself is an empty hand. Salvation is the assurance that God loves me in Jesus. I can't earn it. I can't seize it. It ever remains gift. Even though we often try to buy love, love can never be bought and sold.

Jesus approaches all of life with an open hand—including death. But why? Because of love—because of the Father's love for him. Peter can eventually face death with an open hand because, through Jesus' acceptance of him, God's love seizes him. While Peter can no longer lay claim to Jesus after his three denials, Jesus continues to lay claim to him (Jn 21:15-19). That's grace. That's love. That's salvation. And that's better than a fistful of peanuts—even better than peanut butter.

Jesus' life and call threaten the religious power-brokering peanut gallery. Jesus' gift-based, grace-based life is just too scandalous, just too threatening to their system of guilt and debt, transaction and control. Their ritualism, centered in temple worship (Jn 2:12-22), Sabbath (Jn 5:1-18) and Scripture (Jn 5:39-40), and their nationalism, centered on being physical descendants of Abraham (Jn 8:31-41), enslave them. They don't realize that the temple, Sabbath, Scripture and Abraham find their *telos* in Jesus, and so they cling to them instead of him. That's why the peanut gallery starts plotting to arrest and kill Jesus (Jn 7:45-52; 11:45-57; 12:9-11). Eventually they succeed, but only because Jesus gives himself up to them (Jn 18:4-9) as he entrusts himself to his Father's hands, winning in the end.

Jesus stands in stark contrast to the peanut gallery. Whereas they cling to anything else but Jesus, Jesus clings to the Father. When Jesus rises from the dead to new life as a gift of God, he destroys their system of monkey jars with fistfuls of peanuts. But until then, even in the face of death, Jesus clings to God with open hands because he knows his Father won't abandon him to the grave forever. Even the cry of dereliction— "My God, my God, why have you forsaken me?"—recorded in the Gospels is not the cry of one berating God, but of one bewildered and broken, clinging to God even in godforsaken despair.

I look around me, and I look at myself, and I often see us *Homo sapiens*, the supposedly wise and thinking creatures, making monkey fists at life instead of approaching it with open hands. I guess we're regressing; we're not so wise after all. So much for our survival as the fittest species. We have no room for providence, only paranoia (everything and everyone is against us). We have no time for time, pressing the future into a force that we must control, *now*. (Jesus, on the other hand, waits on God for his hour of glory to approach—Jn 12:27-33.) We make monkey fists on the highway as someone cuts us off, or at the four-way stop where someone takes our turn. Monkey fists at the stock market for shredding our stock values, monkey fists at our children's baseball or softball coaches for benching *our* kids and monkey fists at our teachers or at ourselves for not getting the grades we demand. Monkey fists for God as life doesn't turn out the way we planned. Monkey fists for everyone all around. Closed hands. Closed lives. Closed destinies.

I'm not talking about closed destinies with God but about open lives. I'm not calling for a fatalistic approach to life but for living life with an open hand, palm up. Go ahead and plan, but remember your life is in God's hands.

Such an approach to life is difficult for many of us, however. Realizing that our lives are in God's hands is like coming face to face with bad karma. We're not talking here about the closed cycle of karma but about the open circle of grace and love. We still think that if everything bad that has happened is from God, that God knew about it and that he allowed it to happen. Then we think that God must have been an accomplice.

That's what a friend of mine grew up thinking. He could never fathom how God could stand by while his mother took her own life, committing suicide when he was but a boy. My friend could only approach life and God with a clenched fist, until he read that "Jesus wept" as others wept at Lazarus's tomb (Jn 11:35). While there was a theological explanation for Lazarus's death—God would be glorified through Jesus being glorified in Lazarus's being raised from the dead (Jn 11:4), there was no avoiding the existential trauma associated with Jesus' friend's death. Even for Jesus. Jesus wept. And Jesus died. And they laid Jesus in a tomb. Closed chapter. Questions still unanswered. While my friend's questions about his mother's death still remain, and the tears still flow, he is able to lay them in the tomb with Jesus.

My Japanese wife once told me that I need bigger pockets. She believes that we Westerners often have small pockets for life's big questions. We want everything to be solved and all our monkey-fisted-peanut questions to be answered. Total control. But some questions don't have answers, at least not on this side of the monkey jar glass. We look through that glass dimly.

Jesus dies with a question on his lips, with no answer coming this side of the grave. He dies with open hands because he knows this much: in life and in death—regardless of what happens—he is in his Father's hands. Total submission. Total trust. Total death to himself: "Because it was the Jewish day of Preparation and since the tomb was nearby, they laid Jesus there" (Jn 19:42). Jesus is able to let go even of life itself because he trusts in his Father, and so he places his life and destiny in the Father's hands. I lay myself there—entrusting myself to the loving care of Jesus and his Father. Death held Jesus in its monkey-fisted grasp in the tomb, and death will hold each of us there too—only to be blown away. Jesus' death, our deaths, his question and our questions may be closed chapters, but the book is still open. And we can only turn life's pages with open hands.

So as we move forward in John's Gospel toward Jesus' hour of glorification through the cross, let's not react to and reject him and his Word like so many do. Let's not try to control him or religion. Let's submit ourselves to him and his Word and let go of the peanuts in the monkey jar and be set free (Jn 8:31-32).

REACTIONS
AND REJECTION

John 5:1-12:50

While Jesus may be our last resort, and while he may be our ultimate connection with God, we often react to him and reject him. Perhaps this is because his truth and grace and love are so overpowering and overwhelming. Perhaps it is because of our hardness of heart—we don't want Jesus to get in the way of our agendas. In John 5–12, we find numerous instances where people react to Jesus, even rejecting him. Of course, there are other instances of profound faith in response to Jesus as God's revelation. These faith responses take place in the context of reaction and rejection. I will illustrate this point by drawing attention to Peter in John 6, the man healed of blindness in John 9 and Mary the sister of Lazarus in John 12.

In John 6, Peter confesses that Jesus alone has the words of eternal life. Peter makes this confession, while the crowds and scores of Jesus' disciples abandon Jesus based on his claim to be the bread of life, which people must eat to be saved (Jn 6:60-71). In John 9, the man healed of blindness responds in faith to Jesus' miraculous act of healing and words, even though he no doubt realizes that such faith will lead to his rejection by the leaders in his community (Jn 9:1-41). In John 12, Mary pours perfume on Jesus' feet and washes his feet with her hair, preparing him for burial. Judas reacts to this act of devotion, dismissing it as poor stewardship. Not only that, but Mary's devotion serves as a striking contrast to the reaction of the religious leaders of the people who plot to kill Jesus and Mary's brother Lazarus, whom Jesus just raised from the dead (Jn 12:1-11). Even with Jesus' triumphal entry into Jerusalem in John 12, the account closes with the religious leaders up in arms because they feel there is nothing they can do to stop people from believing in Jesus (Jn 12:19).

There are other examples of rejection, as noted in the introduction to this Gospel: "the Jews'" desire to kill Jesus for healing a man on the Sabbath and for claiming to be equal with God (Jn 5:1-18); Jesus' brothers' rejection of Jesus as the Messiah (Jn 7:1-9); "the Jews'" desire to kill Jesus for claiming to be God—the great I AM (Jn 8:58-59); and again the determination of the religious leaders to kill Jesus because he raises Lazarus from the dead (Jn 11:45-57).

At the close of this section, Jesus speaks of his impending passion and death at the hands of his enemies as his hour of glory through which he conquers the ruler of this world system, Satan (Jn 12:23-33). Moreover, John makes special note in chapter 12 of the unbelief among the crowds and among the leaders (Jn 12:34, 42). Despite all Jesus' miraculous signs, the majority do not believe in him. In highlighting the rejection of Jesus, John quotes from Isaiah 6, as do all three Synoptic Gospels. Jesus' people as a whole reject Jesus as God's prophet and as God himself (Jn 12:37-43; see also Is 6). Whereas Isaiah saw Jesus' glory and spoke about him, even those who do believe in Jesus—and there are many among the leaders who believe in him at this time—do not speak about him or confess him publicly out of fear of the Pharisees (Jn 12:42). Unlike Isaiah, they love the praise of people more than the praise of God (Jn 12:41-43).

Jesus' word of truth will judge those who have rejected him here on earth, for Jesus has spoken only what his Father has commanded him to say (Jn 12:44-50). If Jesus accepts his Father's word and speaks only that word to us, it is vital that we accept him and his word rather than reject them. We can so easily miss the forest while analyzing trees. We think that we are in the position of judge and jury over Scripture and over Jesus, failing to realize that as we stand in judgment over them, we are being judged.

MISSING THE FOREST, MISSING THE TREES
John 5:1-47

Sometimes I get so consumed with something that I miss the big picture. I miss the forest while zeroing in on the trees. One such experience took place on a Sunday afternoon several years ago. In the heat of the day after church, I was outside on a ladder and prepping the house for painting. I had told my son earlier in the afternoon that he and his friend were to keep their bikes away from the car in the garage so they wouldn't scratch the car with their handlebars. Well, sure enough, when I finally went inside the house to eat a late dinner, my wife informed me that my son and his friend had scratched the car with their bikes. And they weren't small scratches either.

I was furious. Even though I was starving for food, my anger was even more ravenous. Boiling over from the heat and the situation at hand, I let my son know how frustrated I was with him for not following my instructions. After hearing me out, my son said to me: "Dad, people are more important than cars." No doubt he had just covered that theme in Sunday School that morning—and although I teach the Bible and theology on a daily basis, I certainly hadn't been covering that theme that afternoon.

It's a good thing I was no longer on the ladder; I would have fallen off. Even though my son was *sooo* wrong for not following my instructions, I was even more wrong for failing to put the car in a relational context. Everything I was not saying but expressing with my off-the-heat-index emotions was telling my son that I valued the car more than him and his friend. I was missing the forest while seeing the trees.

One Sabbath day several centuries ago, Jesus goes to Jerusalem for a Jewish festival and comes upon a lame man on the Sabbath at the Pool of Bethesda (Jn 5:1-5, 9). Perhaps the man had scratched his father's mule when he was a child and his father no longer allowed him to take the mule out for a ride. Jesus comes along and sees the lame man lying there by the pool. Jesus perceives that he had been there a long time—thirty-eight years, to be exact—and so he asks him: "Do you want to get well?" (Jn 5:6).

Now you may be thinking, *What kind of stupid question is that?* Maybe it's not such a stupid question. (And besides, you know it can't be a stupid question. Remember: it's Jesus!) Who knows? Maybe the lame man is enjoying the Miller High Life on welfare. We'll just have to wait and see. In the end, we find out that while this man wants to get well physically, he does not really want to get well spiritually (he stands in stark contrast to the man born blind whom Jesus heals, as recorded in John 9). To make a short story even shorter, Jesus heals the man physically on the Sabbath and then goes on his way without revealing his identity (Jn 5:8-9, 13).

Well, that's where the problem lies—or stands, in this case. Jesus heals the lame man on the Sabbath (Jn 5:9).[1] Working on the Sabbath was expressly forbidden; and to add insult to injury, Jesus has expressly commanded the man to carry the mat on which he laid all those years *on the Sabbath.* The moral matrix power brokers likely took no real notice of the man while he was lame, but now that he can walk, they take a special interest in him. They remind him that the law forbids him to carry his mat, but he tells them in response that he has been commanded by the man who healed him to carry it (Jn 5:10-11).

Now, we come to a really lame question: "Who is this fellow who told you to pick it up and walk?" (Jn 5:12). They are witnessing a walking miracle, and all they can think of is who told him to carry his mat on the Sabbath. While they zero in on the trees (the man is working on the Sabbath by carrying his mat), they take no real notice of the fact that it is this formerly *lame* man who is carrying the mat. For years he could not carry his mat on any day of the week, and now he can. The power brokers badly miss the forest while carefully observing the trees.

The formerly lame man pulls up lame as well when he sees Jesus later in the temple. He, too, misses the forest while looking at the trees. Jesus finds him in the temple and says, "Stop sinning or something worse may happen to you [than being lame]" (Jn 5:14). The man disregards Jesus' warning and walks off on the legs that Jesus healed in order to blow the whistle on Jesus for having done it (Jn 5:15). Jesus' love is amazing. Jesus is controlled by the Father's love and affirmation, and so he can freely confront the man and the rulers so that they might become whole. He knows this man will tell the spiritual police on him for healing him on the Sabbath, and he knows that the power brokers will try to kill him because of his claim to be God's Son (Jn 5:16-18). But Jesus still seeks out the man to warn him about not taking a stand. Later he challenges the power brokers to break it up and to quit stumbling over their human-made traditions and instead to believe the divinely inspired, human testimony to Jesus, so that they might be saved (Jn 5:34). But the ruled man and the rulers of the people fall far short and fail to make right judgments by rejecting Jesus' call.

Among other things, the rulers fail to take account of Jesus' many witnesses (John the Baptist, his works from the Father, his Father, Scripture and Moses—Jn 5:31-47), as required by the law. And while the needling power brokers concern themselves with the praises of their peers, and while the formerly lame man concerns himself with the pressure of the authorities, they crash right into Jesus and come up lame. Why don't they want to get well spiritually?

Perhaps the man doesn't really want to get well because he has been controlled by the system for thirty-eight years. Even though the power brokers had not lifted a finger to help him get well during that time, they still allowed him to live. Now he has to go out and make a living, and all he knows is being controlled and receiving charity. Jesus has made him well, made him walk, made him free, but it sure seems like he'd rather be sick, crippled and enslaved. The religious leaders want to keep control, and Jesus stands in their way. These and other factors keep them from getting well and responding rightly to Jesus; instead, they react to him.

How often do we pull up lame when standing before God and humans? God heals me of sickness and infirmities, raising me to my feet, and then I go and turn my back on God. This man doesn't stand up to the authorities, just as I so often don't. (In John 9, we will find someone who responds rightly to Jesus; the man healed of blindness in John 9 can actually *see* the forest, not just the trees.) This formerly lame man won't stand by Jesus when the pressure is on, for he, just like the power brokers of the people, loves the praises of people more than God. Jesus later says to these leaders of the people who also want to kill him,

> I do not accept praise from men, but I know you. I know that you do not have the love of God in your hearts. I have come in my Father's name, and you do not accept me; but if someone else comes in his own name, you will accept him. How can you believe if you accept praise from one another, yet make no effort to obtain the praise that comes from the only God? (Jn 5:41-44)

Like the rulers of the people accusing Jesus of wrongdoing, the formerly lame man won't make a right judgment because he loves the praises and fears the judgments of humans more than the praises and judgments of God. The persistent sin that Jesus warns him about is that he can't stand up to those who stand against God's judgments because he wants their acceptance more than God's. The "something worse" that could happen to him is that even though he is standing now, he is in danger of standing in God's judgment (Jn 5:19-30).

Psalm 1 talks about the righteous person who obeys God's Word. Jesus, the living Word, epitomizes the person who obeys God's written Word—even as the living Word of judgment. For Jesus always does what his Father does and, as a result of their relational union, the Father entrusts all judgment to Jesus (Jn 5:19-23). Jesus "does not walk in the counsel of the wicked or stand in the way of sinners or sit in the seat of mockers," or fall down on the mat when the authorities start pushing lame sinners around. Jesus' delight is in obeying his Father and doing what his Father does: "his delight is in the law of the Lord, and on his law he meditates day and night." Whereas the righteous stand before God, "the wicked will not stand in the judgment, nor sinners in the assembly of the righteous. For the Lord watches over the way of the righteous, but the way of the wicked will perish" (Ps 1:2, 5-6). Jesus stands with God in the judgment and is the very one through whom God will judge all peoples (Jn 5:24-30).

Jesus judges relationally, not simply behaviorally, looking at people's heart orientation toward God. Do we seek and accept the praise or glory (*doxa*) of people or of God (Jn 5:41-44)? This is Jesus' fundamental concern and is what causes him to care for sinners and cripples even when it leads to his own rejection. Jesus' love of God and care for the crippled man leads him to discount the false judgment by others. Instead, Jesus makes right judgments about them before God, who is pleased with him.

Here we come to a panoramic view of the forest. The law is about relationships—being compassionate toward lame people, and standing for God now, and then receiving his praises when people are called to stand before him in the judgment, when he judges all people through his Son in honor of his Son (Jn 5:22-23, 31-47). As stated in the introduction to this section, we can so easily miss the forest while analyzing trees. We think that we are in the position of judge and jury over Scripture and over Jesus. But we fail to realize that as we stand in judgment over them, we are being judged by God's written Word, which bears witness to Jesus who is God's living Word. In addition, when we stand in judgment over Jesus, we are being judged by the testimony of Jesus' personal witnesses such as the Father, John the Baptist and Moses (Jn 5:31-47). It only took two witnesses to support a claim of judgment in the Old Testament (Deut 17:6). In the case of Jesus, the various witnesses are stacked in his favor.

Do we have a panoramic view of the forest? Do we even see the trees? Do we make judgments relationally? When we miss the forest, we actually miss the trees too. Although my son had disobeyed me by not keeping the bikes away from my car, I realized later that I had disobeyed God by being so consumed with scratches on the car. The car's value is in transporting my kids from place to place, not in its appearance. I hadn't even seen the tree in this case. Although Jesus *appears* to break the law by healing the man on the Sabbath, the rulers of the people fail to see that one of the main reasons the people are to rest on the Sabbath is so that they can continue walking the next week and not fall over from spiritual and physical exhaustion. The Sabbath was made for people, not the other way round (see Mk 2:27). These rulers don't even see the trees. Are we like them, or do we really want to get well?

GREAT EXPECTATIONS
John 6:1-21

John 6 is a key turning point in John's Gospel. The masses and Jesus' disciples have great expectations for Jesus. Will he fulfill their expectations or disappoint them?

Sometime after Jesus has a confrontation with the religious leaders in Jerusalem (recorded in John 5), we find him crossing the far shore of the Sea of Galilee. A great crowd is following him because they have seen his miraculous signs. Jesus sits down with his disciples on a mountainside. In this context, John tells us that the Jewish Passover is near (Jn 6:1-4).

When Jesus looks at the crowds following him, he turns to his disciple Philip and asks him, "'Where shall we buy bread for these people to eat?' He asked this only to test him, for he already had in mind what he was going to do" (Jn 6:5-6). Jesus tests Philip to see if he has confidence in Jesus. Regardless of Philip's response, Jesus plans on performing something big. He's about to provide food in the wilderness for the hungry masses.

Jesus' inner circle of disciples is a bit slow. I mean, his core disciples saw him turn water into wine (Jn 2). They also witnessed the healing of the man by the pool who had been lame thirty-eight years (Jn 5), as well as other miracles. But you have to admit: this is a bit different. "Philip answered him, 'Eight months' wages would not buy enough bread for each one to have a bite!'" (Jn 5:7).

While the crowds and majority of disciples have great expectations for Jesus (they are following him because they have witnessed his miraculous signs), his inner circle doesn't seem to have such great expectations, or if they do, they don't appear so confident that Jesus can meet their expectations. Just as Philip raises concern about the huge challenge before them, Andrew also has doubts about Jesus and his followers having the ability to provide for the crowds. But at least, Andrew recommends that there is a boy who has five small barley loaves and two small fish. Even so, he follows up by asking, "but how far will they go among so many?" (Jn 5:9).

Many sermons have affirmed this boy for graciously handing over his lunch to Jesus. Perhaps it is his lunch, but it is quite a lot for a boy. The child may very well be a vendor. If so, he may have great expectations for bringing in far more than the fair market price for his loaves and fish given the shortage and the market law of supply and demand.

Regardless of the youth's motives, Jesus and his followers probably pay the boy for his food, which they will then distribute to the crowds. Even so, why bother making use of the boy's loaves and fish? How could this boy's goodies help? We're talking about the need for *a lot* of food— for five thousand men (not to mention the women, children and no doubt a few seagulls). Another question arises. If you have read the story before, you may also be wondering why Jesus even resorts to using the boy's loaves and fish: why doesn't Jesus just start from scratch? After all, God created everything through him out of nothing (Jn 1:1-3). Let's pause for a moment before answering this question.

The Old Testament background imagery is pronounced. The reader knowledgeable in the Hebrew Scriptures or Old Testament will find here that one greater than Moses and Elijah and Elisha is in the people's midst. John (and Jesus) wants us to know that Jesus is greater than all Old Testament persons, types, institutions and symbols. He replaces and fulfills and exceeds all of them. Most likely, Jesus doesn't start from scratch because he wants to show that he can multiply food and resources in abundance, excelling the miraculous acts of Elijah and Elisha (1 Kings 17:7-24 and 2 Kings 4:1-36, respectively). Elijah and Elisha each multiply resources for the needy (flour and oil in the case of Elijah and oil in the case of Elisha). Each one of them also raises a boy to life. Jesus exponentially multiplies resources in John 6 and will later raise Lazarus and himself to life. Jesus exceeds the people's expectations of the great prophet to come, if they will only take the time to consider who he truly is and what he ultimately does.

Moving on, we will find that Jesus is greater than Moses and the Passover in John 6. Whereas manna fell from heaven in abundance at the time of Moses, here the bread and loaves are multiplied and distributed in abundance from the hands of Jesus (Jn 6:11; Ex 16:1-36). And just as God tests the people when he gives them the food from heaven (Ex 16), Jesus tests his disciples and the people here to see if they will depend on him and his word.

Jesus' followers don't appear to be trusting very well. I doubt if I would do any better. After all, Jesus is on a prime-time stage now, and the odds against him are greater. Unlike the turning of the water into wine and the healing of the lame man episodes, which only appeared on local stations, Jesus is now on national TV performing an even greater feat. If Jesus can't follow through and deliver, it will be a public relations disaster. If there isn't enough bread and fish to go around to feed the people's faces, there will be egg in his and his followers' faces. What would Jesus' PR disciples say if Jesus can't perform the magic trick? How would they spin it? Perhaps they would say: "People started gorging themselves and wouldn't share," or "Jesus only meant for the morsels to serve as finger food, and the National Guard was supposed to fly in supplies for the main course, so direct your complaint to the Pentagon," or "Barley farmers have just gone on strike, and Jesus, being an old-school Democrat, is a union man; he's cancelled the miracle show until the strike is over," or "Given the dwindling salmon population, Jesus decided not to perform the miracle but to do a mass sit-in by the Sea of Galilee and fast to protest the government's building of more dams."

Fortunately for the disciples, Jesus comes through and delivers: "When they had all had enough to eat, he said to his disciples, 'Gather the pieces that are left over. Let nothing be wasted.' So they gathered them and filled twelve baskets with the pieces of the five barley loaves left over by those who had eaten" (Jn 6:12-13). Twelve baskets. Twelve tribes. Twelve disciples. Fullness and fulfillment.

Sound intriguing? The biblical backdrop is God's provision of manna at the pleading of Moses' people for food (Ex 16). Jesus is that same God, and he is greater than Moses. Jesus fulfills in their day what God did for the people wandering about with Moses in the wilderness on the way to the Promised Land. The symbolism is not lost on the crowds, and so they want to take Jesus by force and make him king, proclaiming him to be the prophet like Moses who is to come into the world (Jn 6:14-15; Deut 18:15).

They have great expectations for Jesus, but Jesus will not allow them to define him with their expectations. Instead, he withdraws again to a mountain to be by himself: "After the people saw the miraculous sign that Jesus did, they began to say, 'Surely this is the Prophet who is to come into the world.' Jesus, knowing that they intended to come and make him king by force, withdrew again to a mountain by himself" (Jn 6:14-15). During the night, Jesus appears to his core disciples, walking on the water to them as they row wind-tossed across a turbulent lake, perhaps leading them and John's readers to recall how Moses led the people across the Red Sea (Jn 6:16-21; Ex 13). One cannot be certain that there is a connection here, but it is possible in the context of John 6, with the very clear biblical imagery of manna and the Passover.

We will deal more with many of these biblical images in "Happy Meals," but in concluding this essay, we should ponder the people's great expectations of Jesus and their desire to make him king by force. Given what Jesus has done for them, I can understand their excitement and efforts. Their situation is pretty dire. They probably don't have much by way of food—certainly not three square meals a day, and their clothing is sparse.

Most of us have so much more than they do, and so our expectations of Jesus are likely less basic and yet probably still as demanding. Most of us probably don't look to Jesus to give us our next meal, but we might look to him to add to our wardrobe or to help us advance our careers and increase our benefit packages. Moreover, we live in a culture driven by consumer demand and untrained desire. So we may be asking Jesus, "What have you done for me lately?" in a very different way. Instead of asking "What will you give me to eat today?" we may be asking him, "Will you help me find a great discount on my favorite brand of jeans?" or "Will you help me succeed in my career or course of studies?" And what if he doesn't help us succeed or get ahead or find the discounted brand jeans we cherish so? What if he doesn't meet our great expectations for what we would make him out to be? Consumer demand means that we will likely try to take Jesus by force and make him king.

Like the people in Jesus' day, we don't realize what life in Jesus is all about—freedom from ourselves and freedom for God and others as we live abundantly by faith in him and his word rather than out of the fear of scarcity.[2] When will we truly realize that Jesus himself—and not the bread or the new jeans or the raise or the career move—is our daily sustenance and significance for life? When will we realize that Jesus is greater than Moses and Elijah and Elisha, and that our expectations for life are often so trivial and that Jesus is so far greater than our greatest expectations?

HAPPY MEALS
John 6:22-71

The crowds are following Jesus around in search of an endless supply of free Happy Meals (Jn 6:22-25). They're not seeking him as an end in himself, but as a means to an end: filling their guts with free bread served fast. They want more and more free food, calling out: "Supersize me!" So when the crowds find Jesus the day after the miraculous feeding of the multitudes, Jesus says to them, "I tell you the truth, you are looking for me, not because you saw miraculous signs but because you ate the loaves and had your fill" (Jn 6:26). Jesus goes on to exhort them to seek for food that is eternal, not the kind that spoils: "Do not work for food that spoils, but for food that endures to eternal life, which the Son of Man will give you. On him God the Father has placed his seal of approval" (Jn 6:27). Jesus will later say that he is the bread of eternal life: "I am the bread of life. He who comes to me will never go hungry, and he who believes in me will never be thirsty" (Jn 6:35).

As in the previous passage, the Old Testament backdrop includes God's provision of manna for the feeding of Moses and the Israelites in the wilderness (Ex 16). I believe Jesus is also alluding to God's provision of water to Moses and the Israelites at the rock at Meribah (Ex 17:1-7), for he talks of taking away their hunger *and thirst* (Jn 6:35). There is more. Jesus also alludes to the Passover celebration in his exhortation to the crowds here (Ex 12:1-30). For he claims, "I tell you the truth, unless you eat the flesh of the Son of Man and drink his blood, you have no life in you. Whoever eats my flesh and drinks my blood has eternal life, and I will raise him up at the last day. For my flesh is real food and my blood is real drink" (Jn 6:53-55). No doubt, John wants us to take note of connections to the Passover (as well as the other Old Testament images) given that he mentions earlier that the Passover is near (Jn 6:4).

The point of this passage is that Jesus is the true manna, the true water from the rock (Paul makes this point about Jesus being the rock from which the water springs in 1 Cor 10:1-5) and the great Passover Lamb. As such, Jesus is the ultimate fulfillment of the Old Testament or Hebrew Scriptures. Along these same lines, Jesus and John would have us know that Jesus is greater than Moses.

But the crowds don't accept this reality. Moreover, they try to get Jesus to compete with Moses. As evidenced by Jesus' conversation with them, they want to know what miraculous sign he will do to show them that he is great like Moses (Jn 6:30-33). But their ultimate aim in requesting a sign is not so that they can believe in Jesus, but so that they can fill their guts with food (Jn 6:26). They're looking for more free bread, not for more Jesus. No wonder they and later Jesus' disciples miss the symbolism and stumble over Jesus' words (Jn 6:52, 60). They can't get their minds out of their guts.

Above I quoted Jesus saying that his flesh is real food and his blood is real drink (Jn 6:53-55). Although Jesus' claims are staggering in their messianic significance and import, Jesus and John are not espousing cannibalism. Rather, Jesus and John call on everyone to believe in Jesus as the Christ through attention to Jesus' claims and signs. Jesus himself says in this passage that the flesh counts for nothing. It is the Spirit alone who gives life (through creating faith in Jesus' words): "The Spirit gives life; the flesh counts for nothing. The words I have spoken to you are spirit and they are life. Yet there are some of you who do not believe" (Jn 6:63-64). Believing and depending on Jesus constitutes eternal sustenance, for Jesus is the bread of life and living water (Jn 6:35).[3] The person who believes in Jesus has eternal life, for Jesus is the bread of life. To believe in Jesus is to eat of him as the bread of heaven, which is his flesh:

> I tell you the truth, he who believes has everlasting life. I am the bread of life. Your forefathers ate the manna in the desert, yet they died. But here is the bread that comes down from heaven, which a man may eat and not die. I am the living bread that came down from heaven. If anyone eats of this bread, he will live forever. This bread is my flesh, which I will give for the life of the world. (Jn 6:47-51)

If only the crowds would realize that Jesus as the food of eternal life is so much more satisfying than the fast, free food that they seek! Although the food Jesus gives them is better for them than McDonald's Big Macs and Filet-o-Fish sandwiches, Jesus *as* food is more nutritional than anything else he can give them to eat. He alone is life-giving. And still, all they want is free, fast food.

We're like that today. While it may not be bread we seek at church, we often gorge ourselves on fast-food spirituality: how to do religion in three easy steps, religious trinkets with all the bells and whistles and celebrity-status Christianity high on glitter and low on the cross. None of this will satisfy, for it is just like fast food. It goes down quickly, but doesn't stick.

Fast food doesn't seem like real food. It goes down fast, and it goes away fast. It often makes me feel heavy, but it never really satisfies me. Maybe that's why there are all the trappings, trimmings and special sauces—colorful cardboard and paper wrapping, toys and trinkets, lettuce, pickles, mayo, mustard and mucho ketchup. That way, we won't notice how little value or specialness special value meals really have. American life and American religion are like that. It's like a giant McDonald's, where everyone goes in search of an endless supply of quick-fix, free, special-value Happy Meals, but where everyone comes away still feeling empty and in short supply of joy.

Now I must admit that sometimes I take my family to a fast-food burger joint when we're on a family outing or vacation. The taste is pretty good, and the price isn't bad. The kids like the trinkets, and I like my kids happy. I have peace of mind in the family van when the kids' mouths are full. Food keeps them quiet and keeps them from grumbling—kind of like the children of Israel on their way with Moses or Jesus to the Promised Land. God's preferred approach is to quiet them with manna burgers; God only uses snakes as a last resort (Num 21:4-9). (With some fast food joints, I've wondered if they've replaced ground cow with rattler.)

Sharing meals together is supposed to be a way of building relationships. But just as American life is like a giant fast-food restaurant, the breakfast bar joining kitchen and dining room in many homes often functions like a drive-up window where people collect their orders to go.

American families rarely sit down together to eat meals. And if they do, they're not really together—each person is doing his or her own thing. Like my family driving down the road in the van with our drive-up window entries in hand, many of us are never content with where we are or what we have—"When will we get there?" "I'm finished with my burger. Can we stop for ice cream?" Our backs to our kids, who are sitting behind us. Music blaring. If only Moses had had a Walkman or stereo speakers to drown out the noise, he wouldn't have had to warn the just-finished-eating-but-grumbling-for-more crowds so often, "If I have to stop this camel and turn around one more time . . . !"

If Moses were leading the people today, it wouldn't be enough to give them quail or manna from heaven or water from the rock. The same thing over and over is never enough, especially today. While the people wanted variety then, we want infinite variety now. Somehow variety seems to take the boredom out of shopping for stuff. When stuff is what we really want, and an infinite variety of it, we will never be truly happy or full of joy. For stuff, by its very nature, never lasts. All that lasts from these fast-food meals are the wrappers I find under the kids' seats every time I look in the van; the toys and trinkets disappear right away.

As in Moses' day, the crowds in Jesus' day want stuff: more and more stuff. Jesus, on the other hand, wants relationship: "Whoever eats my flesh and drinks my blood remains in me, and I in him" (Jn 6:56). The crowds want what Jesus can give them, but do they want *him?* "The Jews" don't accept his word. They don't want to believe in him. They would rather stumble and grumble over his words and raise questions over his pedigree than trust in him (see Jn 6:41, 43, 52, 60-61, for instances in which "the Jews" and/or disciples stumble and grumble over Jesus' words, and Jn 6:41-42, where questions are raised over Jesus as the son of Joseph and Mary).[4] They're cynical and their hearts are calloused, which just goes to show that they do not have the eternal life Jesus offers them. We have this problem in relationships today—not just with God, but especially with God. We use relationships for what they can do for us and what they can get us, but not for what we give to others and receive from them. We keep our distance from intimacy and trust through our cynicism and calloused hearts.

Stuff may cost us a lot to get, and it may cost us a lot relationally. We often want stuff that's sweet, that glimmers and that makes pretty music. And when our relationships threaten to turn sour, lose their shine and sound off-key, we dump them like last year's purchases for upgrades. What's that saying about us? That kind of fast-food frenzy and shopaholism, with large servings of cholesterol and credit card debt to go, should warn us that heart attacks and bankruptcy court await us in the sky—not just the food court in the local shopping mall.

Meaningful relationships are costly. They don't always taste good. Sometimes I have to swallow bitter pills. But sometimes those things we think will taste bad make us feel great and make us whole. I can't imagine Jesus' flesh, blood and bones going down easy. Sometimes one has to gulp hard. But it's worth the effort. Why? Because Jesus is life-giving, and he alone makes us whole. To some people, however, that can sound like a quick-fix answer for a fast-food culture. So let's chew on it a bit more. To do so, we'll have to take a look at filet-o-fisherman Peter.

This chapter, and this passage in particular, is a high water point in the Gospel, signifying that the opposition to Jesus is reaching new heights; really, we find here a point of no return for many, including many of Jesus' disciples who leave Jesus at this juncture. And yet, while "the Jews" grumble and stumble and most of the disciples abandon Jesus because of his hard teaching about eating him, Peter holds tightly to his word: "From this time many of his disciples turned back and no longer followed him. 'You do not want to leave too, do you?' Jesus asked the Twelve. Simon Peter answered him, 'Lord, to whom shall we go? You have the words of eternal life. We believe and know that you are the Holy One of God'" (Jn 6:66-69).

Why can Peter—but not the crowds, "the Jews" and most of the disciples—stomach Jesus' words? For one, Jesus and his Father have chosen him. In other words, it's not because Peter's stomach is tougher, or because he's smarter or more righteous. It's because of Jesus and his Father. Jesus and his Father have chosen Peter and the rest of the twelve, just as Jesus says. The Father who gave Moses and the people bread has sent Jesus to the people as the true bread from heaven (Jn 6:32-33). All whom the Father gives Jesus will come to him, and Jesus will never drive them away (Jn 6:37). No one can come to Jesus unless the Father who sent Jesus draws him or her, and Jesus will raise that person up on the last day (Jn 6:44). And as the Son lives because of the Father who sent him, so the one who feeds on Jesus will live because of him (Jn 6:57). This kind of choosing (election) is hard to swallow for those who would seek after autonomy and the freedom to choose their own destinies. But for those like Peter, who desire intimacy with God that is initiated and sustained by God, it is a life-giving truth.

But Peter has a further basis for his answer. Why does Peter take hold of Jesus' word and Judas doesn't? "Then Jesus replied, 'Have I not chosen you, the Twelve? Yet one of you is a devil!' (He meant Judas, the son of Simon Iscariot, who, though one of the Twelve, was later to betray him)" (Jn 6:70). Spiritual bankruptcy has something to do with it. Peter had made his living as a food provider before becoming a follower of Jesus, whereas Judas makes his living stealing money from the money bag (Jn 12:6). This is bankruptcy of another kind. Judas is in it for what he can get for himself, not for what he can receive from Jesus.

Peter had been a fisherman. His trade demanded sacrifice and patience—lots of patience. He knows what it's like to go without, slaving all night to catch fish and coming away empty-netted. Peter had witnessed the miracle of Jesus filling his net to the breaking point. And it broke him. The story goes that Jesus climbs into Simon Peter's boat one day early on in his ministry and asks him to pull out a little ways from the shore (Lk 5:1-11). The crowds are pressing in around him to listen to the word of God, and Jesus is at the water's edge. After Jesus finishes speaking to the crowds, he turns to Peter, who has been out all night fishing with his crew but who has returned with empty nets, exhausted and empty-hearted. Jesus tells him to go out into deep water and throw out the nets for a catch. Jesus, a carpenter's son and itinerant preacher, is telling a professional fisherman how to fish! Peter is no doubt dumbfounded and exasperated; he bites his lip, however, because there's something about Jesus. And Jesus speaks with such authority. Instead of telling Jesus to jump in the lake, Peter does what Jesus says. What happens? The nets begin to break. Those in Peter's boat call for their partners in another boat to come and help them with the catch. Both boats begin to sink because of the super-sized catch of fish. Luke tells us, "When Simon Peter saw this, he fell at Jesus' knees and said, 'Go away from me, Lord; I am a sinful man!' For he and all his companions were astonished at the catch of fish they had taken, and so were James and John, the sons of Zebedee, Simon's partners. Then Jesus said to Simon, 'Don't be afraid; from now on you will catch men.' So they pulled their boats up on shore, left everything and followed him" (Lk 5:8-11). Talk about reckless abandon, spiritual brokenness and bankruptcy.

Whereas Judas steals from the money bag, Jesus has stolen Peter's heart. Peter has both torn nets and a torn and broken spirit. A broken and contrite heart before God is the most beautiful thing in the world. The true Christ-followers or disciples, like Peter, hold tightly to Jesus' hard teaching, even if they don't get what Jesus is saying.[5] No doubt it's because Jesus holds tightly to them. But it's also because such followers have come to the end of themselves, the end of their resources, the end of self-sufficiency. They have seen how futile it is to go on fishing in oblivion or to wander about in a desert wasteland, hopping from Messiah to Messiah in search of free fast food.

Peter's words quoted earlier are the kind of food that stick to my heart, not just my ribs: "Lord, to whom shall we go? You have the words of eternal life. We believe and know that you are the Holy One of God" (Jn 6:68-69). Peter knows that catch of fish upon fish and infinite free Happy Meal supplies won't do it. Nor will a member's pass to the Fishermen's Wharf Club. Jesus' words alone will do it, for they flow from Jesus' life as the Holy One of God. But Peter's words put him in an exclusive club of those long excluded for holding only to Jesus.

The people in the crowds here may be the same ones who later respond to Peter's and John's words in the Acts of the Apostles, where five thousand are saved (Acts 4:4). But for now, they're not biting. Most disciples abandon Jesus because of his hard teaching, which causes them to stumble. Even many of Jesus' own disciples and one of his apostles, Judas, are mentioned here as reacting to him and rejecting Jesus. They reject him and his claim of coming from God and returning to God through the cross as a dead, battered, bloodied Messiah (Jn 6:58 and 62, along with the imagery of eating Jesus' flesh and drinking his blood, speak to

Jesus being the true bread who comes down from heaven and who ascends by way of the cross). The crowds, "the Jews," most of his disciples and an apostle fail to see him for who he truly is: the one who is greater than Moses, the ultimate bread of heaven and the true Passover Lamb.[6]

The crowds want a super-sized Jesus to cholesterol-attack and destroy the Romans. (As an aside, the best way to defeat America's enemies would be to get them to eat what Americans eat.) Thus, the crowds can't stomach Jesus. They want the free meal on their terms. Most of Jesus' own followers stop following him. They'd rather break than be broken. They'd rather drown in sin than be rescued. But not Peter, the brokenhearted fisherman with torn nets, who has witnessed the breaking and distributing of the bread and fish and who will witness the broken Jesus. Jesus says and does hard things to soften people's hard hearts, though some are further hardened.

Peter has witnessed Jesus bringing forth abundance time and time again. So he can trust him here. I can trust Jesus too. When Jesus breaks me, he does it to bring life. Jesus has no trouble giving free food to people, and lots of it, but he always presses home the point that we must seek after the free gift of eternal life—himself. When Jesus breaks me just as he did Peter, he wants me to move beyond my attempts at self-sufficiency so that I cling to him and his word in faith.

This *is* a hard teaching. Who can accept it? (See Jn 6:60.) My flesh can't accept this teaching. The hard-of-heart disciples who raise the question before abandoning him can't accept it. Only those whose hearts have been broken by Jesus' difficult but life-giving teaching and way can accept it. But why does adherence to Jesus involve so much effort? Why can't we put Jesus in the blender, or mix a little bit of him into our strawberry shake? Wouldn't it be better to just wait for that new product with the ad that will say, "Three steps to complete union with Christ—now! Why wait when it can all be yours for just $39.95? The phone lines are open. Order *Jesus Juice* today, and be divinized tomorrow."

We want everything yesterday, and yet we want it fresh. *Fast* food symbolizes everything we prize with the promise of getting it all now. And yet it seems like all we do is wait. The drive-up window line at the burger joint is backed up for blocks, and I've been on hold at 1-800-JC-

Juice for such a long time. In contrast, Jesus never promises to make our journey easy and never provides us with a drive-up window option. He warns us that there will be plenty of waiting and hoping going on.

We can't understand that the best things in life often take the most time to make. And besides, we've been in this mess of negative consumption a heck of a long time—going way back to the garden burger grease pit Adam opened in Eden and franchised just east of it. There are no quick fixes; just fast food. And that won't help us in the long run.

Jesus alone has the words of eternal life, but it will mean death to my flesh. We don't feed on him to suffer. But feeding on him entails suffering with him as we suffer the death of our flesh. It's part of the package—his very own special value meal. We are what we eat. If we feed on Jesus and identify completely with him, we will become like him. Jesus doesn't promise us free fast-food Happy Meals, but he does promise to lead us into freedom through the joyful meal of exchanging our lives for his, drinking from his cup and feasting on him and his Word in faith. Entering into his free-of-charge detox program is better than any "detox diet." While it will certainly cost us our fleshly lives, just think of all the money we'll save on doctors' bills. So go ahead: super-Jesus-size me![7]

A FAILED CANDIDACY
John 7:1-44

By all accounts, it's a failed candidacy. Up until now, Jesus is the front-runner in the race for Messiah. But right when he has the people eating bread and fish from his hand, he tells them that the answer to the world hunger problem is to eat his body and drink his blood. A scandalous teaching that will certainly make the tabloid news front covers: "Jesus a Cannibal—Tells the Crowds, 'Eat My Flesh.'"[8] Try as hard as they can, his campaign spin doctors will not be able to talk this one down, even if he claims that he didn't inhale.

It sounds gross today, and it sounded gross then. Many on his campaign team, including Judas, couldn't believe it—we sense that the tensions between Jesus and Judas are beginning to surface (Jn 6:70). Every time Jesus soars ahead in the polls, he pulls a Dan Quayle and says something that sounds so unpresidential. Political opportunists like Judas start wondering if we've got the wrong person picked for the Messiah. At the very least, Jesus is in the wrong place, and his timing is all off. We will come to the matters of location and timing a little later on in this essay.

Why might Jesus not be the best choice for Messiah? Because he's from Nazareth. It's kind of like being from Arkansas: hick country, or so many seem to think. And he and his family line have no social clout. They have no money. Most candidates can buy a few million votes by putting their own millions to good use and paying for TV ads. But not Jesus. All he's got is what's on his back and in the money bag, and we already know Judas keeps helping himself to that.

And as a backwoods hick from Nazareth, Jesus has no power base. He never makes his peace with the back-room power brokers and king-makers in the big city. In fact, he only provokes and angers them, never holding to the party line.

The only thing he had going for him until now was that he appeared to be the people's candidate, since he's not a Washington or Jerusalem insider. Although many confuse him with Santa Claus come Christmas-time, Jesus refuses to play Santa or promise to give them whatever they wish for. We like candidates who make us feel good about ourselves, who tell us what we want to hear. Although he never said he would raise taxes, he refuses to promise a chicken in every pot and a car in every garage. Instead he promises supporters that "whoever believes in me, as the Scripture has said, streams of living water will flow from within him" (Jn 7:38). Not very tangible results. The only times he performs miracles is out of compassion, never for self-promotion. In fact, as witnessed in the Synoptic Gospels, he often tells those witnessing his healings to keep the miracles to themselves. He doesn't ever seem to want to make the evening news.

Staying with the Samaritans in John 4 was a bad move. He should have joined the royal official noted in the same chapter at his summer home on Martha's Vineyard for a few days instead. And he should have spent far more time in Jerusalem than in Galilee and other unseemly places like Samaria.

This point leads us to his conversation with his brothers. While his brothers are no help to him, still they are right. No one running for Messiah hides! Recall how in John 6:14-15 Jesus withdraws from the crowds when they want to come and make him king by force. The savvy and successful candidate goes public with his campaign on center stage in Jerusalem of Judea (not Galilee; see Jn 7:1) and at prime time during the Feasts (such as the Feast of Tabernacles which is near; see Jn 7:2).[9] "'You ought to leave here and go to Judea, so that your disciples may see the miracles you do. No one who wants to become a public figure acts in secret. Since you are doing these things, show yourself to the world.' For even his own brothers did not believe in him" (Jn 7:3-5). Even Jesus' brothers react to him and don't accept him.

Jesus' answer to them is classic red-letter Jesus: "The right time for me has not yet come; for you any time is right. The world cannot hate you, but it hates me because I testify that what it does is evil. You go to the Feast. I am not yet going up to this Feast, because for me the right time has not yet come" (Jn 7:6-8). The more he speaks, the more his campaign finances move toward the red.

Jesus' time or hour has not yet come. He has not yet been glorified. For them, any time is right. Jesus keeps talking like this. He never seems to seize the moment. And the opportunity to take control of his own political destiny is slipping through his fingers.

It must be very difficult for Jesus' closest followers. Their own political ambitions and fortunes are so wrapped up with his. I know that as I get older, I see opportunities to rise on the religious scene come and go (most of the time, go!). My window of opportunity to make it big, for good or for bad motives, gets narrower by the moment. Their own window of opportunity is narrowing now too. And probably the biggest frustration for them is that Jesus is the most qualified person to be president or king: he's the best public speaker, the biggest wonder worker and even the most sensitive of the candidates to the people's needs. Just think what he could do to alleviate world hunger!

But Jesus doesn't seem to want to be elected. In fact, if one listens closely to all his past messages, he never did. We put him there. It's not that we wanted *Jesus* to be president. *We* wanted to be working the control room in the West Wing, and we thought our best opportunity to gain control of all the world's problems (i.e., other people) was through him. We should have chosen someone else with whom to throw in our political lot; now we're throwing it all away.

Jesus never positioned himself as the savior of conservatives or liberals, or of moderates for that matter. So he has never gained ground with a major voting bloc. While he has never been accused of playing to the political winds of change, he is accused of deceiving the people and disturbing the peace. So much for the stump speech the "sons of thunder" (James and John) have written on world peace to be delivered at the Passover Feast. While Jesus has given every appearance of being shrewd as a serpent and innocent as a dove throughout his career, playing the independent card doesn't play too well in a two-party system of Pharisees and Sadducees. There's no evidence he has ever ridden on an elephant, and the donkey's foal on which he later rides into Jerusalem is too young to vote. As time marches forward, and as Jesus nears Jerusalem, some wonder if he has what it takes to win. He has even started to talk about conspiracy theories and assassination plots on his life. "'Has not Moses given you the law? Yet not one of you keeps the law. Why are you trying to kill me?' 'You are demon-possessed,' the crowd answered. 'Who is trying to kill you?'" (Jn 7:19-20; see also Jn 7:1, which speaks of the reason that Jesus stays away from Jerusalem at first: the authorities in Jerusalem want to take his life). Jesus appears to be unraveling before their very eyes! As the old saying goes, "If you can't take the heat, get out of the kitchen." No wonder he doesn't promise a chicken in every pot.

Actually, the pressure must be nearly unbearable for Jesus. The closer he gets to Jerusalem and the center of power, the heavier is the burden on his soul. Whereas his followers would use his position to bring about good, remove evil and eradicate world hunger, he knows of a far worse hunger that can never be satisfied until streams of living water—the Spirit—flow from within us all:

> On the last and greatest day of the Feast, Jesus stood and said in a loud voice, "If anyone is thirsty, let him come to me and drink. Whoever believes in me, as the Scripture has said, streams of living water will flow from within him." By this he meant the Spirit, whom those who believed in him were later to receive. Up to that

time the Spirit had not been given, since Jesus had not yet been glorified. (Jn 7:37-39)[10]

The glorification here will follow on the heels of his defeat in the opinion polls and voting booths across the nation. Sometimes the best thing that can happen to a politician is to lose an election. The political revolutionary can often effect more change as an outsider, keeping pressure on those inside. The back-room power brokers can never compromise the revolutionary's message if he stays an outsider. And while they may try to silence his or her voice, it doesn't work in the case of Jesus. By assassinating him, they only make it possible for the pundits and the people to hail him as the original Comeback Kid, once his theo-political fortunes rise from the dead. I guess Jesus has friends in high places after all.

THE MATRIX
John 7:45-53

Things are not as they appear. Nicodemus comes to find this out. A mob that supposedly knows nothing of the law and is cursed believes in Jesus and is blessed, whereas the chief priests and Pharisees who think they know everything are blind and are cursed even though they appear blessed (Jn 7:48-49).[11] This is the way things are in the Matrix. Life in the Matrix is an illusion.

The movie *The Matrix* chronicles a time in the future when machines create a simulated world to control humans using their bodies' natural energy as a power source to fuel their own ambitions of world domination. People are blind to the Matrix, living a lie.

We will come back to Nicodemus, but it is not simply in this account in John 7 that we find that things are not as they appear. This theme runs throughout John's Gospel. People claim to be free but are enslaved (Jn 8:31-36). People think they walk in the light but are shrouded in darkness (Jn 3:19-21). Some who are esteemed as honorable authorities and gatekeepers and who are paid to protect the masses are ravenous wolves, thieves and robbers who will tear the masses to pieces (Jn 10:1-21)—real-life versions of *The Matrix's* Agent Smith. They and we, too, are living a lie. We are all living in the Matrix.

John the Baptist and John are like ancient versions of Morpheus, who tell us we need to be free. But we can't free ourselves; we're not in control. We can't free our minds or our souls, no matter how many red pills we take, if we are not talking about faith in God's chosen one as the red pill. We can only be free if the chosen one sets us free.

But who is this chosen one, and how does he set us free? He's an ancient version of a computer hacker, wanted by the law for breaking the codes—the moral (immoral) laws and traditions that control us. How does he break these coded chains? Not by guns or martial arts, as in the movie *The Matrix*, but by dying to the power games that enslave us and by offering sacrificial love as our redemption. It's all so contrary to our experience. But we must remember: things are not as they appear.

Faith in his Word moves us beyond appearance to reality. We can't see without faith, but we only have faith if we trust, and we only trust if we are loved. And John's Gospel tells us that we are loved, even if you can't imagine that can be true based on your experience or based on what others tell you. So imagine it based on what God's Word tells you: "For God so loved the world that he gave his one and only Son [the chosen one] that whoever believes in him will not perish but have eternal life" (Jn 3:16). Though you may think what you are imagining in this text is simulation, it is reality.

Imagining life in view of the light of God's true love, poured out in Christ's sacrifice, is a matter of life and death. But many would rather not come into this light for fear that their evil deeds will be exposed. They would live the lie rather than walk in the truth (Jn 3:19-21). John's Gospel tells you that you have a choice to make. You can open your eyes, discover the Matrix and learn how to get out of it—or you can continue living the lie. It would be so much easier simply to take the blue pill and wake up to find that everything is just like it always was—that is, before you started deciphering the code while reading John's Gospel.

I wonder what it is like for Nicodemus when, after his late-night conversation with Jesus (recorded in Jn 3), he realizes that this young upstart outsider from Galilee is actually the truth, whereas he and his fellow power-brokering insiders are living the lie. In John 7, we find that Nicodemus is beginning to see things for what they really are. Nicodemus seeks to defend Jesus against his fellow Pharisees and also the chief priests, who want to arrest Jesus (Jn 7:32). Nicodemus says: "Does our law condemn anyone without first hearing him to find out what he is doing?" (Jn 7:51). Their response: "Are you from Galilee, too? Look into it, and you will find that a prophet does not come out of Galilee" (Jn 7:52). (They fail to realize that Jesus is from Bethlehem in Judea, but I doubt they even care to check the sources; see Jn 7:40-44.) The verse following says that "each went to his own home" (Jn 7:53). I wonder if Nicodemus sleeps at all this night. He is beginning to realize that he must choose a side. One way or another, the consequences will be enormous.

The pressure his fellow Agent Smiths will put on him will be severe. It is their job to eradicate anyone or anything that would interfere with the simulation of reality that they preserve. In this simulated universe with its projection of illusion, light is darkness and darkness is light, life is death and death is life, glory is shame and shame is glory, insiders are outsiders and outsiders are insiders. The external façade of sweet niceties and everyday normalcy shrouds the internal reality of cancerous abnormality and hostility that lead the people to seek Jesus' death.

No wonder Jesus doesn't entrust himself to anyone except his Father, for he knows what is in a person's heart (Jn 2:24-25). All too often we look on the outward appearance rather than make right judgments, and we trust in flesh rather than in God. But where does focus on the outward appearance and trust in the flesh get us in the long run? It gets us more and more entrapped and enslaved in the Matrix.

It can get so overwhelming, and it can make you paranoid. Besides having to be conscious of Agent Smith's whereabouts, you also have to account for Cypher—the Judas friend. He'll kiss you on the cheek and stab you in the back right after you drink from the same cup with him. So who's got your back?

Nicodemus isn't like Judas. He's no backstabber. Nicodemus sides with Jesus' cause in the end and helps Joseph of Arimathea bury him (Jn 19:38-42). But still, Nicodemus can't raise Jesus from the dead; nor can any of his disciples. Deliverance will have to come from outside the simulated world of the Matrix. And so it is with us.

While you and I no doubt have friends who will side with us to the

end, they can't raise you and me from the dead. Our hope and help will
come from outside the Matrix. As with the movie *The Matrix*, things are
not as they appear. But unlike the movie, it's not by winning at the power
games but by *dying* to them that we live. It's as we trust in Jesus (as opposed to ourselves) that we are redeemed: his sacrificial love flows from
the world above to free us from this simulated world of total domination
below; in him we are resurrected by his Father from the dead.

So put away the blue pill. While you're at it, put away confidence in
yourself. There's no place for a Neo complex in Jesus' universe; neither
Neo nor you can free your mind. You can only be free as Jesus calls you
to do the inexplicable, as you let go of control and become controlled by
him. You can be free only as you take the red pill of faith and tumble
down the "rabbit hole" that Morpheus talks about and wake up in Jesus'
embrace. It's only as you hold to Jesus' teaching and as you are held by
his Father' affectionate gaze that you will be free from Agent Smith,
paranoia and blind fate.

I imagine that you may feel a bit like Alice at times, as John's Gospel
reveals to you more and more that things are not as they appear in this
world. Don't worry, Alice. He'll catch you. So then: do you want to know
what the Matrix really is? Do you want to see how deep the rabbit hole in
the ground goes? Do you want to stay in Wonderland? If the answer is
yes, then go ahead: take the red pill.

TWO TO TANGO
John 8:1-11

We live in a blame-game culture in which it's always the other person's
fault and in which litigation news and shows capture people's imaginations. By all appearances, you would think that it only takes one to do
the tango.

So it is with the tale of the woman caught in adultery in John 8.[12]
While the earliest manuscripts do not include this episode, the story
resonates well with everything we know of Jesus and those trying to
bring him down. Jesus' opponents bring a woman caught in adultery to
Jesus and throw her down at his feet. They want to test him, trying to get
him to oppose the law, in order to accuse him and do away with him. "In

the Law Moses commanded us to stone such women. Now what do you say?" (Jn 8:5).

The woman's life is in Jesus' hands. So is Jesus' life. Jesus does not respond immediately. He knows it's a trick. Instead he kneels down and begins writing in the sand. The woman's accusers don't let up. They keep on with their questioning. Finally he stands up and says to them: "If any one of you is without sin, let him be the first to throw a stone at her" (Jn 8:7). Then Jesus bends down again and continues writing on the ground.

The woman's accusers are now speechless. One by one they drop their stones and their charge against her and walk away, the older ones first. (The older ones probably know better; they likely have accumulated a larger pile of sins, and it was also customary for the oldest accuser to throw the first stone.[13]) After they are all gone, the Lord says to the woman still at his feet: "'Woman, where are they? Has no one condemned you?' 'No one, sir,' she said. 'Then neither do I condemn you,' Jesus declared. 'Go now and leave your life of sin'" (Jn 8:10-11).

Jesus does not ignore what she has done. While Jesus does not condemn her, he does not condone her sin, either. He tells her to go and sin no more. We often forget that part of the story. However, the million-dollar question was: What was Jesus writing in the sand? The sins of the persons who had accused her? Perhaps each one of them had slept with her or someone like her before. And since she had been caught in adultery, where was the man with whom she had just slept (Jn 8:3)? It takes more than one to do the tango. The law of Moses required that both parties be brought forth to be stoned, not just the woman (Deut 22:22).

Jesus upholds the law, not the accusers or the accused. He walks in the light, for he is the light, as the next account makes clear. The rest—accusers and accused—walk in darkness. And yet, Jesus brings his light into the darkness and becomes the guilty party, even though he is completely faultless.

But still we go on with our blame game. We keep acting as if we were the victims and as if everyone else were the victimizer. We don't mind throwing stones. But we forget the old saying: "People who live in glass houses shouldn't throw stones." (Translation: Don't accuse and criticize others when you have faults of your own to address.)

If the million-dollar question is, "What was Jesus writing in the sand?" the *ten*-million dollar question is, "Why do we like playing the victim card, accusing others of victimizing us, when the only truly innocent victim, Jesus, doesn't play the blame game with us—his victimizers—but forgives us?"

We're all implicated. We're all doing the tango together—not just one of us, not just two of us but all of us. We keep dancing with the devil by playing the blame game when we could be dancing with Jesus, who sheds light on our situation and helps us to see that we've been doing the tango—stepping on one another's toes. He helps us to see that we need to accept his forgiveness and forgive others so that we can dance to a new tune with Jesus as the lead partner. So shall we dance?

FALSE REDEMPTION
John 8:12-59

On the Web, people go to chat rooms, constantly changing their identities while searching for meaningful relationships. Others are constantly updating their Facebook statuses, asking their list of contacts to check out their latest and greatest. The rapid-fire responses they receive affect the images of themselves they wish to project in the future.

Others go to department stores to buy brand-name items to gain significance in the eyes of others. The thinking goes that I can never get a boyfriend or girlfriend unless I buy this product. The market is always changing. Our identities are always changing. In a free-market system, a product has no value unless people buy it, and you have no value unless you buy the bestselling item. The hot commodity today is cold tomorrow. You have to buy the latest thing to stay hot.

We think we are free, but we are enslaved to what peer responses and supposedly free and liberating markets make of us. As a paid theologian, I can't afford to buy many brand-name items or to find my worth in the accumulation of more and more stuff. And I am Web-challenged, finding blogging mind-boggling. So I have to find my significance elsewhere, hoping to write that book that will put me over the top and win for me widespread acclaim. But what if it never happens?

What if we never find what we're looking for in chat rooms, shopping malls or Amazon's book rankings? When we find our identity by changing our identity to meet others, by buying brand names to gain significance in the eyes of others and by trying to achieve acclaim by what we accomplish, we lose our identity.

In contrast to us, Jesus is secure in his identity. How can it be otherwise? Jesus says in John 8 that he is from above and that his accusers (and the rest of us) are from below (Jn 8:23). Unlike his accusers (and the rest of us), Jesus knows where he comes from and where he is going (Jn 8:14). Jesus comes from the Father (Jn 8:16, 23), says only what the Father has taught him to say and does only that which pleases the Father (Jn 8:16, 25-29). (While Jesus comes from above and seeks only to please his Father, we often seek to please those around us, those from below—see Jn 8:42-44 and Jn 5:41-44.) Jesus will also return to his Father through the cross to which the Father sends him (Jn 8:21, 28-29).

Jesus knows who he is, knows where he comes from and where he is going. No wonder Jesus says, "I am the light of the world. Whoever follows me will never walk in darkness, but will have the light of life" (Jn 8:12).[14] Jesus is the light, and I can know where I am going as I walk in his light, just as he knows where he is going as the light. But if I don't follow him, I will walk in darkness, always stumbling in the darkness, lost and blind in cyberspace.

So, which course will we take? Where will we go in search of our identity? If we believe in Jesus, we know his Father too (Jn 8:19). If we reject him, we reject his Father too. If we believe in Jesus as the light, we will walk in the light of life. Apart from faith in Jesus and his word, we will die in our sin of false redemption (Jn 8:24). If we want to remain lost and blind and ultimately alone, we should keep searching, infinitely searching, for redemption here below. We should keep chatting incessantly and changing our profiles and statuses. But if we want to truly find ourselves and never be alone, we must respond to Jesus' word and believe in him, for he is secure in his identity in relation to the Father and is never alone. He always says and does what pleases his Father (Jn 8:28-29).

As a result of Jesus' teaching, many of the people believe (Jn 8:30)—at least for a little while, as they add Jesus as a Facebook friend. But Jesus is not content to be on our Facebook list of friends. He wants to reside in our hearts. So Jesus tells the people who have come to believe in him: "If you hold to my teaching, you are truly my disciples. Then you will know the truth, and the truth will set you free" (Jn 8:31-32). Let's pause for a moment. Just like this essay, John 8 is filled with identity questions and answers surrounding who Jesus really is and who the people truly are. We will find out soon enough how ephemeral these new disciples' faith is, even while we realize more and more how constant Jesus is as the great I AM, who is the light of the world (Jn 8:12; 8:58). Even those who come to believe in Jesus here refuse to deal with who he truly is, and who they truly are—living under the illusion that they are free through false forms of redemption. (See Jn 8:31 for the reference to those who believe in Jesus and their response throughout the following verses in Jn 8:33-59; there is no break in the text.) No matter whether we are religious leaders or disciples, we must guard against rejecting Jesus' teaching, for his word reveals his true identity and our response to his word exposes our own. In this passage, Jesus' supposedly new disciples turn on Jesus when his words penetrate their hearts and lives, exposing their pretense and false forms of piety and identity and false hopes of redemption.

Jesus gets beyond the façade of the false forms of faith in which these faulty "believers" place their hopes. They immediately react to Jesus and his word when Jesus says to these new disciples that they must hold to his teaching to become free: "They answered him, 'We are Abraham's descendants and have never been slaves of anyone. How can you say that we shall be set free?'" (Jn 8:33). Their identity and security are bound up with their ancestry and nationalism (Jn 8:31-41) as well as their peers' assessment of them (Jn 5:41-44).

Here in John 8 we see evidence of these supposed disciples' nationalistic and patriotic pride: they are children of Abraham, and they claim that they have never been slaves to anyone. (How quickly they forget that for much of their history they have been subdued, including now by the Romans.) For us today, national identity and security are often bound up with consumerism. As President Bush told the nation after September 11, "Don't let the terrorists win. Go out and shop." Against the backdrop of President Bush's challenge, a cartoon in the *New Yorker* showed a man at a bar saying to another, "I figure if I don't have that third martini, then the terrorists win."[15] Most of us put our hope in things like patriotism, consumerism, alcohol and even our number of Facebook friends—anything but God.

Why is it that "the Jews" who have come forward for the altar call in John 8 get so freaked out when Jesus tells them that they must hold to his teaching to be truly free? We think we can only be free if we let go. But Jesus tells us that we can only be free if we hold tight to him and his word. It makes sense that Jesus would tell the people that they must hold to his teaching to be free and to find life. After all, he is the Word of life through whom God created all things. He is the very self-expression of God, and he himself only finds his existence and meaning as God's self-expression. As we hold to the word of the Word, living as an expression of his life, we find our own existence and meaning. Outside him and apart from dependence on his word, we are enslaved and die in bondage to our false forms of redemption. (See also "Burnout," which develops John 15's discussion of the vine and branches.)

So, why do these new believers get so freaked out? Is it because Jesus—like his cousin John the Baptist—never read the book about how to win friends and influence people so they end up calling the people such things as the devil's children (Jn 8:42-47)? Why does he try to get under their skin in the first place by talking about freedom and slavery? Why can't Jesus simply let it lie, being satisfied with the number of decision cards he has received after the altar call? It's because you can't have meaningful relationships with decision cards and with people who lie about where they're really at. That's why Jesus speaks so forcefully to those who have filled out their decision cards during the altar call and yet hold back from giving their hearts to him in dependence on his word:

> Jesus said to them, "If God were your Father, you would love me, for I came from God and now am here. I have not come on my own; but he sent me. Why is my language not clear to you? Because you are unable to hear what I say. You belong to your father, the devil, and you want to carry out your father's desire. He was a murderer from the beginning, not holding to the truth, for there is no truth

in him. When he lies, he speaks his native language, for he is a liar and the father of lies. Yet because I tell the truth, you do not believe me! Can any of you prove me guilty of sin? If I am telling the truth, why don't you believe me? He who belongs to God hears what God says. The reason you do not hear is that you do not belong to God." (Jn 8:42-47)

The people assume that they have God as their Father. They do so given that they are physical descendants of Abraham, the father of the nation. But they react to Jesus and ultimately reject him. Given their response, they prove themselves to be children of the devil, the father of lies, who rejects the truth of Jesus. God accepts Jesus, and has sent Jesus (Jn 8:42). Abraham also looked forward to Jesus' day (Jn 8:56). In fact, as we shall see later in this passage, Jesus is the God of Abraham (Jn 8:58). But the people who filled out decision cards can't really hear Jesus or believe in him because of their false allegiances, false sense of national pride and their desire to carry out the desire of their father, the devil (Jn 8:40-41, 44).

"The Jews," who at first appear to believe in Jesus, cannot hear Jesus because they do not have God's love in their hearts but only the desire to carry out the work of the devil. They are the devil's children because they will not accept the truth that they are enslaved and in need of the redemption that Jesus alone can provide. Yet even though these people who came forward at the altar call live the lie and reject Jesus, Jesus does not reject them. Instead, he truthfully challenges them to respond to his gracious love and longing for relationship.[16]

Jesus wants them to be free, but the people's false forms of redemption bound up with their allegiance to the father of lies makes it impossible for them to receive Jesus as their Messiah and be true children of Abraham (Jn 8:31-59). Their hopes are in their national heritage. They're living in the past, which is a dead-end street. As father of the nation, Abraham is worthy of honor. Following Abraham's example, Abraham's nation is to be a people of faith—looking forward to the Messiah, just as Abraham longed for Jesus' day (Jn 8:56). Now that day has come, and the people don't want their long-awaited deliverer. Sure, they believe in Jesus: as someone worthy of great respect, as a great teacher and maybe even as a messianic figure. But they do not believe in the kind of Messiah who delivers them from themselves, from their sin and from their alienation and sickness unto death. Once Jesus crosses that line and claims to be their all in all rather than someone who simply has a special little place in their hearts, they reject him.

What proof does Jesus have that those who have come forward for the altar call are enslaved to sin? Whatever heart clues he perceives, these supposedly new converts manifest their hearts' motives when they react to his call to hold tightly to his word and eventually try to stone him (Jn 8:59).

The people don't want liberation if that means they have to look only to Jesus. Jesus challenges them where it hurts most—their enslavement (Jn 8:31-36). They have been enslaved for most of their history as a people—under Egypt, under Assyria, under Babylonia, under Persia, under Greece and now under Rome. Jesus pricks at their false form of redemption—national heritage and security. Even though patriotic pride is a good thing, it's a bad thing when it's an end in itself. They must find their end in him, by being enslaved to him and his liberating word.

Jesus tells them at the end of this account the same thing he is telling us: "Before Abraham was born, I AM" (Jn 8:58). "Before the nations of Israel and America were born, I AM. Before you were loved or hated, famous or infamous, loaded with stuff or empty-handed, popular or unpopular, I AM." Jesus isn't surfing the web of fickle relationships for his identity. He knows who he is in relation to his Father, and so he is more than able to give us relational security. Jesus doesn't need to get stoned to find himself, so he can handle it when they or people today throw stones at him. "Before _____ (whatever your false form of redemption), I AM."

But can you handle these questions that Jesus throws your way? Jesus is basically asking us: "Who are you? Even more to the point, *are* you? Do you even exist? Or do others exist through you? Are you still enslaved to finding out who you are apart from me? It's only when you find yourself in relation to me that you truly become you."

The Word of creation and Israel's redemption, who told Moses that his name is "I AM" and who told Pharaoh through Moses, "Let my people go" (Ex 3–5), calls on the Pharaohs that enslave people then and now: "Let my people go!" But too many of us then and now would rather stay enslaved in Egypt and take every opportunity to go back there.

Jesus offers the people freedom from false aspirations bound up with false identities. But the people would rather be enslaved to false forms of redemption than live. Why is this? It's too threatening, too destabilizing, too vulnerable and too violating. A wise person once told me that people find most difficult to pursue that which they want most: intimacy. Rather than pursuing lasting identity from above in relation to Jesus and his Father, we settle for false forms of redemption here below such as our comforts, careers, fickle peer pressure, casual Internet friendships in which people respond positively to our updated profiles, and our countries' status on the world stage. How can we settle for that which is fleeting and ultimately impersonal rather than pursue lasting, relational identity with God through his Son, who with his Father is the Great I AM?

Before my comforts, Jesus is. Before my career, Jesus is. Before my casual Internet friendships and "my country 'tis of thee, sweet land of liberty," Jesus is. Before all our attempts at finding false redemption, Jesus is. Jesus is the great "I AM." As the great I AM, Jesus is our all in all.

John makes this point about Jesus being our all in all throughout his Gospel, and not just here. As the great I AM, Jesus is greater than Abraham and Moses (Jn 8:58 and Jn 1:15-17; Jn 6:1-21). As the great I AM, Jesus is the bread of life (Jn 6:35). Jesus is the light of the world (Jn 8:12). He is the gate (Jn 10:7, 9), the good shepherd (Jn 10:11, 14), the resurrection and the life (11:25), the way, the truth and the life (Jn 14:6) and the true vine (Jn 15:1, 5). And because Jesus is all these things and more, you *are* and I *am*. The "I AM the bread of life," the "I AM the light of the world," the "I AM the gate," the "I AM the good shepherd," the "I AM the resurrection and the life," the "I AM the way, the truth and the life" and the "I AM the true vine": this is our all in all. In Jesus, we find meaning and hope and purpose and identity. So we must live freely by holding tightly to him—enslaved to our true redemption.

A NEW HOOVER
John 9

I'd hate to be the vacuum cleaner salesman who comes to someone's home, dumps coffee grinds, cooking oil and grease on the carpet for his demonstration and then fails to clean up the mess. The ensuing scene would make for a great one-act play titled *The Death of a Vacuum Cleaner Salesman.*

Some of us have been playing the part of a vacuum cleaner salesperson with our "Before (I met Jesus) and After (I met Jesus) sales pitch." We promote Jesus like he's a new and improved Hoover, who will suck out all the messiness and dirt from our lives—only to find out, to our horror and dismay, that he actually makes things messier.

The Bible doesn't read like a sales pitch, however. It's about life, not an appliance. There are no guarantees in the Bible against messy spills. With this in mind, let me introduce you to the man born blind in John 9. Jesus heals him of his blindness, but the very means Jesus uses to heal the man of his blindness should tell you that his life is about to get messier. Not only does opposition to Jesus increase as a result of this man's healing, but also this man healed of blindness will face opposition because of his healing and identification with Jesus. Life is going to get messier.

Jesus spits on the ground to make mud, places the mud on the blind man's eyes and has him go to a pool to wash (Jn 9:6-7). Couldn't Jesus have chosen some other means? Knowing Jesus, however, he wouldn't choose some other means. Why would he, given how he and his Father tend to operate? Just think for a minute. Jesus' whole life is a bit messy, from beginning to end—from being a baby thought by many to be born out of wedlock on a not-so silent night, to being a supposed messianic pretender dying a criminal's death on an old rugged cross.

Life was so much easier for the man born blind before meeting Jesus. He depended on his parents from birth, and on the Jewish welfare system too. He didn't have to do much, just as he didn't have much to do. But now his life changes drastically, suddenly. It gets messy.

The power brokers are preoccupied with the claim that the man was healed on the Sabbath; they do not rejoice over the fact that he can now see. In fact, they choose not to believe at first that this was the man born blind (Jn 9:13-19). This formerly blind man sees things much more clearly than they do. Their power tactics marked by do-gooder rule-keeping on the Sabbath cloud their judgment and blur their vision. And Jesus is always trying to rub dirt in their eyes on the Sabbath so that they can finally see. Jesus performed laser eye surgery on the man born blind while seeking to do open heart surgery on their hearts.

The man's spiritual insight is much better than his opening theological response would indicate, but his theological logic gets better as the debate goes on. When the moral matrix law brokers say that Jesus is a sinner, the man responds: "Whether he is a sinner or not, I don't know. One thing I do know. I was blind but now I see!" (Jn 9:25) When they keep pressing him about the manner of his healing, he replies: "I have told you already and you did not listen. Why do you want to hear it again? Do you want to become his disciples, too?" (Jn 9:27).

Now things get *really* messy. The law brokers start hurling insults at him, knocking him for his lack of theological training and questioning his spiritual pedigree (and that of Jesus). But that doesn't stop him—he sees too clearly and innocently to stop. It's as if he doesn't know any better. When they say that they listen to Moses but don't know where Jesus is from, the man replies:

"Now that is remarkable! You don't know where he comes from, yet he opened my eyes. We know that God does not listen to sinners. He listens to the godly man who does his will. Nobody has ever heard of opening the eyes of a man born blind. If this man were not from God, he could do nothing." To this they replied, "You were steeped in sin at birth; how dare you lecture us!" And they threw him out. (Jn 9:30-34)

The man healed of blindness wins the debate, but they're sore losers. So they do what they always do when someone goes over to Jesus and shows them up: they throw him out of the synagogue. Now you may be thinking, "No big deal. He can go to the Baptist or Lutheran synagogue across the street or next door. Who knows? He might even like the new synagogue's sound system and theater seating more." But it's not quite like that. When you get kicked out of the synagogue in Jesus' day, you get kicked out of society.

When I was in junior high, I once got kicked out of my Lutheran confirmation class for fighting with another boy. I don't think the fight had anything to do with Jesus that morning. After being dismissed, I went home and shot baskets, letting my parents sort it out with the pastors. My parents didn't have to fear that they would be kicked out of church, or out of town or out of the middle-American German Lutheran culture with its Oktoberfests and lederhosen. But in John 9, this man's parents fear being kicked out of Jewish culture. They know that anyone who fights the law brokers over Jesus gets kicked out of Jewish culture (the synagogue community) for not being kosher. The parents fear this fate; so they force the issue on their son (Jn 9:18-23). But he doesn't care. Jesus healed his eyes of blindness, and these religious leaders don't even care! All they care about is their Sabbath laws and their authoritative position over the people, not about him. So he has nothing really to lose if he loses favor with them.

When Jesus hears that they have thrown the man out of the synagogue, Jesus finds him and asks him, "Do you believe in the Son of Man?" (Jn 9:35). When Jesus reveals to him that he is the Son of Man, the man healed of his blindness believes and worships Jesus (Jn 9:35-38). Jesus closes off the episode by saying: "For judgment I have come into this world, so that the blind will see and those who see will become blind" (Jn 9:39). When some Pharisees ask him if he thinks they're blind, Jesus says, "If you were blind, you would not be guilty of sin; but now that you claim you can see, your guilt remains" (Jn 9:41).

If you've never been blind, you've never been able to see. Only those who know they're blind will someday receive their sight. This is what Jesus is talking about. What *we're* talking about in light of what happens to the man in John 9 is that the lives of those cured of blindness get messy. "Ignorance (blindness) is bliss" is the motto for those who like their lives squeaky clean.

Now those who claim to see spiritually because of Jesus, if they think Jesus takes away the messiness from their lives, are actually walking around with dried mud on their eyes. Sure, he heals us of our spiritual blindness. Praise God! But those who see clearly also begin seeing life for what it really is; and so, they see that it gets messier by the day.

Blind man, meet Rachel. Life wasn't all that hot before she became a Christ-follower. And it's not so hot now either. She says that mediocrity sums it up—mediocre grades, mediocre writing skills and mediocre boyfriend—before she became a Christian and after she became a Christian. Nonbelieving friends at work ask her why she keeps going on with this Jesus thing. They think it's just a phase she's going through in hopes of finding that new and improved Hoover to clean up her life. But she can't let Jesus go. This intrigues them. They can't comprehend or understand her faith. It's not prepackaged. She doesn't give them sales pitches. Somehow Rachel sees that Jesus is the Son of Man who enters this world to make the blind see; she was blind, but now she sees.[17] Rachel now sees Jesus for who he is, not for what people would package Jesus to be. Her Jesus ain't no Hoover.

Meet Rob. Rob went from filthy rags to riches and now is back in rags again. A bad car accident wrecked his vision, and the Pharisee-like insurance company officials only care about making sure they don't have to pay for damages. Instead of denying that he is blind (which is what the Pharisees do for a time; see Jn 9:18), they tell Rob he's not all that blind. "You're not that bad off," they say. "It could be worse." Actually, it was worse, and it's getting worse again. Rob was abused sexually—even violently—throughout his youth and young adulthood; he was a plaything for other men as well as for women, both inside and outside the home. But then Rob met Jesus. Jesus got rid of the abusive people in Rob's life, taking ownership of Rob's body and soul. Rob's past no longer defined him. Praise God! While his past no longer defined him because of Jesus, Rob's family disowned him because of this same Jesus, just like the man healed of blindness in John 9 and likely many of John's first readers. Perhaps you, too, have experienced similar rejection.[18] Cut out of the family will, Rob lost his portion of a sizeable family inheritance; through it all, his eternal inheritance sustained him. Though deemed a failure by his family, Rob became a Christian success story after meeting Jesus. Like so many others, Rob went to Bible college. After college, he went to work in Silicon Valley, where he climbed the corporate ladder. But then the car wreck happened, and Rob's life tumbled down. Now he says: "I could see, but now I'm blind." Even so, Rob has no intention of taking Jesus back to the Hoover store to customer returns. In fact, he has destroyed the receipt. Rob sees with the eye of faith who Jesus really is; he doesn't try to sell Jesus or gift-wrap him. Jesus is the Son of Man, who causes the blind to see. And when we come to see, we find that Jesus messes with our lives, not cleaning everything up just now. As far as Jesus is concerned, he comes to judge the world to make those who claim they can see spiritually blind and to make those who know they are spiritually blind see spiritually (Jn 9:39). And so, as he judges, Jesus is going to make things a whole lot messier before he will get around to cleaning things up. Jesus ain't no Hoover, and Rob sees this.

There's more to this Jesus thing than meets the eye. The problem with many of us is that we expect God to clean up all the messiness of life—our questions, our relationships, our lives, our careers, our eyes. Rachel and Rob got burned by the Hoover salesman with his unfulfilled promises. They waited for the longest time for the repair-service god to fix the vacuum and clean up the mess. But then they came to see that if the repair-service god shows up to fix the problem, he'll try to clean out Jesus, too, because Jesus only traffics in messy lives and truths. They'd rather have Jesus than clean, beautiful and perfect lives, since for them the reality of the messy Jesus is beauty and perfection. What about for you? Why don't you go and wash the mud off in the pool? And the next time the vacuum cleaner salesperson comes to the door, tell him you'll take life with Jesus—messy as it is.

TV PREACHERS
John 10

As the Son of Man, Jesus sees things for what they are and knows what people are really like from the inside out.[19] As the judge who makes the blind to see and those with sight blind, Jesus makes right judgments about the TV-preacher equivalents of his day, seeing them for what they are—wolves in sheep's clothing. In John 10, we find Jesus contrasting himself with them. Who are they? They are the shepherds of Israel in John 9 who kick the man healed of blindness out of the synagogue. They don't realize that they are blind guides and are completely lost; they are blind guides leading the blind astray.[20] Jesus alone is the good shepherd. He alone sees them for what they truly are—wolves in sheep's clothing. One of the biggest stumbling blocks to faith in any age is faith-healing, TV-preaching, pension-stealing evangelists. Jesus has their kind in mind when he says, "I am the good shepherd. The good shepherd lays down his life for the sheep" (Jn 10:11). He also has in mind Ezekiel 34, in which God says that he will remove the bad shepherds of Israel who do not care for his people. He will come and shepherd them himself. Whereas they lay down the sheep's lives for themselves, he will lay down his life for the sheep.

Pension-stealing TV preachers and bad shepherds alike are thieves and wolves. Then there are the hired hands. "The hired hand is not the shepherd who owns the sheep. So when he sees the wolf coming, he abandons the sheep and runs away. Then the wolf attacks the flock and scatters it. The man runs away because he is a hired hand and cares nothing for the sheep" (Jn 10:12-13).

I don't consider myself a wolf or a thief, but I sometimes wonder if I'm a hired hand. While Jesus alone is the good shepherd, and this passage is about him, there are implications for how his under-shepherds are to serve. As a religion professor, I make a living off of religion and spirituality. But does it own me? Do the people own me, or do they simply pay me? These questions are often viewed negatively in our CEO world of church growth, in which everything is about boundaries and chains of command. The church is full of business models, but do we have many good models of how to shepherd people and lay down our lives for them?

I remember a time during my course of doctoral studies in theology in England, when I was frustrated over not having more opportunities to serve up front in my church there. I remember sharing with a fellow doctoral student about my frustration, indicating that I *deserved* to serve up front more given all that I had done and all the training I had received academically and practically. My friend, who had grown up in a family famous for pastors, replied that he did not want to minister "up front" because he was afraid he would ruin people. He had experienced disillusionment due to observing how some ministers his family knew did not come to serve but to be served and to give up their people's lives as ransoms for their own, ruining the sheep. While I believed I was deserving of serving the people, my friend did not feel worthy to serve them. While I was afraid of *missing out* among them, he was afraid of *messing* them *up*. Was *I* rebuked?! I had the mentality of a hired hand, and he had the mindset of an under-shepherd. While I cared for my own advancement, he cared for the people's welfare. I am glad to report that my friend now serves as a pastor, shepherding God's people. Those under his care are in good hands. My friend won't leave them when the wolves and thieves appear.

Many sheep are dumb, though. They follow wolves in sheep's clothing. By John 9 and 10, most of Jesus' disciples have abandoned him (here I am thinking of the majority of disciples' abandonment of Jesus in Jn 6). You would think that all those who witnessed the healing of the man born blind (Jn 9) would have believed in Jesus, especially the man's parents! But they're more concerned about remaining in the synagogue—remaining cultural insiders—than they are concerned with entering Jesus' pen of protection for his sheep. By all cultural appearances, they appear shrewd. The religious leaders—ancient TV evangelists—offer them prosperity and wonderful lives. Jesus, on the other hand, offers them communion with him—outside the security and significance of the synagogue's walls. Which would you choose? Whose voice do you find more compelling—Jesus' or theirs?

Don't let the big hair and antics fool you—and don't let the *lack* of big hair and antics fool you either. Not all imposters are TV preachers, nor are all TV preachers imposters. You don't have to have all the TV preacher trappings to trap people. Any "preacher" who would lure you away from finding your sole significance and security in Jesus' care is functioning as a "TV preacher," as I'm using the image here. I doubt very many of the religious leaders really looked and acted like those TV preachers today who offer you prosperity if you believe—and if you send them your first fruits and last fruits. They scream and cry, threaten and plead, rant and rave until you call them, incessantly reminding you the phone lines are open. The thieves and wolves in Jesus' day were more refined and digni-fied than that. They were national and religious heroes because of their historic war on Roman imperialism and paganism. What connects them to these TV preachers is their message of comfort and peace and prosperity for all who adhere to the insider system rules. *Only those who prosper these preachers will find prosperity with God,* so such folk religion goes. The reason that they exclude Jesus from their club is because he doesn't play by their rules for finding peace and prosperity.

Jesus is a faith healer who offers peace and prosperity. But the peace and prosperity he offers is not as the world gives. Jesus doesn't promise us fame and fortune, and he doesn't promise healing for everyone. He also doesn't make money from faith-healing religion. Jesus is not like the cult leader famous among the rich, L. Ron Hubbard, who supposedly said, "If a man really wants to make a million dollars he should start his own religion."[21] Whether or not Hubbard said it is not the most important issue; many others have basically said it or have thought it and lived it out across the landscape of religion throughout history.

Not only is Jesus *not* making money from his work, but he's also about to lose his shirt and even his life for healing people on the Sabbath. You could think that Jesus is a bit clueless, even dumb. Why can't he be more careful, checking which day of the week it is before he goes about healing people? But Jesus does know, and he intentionally heals people on the Sabbath so as to test and try them with a spiritual gut check. Their priorities are not his: for Jesus, the Sabbath was made for humans, not humans for the Sabbath. Moreover, the Sabbath was made for God, not mammon and money—as he rebukes the rulers in John 2 for turning his Father's house into a market (Jn 2:16). Jesus risks it all as the good shepherd so that people don't lose their lives at the hands of the thieves and wolves.

In John 9, which serves as the backdrop for this passage (see the allusion to Jn 9 in 10:21), Jesus cares for the man born blind, healing him on the Sabbath. Whereas Jesus cares for him, and so heals him, the rulers of the people only care about the man after Jesus has healed him. And all they really care about is that Jesus has healed him on the Sabbath. A big no-no. They will do anything to keep the people playing by the insider rules. And so in turn, they kick the man out because he defends Jesus and refuses to play by their rules.

The formerly blind man doesn't listen to these spiritually blind guides because he's got spiritual sense. He knows they're clueless. They can't see God working in their midst, and they can't hear the man's clear logic. While the rulers cannot hear the man and cannot see the miracles Jesus performs by the power of God, this man hears the voice of the one who has healed his eyes and believes. This man listens to Jesus, for he knows the good shepherd's voice. Jesus has this episode in mind when he says in John 10:

"I tell you the truth, the man who does not enter the sheep pen by the gate, but climbs in by some other way, is a thief and a robber. The man who enters by the gate is the shepherd of his sheep. The watchman opens the gate for him, and the sheep listen to his voice. He calls his own sheep by name and leads them out. When he has brought out all his own, he goes on ahead of them, and his sheep follow him because they know his voice. But they will never follow a stranger; in fact, they will run away from him because they do not recognize a stranger's voice." Jesus used this figure of speech, but they did not understand what he was telling them. Therefore Jesus said again, "I tell you the truth, I am the gate for the sheep. All who ever came before me were thieves and robbers, but the sheep did not listen to them. I am the gate; whoever enters through me will be saved. He will come in and go out, and find pasture. The thief comes only to steal and kill and destroy; I have come that they may have life, and have it to the full." (Jn 10:1-10)

The rulers who oppose Jesus and this man are those who have come before Jesus—they are thieves and robbers. Although they kick the man out, he becomes a true insider by believing in Jesus. He finds security in the good shepherd's sheep pen and in his pastures. The man does not recognize these strangers' voices, in part because he knows these strangers don't have his best interest at heart. He knows Jesus has his best interest at heart and so goes outside their camp to be with him.

Jesus has other sheep: "I have other sheep that are not of this sheep pen. I must bring them also" (Jn 10:16). All his sheep listen to his voice (Jn 10:16) and not these strangers' voices. Jesus is speaking here of the non-Jewish people, who will also believe in him throughout the ages. Whether Jewish or Gentile then, Jesus is speaking to you. Are you listening for his voice?

Many people make light of big-hair and big-antic TV preachers. But unless we're listening to Jesus' voice, we're really listening to them. In fact, I once was asked to speak on Trinity Broadcasting Network, the largest Christian television network in the United States (perhaps it's because of my blow-dried hair!). Whereas some of my peers teased me, thinking it strange that I would go on the air there, a godly friend of mine living in an intentional community in an impoverished part of Portland challenged me to make the most of the opportunity. He said that his crack-addicted neighbor watched TBN to find spiritual healing and hope since the evangelical church in their neighborhood considered her an outcast. My friend challenged me to shepherd her with my words—making Jesus known in such a way that she could listen and understand and believe. In the end, "TV preachers" here stand for all those who steal people's hearts with religion for love or for money, for power or for fame, keeping outsiders outside and promising their sheep an insider's life with God while fleecing them for their own gain.

How do we know which is Jesus' voice then? His is not the voice of one who tells you to lay down your life for him so that he can save his own skin. Instead, Jesus obeys his Father's voice by laying down his life and taking it up again: "The reason my Father loves me is that I lay down my life—only to take it up again. No one takes it from me, but I lay it down of my own accord. I have authority to lay it down and authority to take it up again. This command I received from my Father" (Jn 10:17-18). He is the one who lays his life down for his followers. Whereas the thief comes to steal, kill and destroy, Jesus comes to give life to the full. Listen for his voice.

The story of a friend bears witness to the fullness of life Jesus brings in contrast to the kind of life the thief takes. This tale may help you learn how to discern Jesus' voice better. My friend spent much of his life, up until recently, trying to prove himself to the Christian authority figures in his life. He is very talented and has a lot of ministry experience, and so he always thrived in his studies and service. Then he hit rock bottom, "falling out of favor" with those responsible for him due to sin in his life. This sin damaged him, his family and his church family. He has gone through restoration and is now in full fellowship with his family and church. God has taught my friend a lot about God and about himself through his agonizing journey. My friend is far less inclined now to connect his significance and worth to what he can produce—whether as a Christian or as a professional. This past year, my friend shared with me about how he was at a Christian men's meeting at which everyone introduced himself. As each man shared, he would say something like, "I'm Jim, and I'm a stockbroker. But I'm really a Christ-follower." When it came time for my friend to share, he said, "I'm Steve. Christ-follower?" Pause. "The Lord is my shepherd. I shall not want." He could not muster the spiritual moxie to say that he was a Christ-follower, given what he had done. He didn't think he was good enough to consider himself a Christ-follower. He had no ground for boasting that he was a follower of Christ. All he could boast in is that Christ leads him and takes care of him. And so he found great comfort and healing in saying simply, "The Lord is my shepherd." There is nothing my friend could do to make this happen. He did not call Jesus. Jesus called him, and my friend heard his voice.

Jesus' voice is quite different from the voices that played in my friend's head for years—voices telling him that his worth depended on proving to those responsible for him in ministry that he was a legitimate Christ-follower and that he would benefit them. Those voices in his head served the thief well, as he sought to steal, kill and destroy my friend's life. Jesus isn't simply responsible for us. He cares for us and lays down his life for us. He's the kind of shepherd who leaves the ninety-nine "good sheep" to go after the one "bad sheep" who has wandered away, risking his life to save it rather than sacrificing us to save himself.

TV preachers come in different forms, shapes and sizes. Sometimes you'll find them on TV saying, "God will heal you if you have enough faith," or "God will bless your life abundantly if you call right now and give your pension check to me." Sometimes you'll find them in your head saying, "God will love you if you live a successful Christian life and don't mess up (and if you benefit my ministry)." Their message is always *quid pro quo*: give to God (and them) in order to get from God. But Jesus doesn't act that way.[22] Jesus reaches out to the blind man to heal him before the blind man has a chance to beg for healing. And even though the blind man has to obey to get healed in this case, it's a foregone conclusion that he will do as Jesus says. The man's healing is not an achievement based on his obedience; rather, his obedience is a response of trust to Jesus' call. His obedience flows from Jesus' compelling and loving call on his life. Jesus calls his sheep, leads his sheep and loves his sheep. The Lord shepherds me. I shall not want.

What do you want? Whose voice do you listen to? Do you listen to Jesus' voice, or do you reject his word? John 10:19-21 reveals that "the Jews" or Jewish leaders are divided once again over Jesus' words.[23] Some claim he is "demon-possessed and raving mad," so "why listen to him?" Others argue that a demon can't open a blind man's eyes (Jn 10:19-21). In the end, you'll have to decide who to listen to—Jesus or the TV preachers. In the end, you'll need to ask if you have eyes to see. In the end, you'll need to ask if you have ears with which to listen to Jesus' words. If not, you are not his sheep, for sheep know their shepherd's voice. If not, perhaps it's because you've listened to TV preachers for far too long and can no longer discern Jesus' voice.

If you have ears to hear, you'll listen to Jesus and believe and follow hard after him. And if you do, it's because you are in Jesus' and his Father's hand, for they are one:

> Jesus answered, "I did tell you, but you do not believe. The miracles I do in my Father's name speak for me, but you do not believe because you are not my sheep. My sheep listen to my voice; I know them, and they follow me. I give them eternal life, and they shall never perish; no one can snatch them out of my hand. My Father, who has given them to me, is greater than all; no one can snatch them out of my Father's hand. I and the Father are one." (Jn 10:25-30)

If you have eyes to see and ears to hear, you will look and listen to Jesus and follow hard after him.

If you have eyes to see, you will believe in Jesus because of his miraculous signs that he performs over and over again. Don't be like the Jewish leaders who, at the Feast of Dedication, ask Jesus to speak plainly and to tell them if he is the Christ—when he has been telling them all along through his miraculous signs that he and the Father are one. Don't be like these leaders, who, as soon as Jesus says that he and the Father are one, pick up stones to stone him (Jn 10:22-33).[24] If you have ears to hear, you will decide to listen to Jesus. If you are his sheep, you will not try to trap him in his words, for you are held firmly in his hand.[25]

If you have eyes to see, you will believe in Jesus because of his miraculous signs at the very least (Jn 10:37-38), such as the sign of healing the man born blind (Jn 9; also Jn 10:21). Jesus is the Christ. He is the Son of God, as evidenced by his miraculous signs: "Do not believe me unless I do what my Father does. But if I do it, even though you do not believe me, believe the miracles, that you may know and understand that the Father is in me, and I in the Father" (Jn 10:37-38).

Jesus tells these religious leaders who are fixated with miraculous signs to believe him because of the signs even though they do not believe his word. But no matter what Jesus says or does, they still don't believe. Instead, they try to seize him, and so they are left with no excuses. Their reactions and ultimate rejection of Jesus' signs and words bear witness against them and their prosperity gospel ways.

While they have always tried to control religion, they cannot control Jesus. Just as faith eludes them, Jesus eludes their grasp (Jn 10:39). So Jesus goes away across the Jordan to the place where John was baptizing in the early days. In that place and that time, many common Jewish people come to him and believe in him because of John's earlier testimony and because of Jesus' miraculous signs (Jn 10:40-42).

What about in *this* place in *this* time? Do Jesus' miraculous signs and words elude us? Are we mesmerized by other sights and lured away by other voices? Are we like the power-brokering TV-evangelist types of Jerusalem in Jesus' day, who cannot make room for Jesus in their hearts because of their fear of losing control? Or are we Jesus' sheep—like the people who follow Jesus out to the wilderness where John preached in the early days?[26]

You may joke about how raving loony many TV preachers in our own day appear and sound, but you can't knock their success given the standards of measurement. Like the prosperity gospel preachers of Jesus' day, they're wired the same way we all are: quid pro quo. Give to God to get from God; God helps those who help themselves. It makes so much sense. That's why they're so successful.[27] And that's why Jesus is often out searching for sheep in the wilderness, reaching over mountain ledges and pulling up sheep like the blind man and my broken friend and others in need of a good shepherd, many of whom have been left for dead by false teachers and bad shepherds. Jesus appears demon-possessed and raving mad in a world filled with quid pro quo TV preachers. But actually, he's very sane and sound, and he's no control freak. That's why he can go off to the wilderness and minister to the masses who come to him to find life.

Jesus doesn't do quid pro quo. He doesn't perform his miraculous signs only after we believe in him. He performs his signs regardless of whether or not we believe, and he performs them in order to get *us*, not something from us. He simply wants life with us—for eternity. Whose voice will you listen to? Who will you follow—the TV preachers or Jesus? There's more than a pension check or bank account at stake here. We're talking about your life itself—eternal life. So perhaps it's time to change the channel on your TV and activate closed captioning. Jesus' lines are always open to you. In fact, he's been calling you, but your line's busy. Get off the phone and listen for his call.

REVISITING LAZARUS'S TOMB IN AN AGE OF PAIN
John 11

We now move from a discussion of Jesus performing various miraculous signs so that people might believe in him to a discussion of Jesus performing the greatest sign of all prior to his resurrection. Jesus knows the miraculous sign he is about to perform, the reaction and increased opposition that will result from it and the response of faith of multitudes of people. The reactions and rejection come to a fever pitch here in this chapter and the one that follows. In anticipation of these coming events, you would think Jesus would have his retributive, Rambo-like war paint on. Instead, we find him weeping.

◆ ◆ ◆

Just two words. The shortest verse in the Bible: "Jesus wept" (Jn 11:35). Jesus doesn't offer a word of explanation for his tears, but his tears create oceans of questions. His actions that follow are answers filled with life and meaning in the face of death. Why does he weep? Is it because of Martha's and others' unbelief? Is it because of Mary's and the people's grief bound up with the ravages of death? Perhaps a combination of the two?[28] Whatever the reason, Jesus weeps, being deeply moved by the events and encounters surrounding Lazarus's death.

I think Jesus weeps because of the people's grief *and* their unbelief; it must grieve him to know that his delay inspires such torment. It even inspires torment in his own soul; for he loves his Father and he also loves Lazarus (Jn 11:4-5, 36). And while the God revealed in Jesus can make sense of these things, even bringing about good through evil, God's knowledge doesn't keep God from identifying with us fully in our pain: "When Jesus saw her weeping, and the Jews who had come along with her also weeping, he was deeply moved in spirit and troubled" (Jn 11:33).

Jesus could arrive sooner and heal Lazarus, but he doesn't. There are a lot of things God could do, but for whatever reason won't do. John actually tells us that the reason that Jesus doesn't arrive earlier to heal Lazarus is so that God's glory would be revealed (Jn 11:4, 6, 21, 32). Raising Lazarus from the dead will be the greatest sign of Jesus' glory prior to his own resurrection. God has a way of bringing great good out of horrible tragedy. But no matter how well we know this to be true, it doesn't keep us from experiencing grief. In fact, this understanding can actually intensify our pain. For sometimes in our darker moments we honestly or cynically ask, "Couldn't God have chosen some other means through which to glorify his name?"

It's hard to imagine how God could be glorified through the suffering that so many innocent lives endure. I understand that the word *innocent* is a relative term; no one besides Jesus is really innocent, not even Jesus' friend Lazarus. But besides Lazarus, the little girl in the book *The Shack* comes as close as anyone imaginable to rightly wearing that adjective. In the novel, Missy, a very pure and innocent little girl, is violently raped and murdered. The serial killer who murders her isn't seized until a few tormenting and agonizing years have passed.[29]

I don't really know why God allows bad things to happen to good people, or good things to happen to bad people. I don't want to rationalize people's pain away, or to tie up loose ends in nice little religious bows. The skeptic David Hume famously addressed this subject. Here is the age-old question he engaged: "If God is good and all powerful, where does evil come from?"[30] Good question. I'm not sure I have an answer that makes sense of his question existentially. But I am well aware of its import in an age consciously and overtly marked by pain and suffering, and in which people increasingly challenge the Christian claims of the goodness, power and even the existence of God.[31]

I'm not one to remove either of the points of tension in the question set forth above: either saying that God isn't all-good or that God isn't all-powerful. I believe God is both all-good and all-powerful—and at the same time, through all of history's events. I'm not saying that I can offer you convincing proofs as to how this can be, but what I do know to be so isn't accounted for in Hume's question: namely, Jesus' own existential suffering that requires me to reframe my theology and my own experience of suffering. "Jesus wept": while I don't have all the answers, Jesus lives the question and is himself the answer to our greatest pain and suffering. He who knows no sin as the all-powerful and all-good God becomes human to identify with us in our need, as John's Gospel discloses.[32] He becomes sin so that we can become God's righteousness, as Paul says (2 Cor 5:21).

I like how William P. Young says in *The Shack* that we need to take ourselves out of God's judgment seat and stop playing God.[33] One reason that I think we need to get out of God's judgment seat is because God himself did. Karl Barth wrote that the judge was judged on our behalf.[34] The little girl didn't experience something that Jesus himself did not experience. Jesus was there, as Young writes. And Lazarus didn't go through anything that Jesus himself did not endure. Lazarus's death was a foreshadowing of Jesus' own death and the chief reason that the religious leaders wanted Jesus killed (Jn 11:45-53). So, if you're going to judge God, keep in mind that God himself got out of his judgment seat to be judged with you—and even by you—as the chief of sinners. God feels your pain far more than you can imagine.

Not only does Jesus identify with us in our sin and suffering; Jesus also causes us to identify with him by participating in his glory. Although I do not wish to justify innocent victims' suffering, the victory that they experience in being identified as participants in Jesus' crucified and risen glory is a mind-boggling privilege, especially as their participation magnifies Jesus' passion-filled glory. This is true of Lazarus's suffering, death and resurrection, and it's true of the suffering, death and resurrection of little ones like Missy in *The Shack*.

I don't get any sense from John's Gospel that Lazarus or his siblings play the victim card with Jesus. In chapter 12, Martha and her siblings throw a party in Jesus' honor. Mary, Martha's and Lazarus's sister, pours expensive perfume on Jesus' feet and wipes his feet with her hair. Martha does the serving, while Lazarus is found reclining at the table. I get the sense that they are filled with gratitude for what Jesus did in raising Lazarus from the dead, not grudging respect.

Now if you or I were Lazarus, we might be bitter about the sickness, the death and the four days in a tomb while wrapped in burial linens and cloth—all so that Jesus can bring glory to God and so that there could be a sign of Jesus' own death and resurrection. Our bitterness may intensify when we find out that our death and resurrection have made us dangerous to the authorities. As a result of our resurrection, many people believe in Jesus, and the religious power brokers want us dead—again. We may feel that Jesus owes us something for "using" us in this way. But not the real Lazarus or his siblings. Instead, they honor Jesus. As Mary prepares him for burial by pouring the expensive perfume on Jesus' feet and wiping his feet with her hair, they bear witness to Jesus' own victimization that will lead to ultimate victory (Jn 12:1-11).

It's also worth pointing out here that Jesus himself never plays the victim card in the Gospels. Although he does pray that the cup of God's wrath might pass from him (Mt 26:39-42) and he does cry out in agony and ask God in despair why he has forsaken him (Mt 27:46), it only goes to show how human he is and how real the pain and suffering are. Far from playing the victim, Jesus, on the way to the cross and long after the resurrection, plays the victor card. Jesus overcomes the world (Jn 16:33)!

It's hard to imagine anything more dehumanizing than when those who were once victimized constantly play the victim card. These individuals don't realize how they are allowing themselves to be victimized over and over again. It's equally hard to imagine anything so humanizing and uplifting to a person's well-being and dignity than finding victory in Jesus in the face of victimization. I rarely come across such individuals, but when I do, I am always struck by how powerful and glorious God's grace and love are as these attributes are manifested through these victors' lives. Such persons remind me of Jesus more than any others and participate fully in his relational glory.

I have played the victim card, agonizing and complaining about what others have wrongly done to me. In the midst of being tempted to play the victim card, I am thankful for those friends who remind me that there is no victory in playing the victim's role, no wholeness or healing, only emptiness and despairing sickness. Such friends serve as agents of God's healing power in my life.

One of my friends whose life experience encourages me to look for victory in Christ in the midst of victimization is a medical doctor, Michael Tso. Michael is on staff at His Mansion Ministries in New Hampshire, which helps young people broken by addictions and substance abuse problems. Sometimes the staff members at His Mansion are overwhelmed as they try to help beautiful but broken people in the midst of victimization seek wholeness and find victory through Jesus. While the staff members witness many personal victories among those entrusted to them, they also witness glaring failures, such as when people turn away from help, betray their caregivers or leave forever. I am encouraged that in the midst of the obstacles and stresses and perplexities of everyday life at His Mansion, Michael is becoming an even greater witness to Jesus' healing touch, relying on Jesus for the compassionate care that he alone can give and then sharing it with others. He and the other staff members see their work as a participation in Jesus' healing ministry, whereby Jesus performs miraculous "signs" of healing broken lives in their midst.

Michael shared with me how a friend of his once ministered to him, and how this friend's impact on his work and ministry continues to this day. The friend in question was a young married man who was dying of cancer. Michael recounted how, on one occasion, he was helping his friend get comfortable in his hospital bed; the cancer that racked his body was everywhere, and he was constantly in pain. After twenty minutes of trying to help his friend gain some level of comfort, Michael was about to leave when the young man turned to him and asked, "Can I pray for you?" Michael couldn't believe it. Here was this man in so much pain and facing death, and yet he had the presence to concern himself with Michael's welfare. No doubt, it was this young man's awareness of God's providential presence and constant care for him there at the hospital that caused him to live victoriously even as he endured such cancerous victimization.

Coincidently or not, the hospital where the man stayed is named Providence. It's also worth noting that Michael doesn't consider himself a caregiver, but rather someone who comes alongside hurting and broken people and loves them with the love of Jesus. His boss at His Mansion, Stan Farmer, says that he firmly believes that the healing that takes place at His Mansion is as much for the staff as it is for those who come seeking it. It's a place of hope and healing for all, as Jesus raises victimized lives from the dead and gives them victory.

A thankful, heaven-minded and other-centered spirit is a key mark of the person who lives victoriously in Christ. Just before Jesus commands death to release its grip on Lazarus and calls Lazarus to come out of the tomb, he thanks his Father for always hearing him (Jn 11:41-42). While the cynic might say it's easy for Jesus to be thankful when it's someone else who has undergone death and four days in a tomb (Jn 11:39), the cynic fails to account for the fact that Jesus' act of raising Lazarus from the dead is the chief reason that Jesus' enemies seek his own death and that it will lead shortly to his own three-day stay in a tomb. Jesus' awareness of the Father's care for him makes it possible for him to reach out and care compassionately for others like Lazarus and us—raising Lazarus from the dead, and Jesus dying for you and me.

By the end of *The Shack*, the father of the little girl has a thankful and trusting spirit. It's not that he's thankful for what happened to his daughter, but he's thankful for the triune God's victorious presence in his life in the face of such horrible victimization.

Have you been victimized in life by death? Have you met Jesus at Lazarus's tomb, or at Young's shack and the nearby gravesite cave or at "His Mansion," where you are forced to deal with the skeletons in your closet? Are you like Martha who wants a miracle to occur—but on her own terms? Martha wishes Jesus would have come before her brother had died and healed him in his sick bed. But since Lazarus has been dead four days, Martha is afraid of the odor that would pour out of the tomb were the stone rolled away (Jn 11:38-39). After all, what would the neighbors say? But as Jesus says to Martha, so he says to you, "Did I not tell you that if you believed, you would see the glory of God?" (Jn 11:40). I'm not saying Jesus will raise you or your loved one from the grave just now, but that he'll raise you spiritually from the dead and give you new life in the face of victimization. That's one of the greatest miracles imaginable. The bodily resurrection from the dead will surely follow, when God makes all things new. But now is the time to respond to his call, as he performs the present miracle of removing the stone that seals your heart and raises your soul to new life.[35]

> So they took away the stone. Then Jesus looked up and said, "Father, I thank you that you have heard me. I knew that you always hear me, but I said this for the benefit of the people standing here, that they may believe that you sent me." When he had said this, Jesus called in a loud voice, "Lazarus, come out!" The dead man came out, his hands and feet wrapped with strips of linen, and a cloth around his face. Jesus said to them, "Take off the grave clothes and let him go." (Jn 11:41-44)

Jesus calls to you now. Take off your grave clothes and go.

CONSPIRACY THEORY
John 12

John 12 reads like a conspiracy theory. John wants the reader to know the *real* reasons for Jesus' death. Jesus isn't killed to keep him and Mary from having a child and ruining it for the Catholic Church, as some *Da*

Vinci Code–like bestseller might claim. Nor is he killed because he keeps money from the poor, as some socialist defending Judas might argue. Nor is Jesus killed in protest by a group of animal rights activists for riding a donkey's colt into a violent mob, as still other conspiracy theorists might concoct.

Let's get the facts foreshadowing Jesus' death straight. Mary pours expensive perfume on Jesus' feet at a dinner six days before the Passover, not as part of some wedding ceremony but in extreme devotion to prepare her Lord for burial. Judas complains that the perfume should be sold and the proceeds given to the poor, not because he cares for the poor but because he wants to pocket the money for himself (he is responsible for keeping the money bag and often pilfers from it). The crowds on the road leading into Jerusalem are not screaming in anger or stabbing one another with swords and spears; they are shouting for joy while waving palm branches and casting them on the road in homage to Jesus, their coming king.

The real conspiracy surrounding Mary is that we often refuse to pay homage to Jesus in such dramatic ways; we're so unlike Mary. Like Judas, we ridicule and sabotage the worship of Jesus by Mary and those like her (Jn 12:4-6). The real conspiracy displayed at this point in John 12 isn't taking place on the surface or on the page. It is taking place in the hearts of the respondents—including the readers, as we react to Mary's act of supreme devotion to Jesus and to Jesus himself. We the readers tend to praise Mary—who is safely dead—for her extravagant demonstration of love for Jesus. But we tend to behave like Judas, both in our carefully controlled piety and in our dismissal of tactile, costly worship when we encounter it in whatever form. In the same vein, we praise Mary's radical faith as expressed in people such as Mother Teresa, who lived among lepers out of devout love for Jesus—just as long as they are dead or at least safely tucked away in some ghetto in India.

Here's what the text in John 12 recounts of Mary's own act of worship:

> Six days before the Passover, Jesus arrived at Bethany, where Lazarus lived, whom Jesus had raised from the dead. Here a dinner was given in Jesus' honor. Martha served, while Lazarus was

among those reclining at the table with him. Then Mary took about a pint of pure nard, an expensive perfume; she poured it on Jesus' feet and wiped his feet with her hair. And the house was filled with the fragrance of the perfume. (Jn 12:1-3)

Like Judas, we may ridicule Mary for her act of extravagance, which costs her a great deal—not only in terms of losing her savings but also in terms of losing face. How impractical! How outlandish and wasteful! But at times authentic worship will appear as impractical, as outlandish and as wasteful as it does here—just like God's grace, which is poured out lavishly on unworthy sinners like Mary, you and me.

Mary knows how to worship. She puts her heart and soul and finances into it, and she doesn't care what others think of her. Remember Martha's rebuke of her in Luke's Gospel for sitting at Jesus' feet and listening to him teach? Custom dictates that a woman's work lies in the kitchen with Martha, getting ready for dinner, rather than listening to the rabbi with the men. Actually, it is more than seeking instruction in Mary's case. It is devotion; she hangs on every word that Jesus speaks (Lk 10:38-42). In John 12, Mary doesn't simply pour perfume on Jesus' feet. She washes his feet with her hair. Surely a washcloth and a towel are available. Why can't she use them? Conspirators ask these kinds of questions. Another way of framing the question is, "How can we worship Jesus without having to be undone and lose it all in the process?" Mary doesn't ask or answer these questions. She's too awestruck, consumed, overwhelmed, undone. Like John the Baptist, she realizes she is not worthy to untie the thongs of the Lord's sandals. As the Baptist says, "I baptize with water, . . . but among you stands one you do not know. He is the one who comes after me, the thongs of whose sandals I am not worthy to untie" (Jn 1:26-27).

Mary and John the Baptist are not groveling in the dirt or carrying on as if they are slimy slugs with no sense of self-worth. Rather, they realize how great and awesome and amazing and worthy the Lord is, and they can do nothing more than bow and prostrate themselves in his presence. I don't pity Mary and the Baptist. I pity all those Baptists and Lutherans and Catholics who no longer feel the same way—who have lost that sense of wonder and who throw only their money in the offering plate and not their souls and bodies too. I pity myself, and admire Mary and John the Baptist. I hope you're like Mary and John and not like the rest of us, who conspire against the Lord in our spiritual state of complacency.

I hope you're not like Judas either, for he cannot stand the aroma of perfume as it fills the house. He can't get away from the smell, as it permeates everything around him. As delightfully intoxicating and as pleasing to the senses as the aroma is, it makes Judas nauseated. He has an allergic religious reaction: "But one of his disciples, Judas Iscariot, who was later to betray him, objected, 'Why wasn't this perfume sold and the money given to the poor? It was worth a year's wages.' He did not say this because he cared about the poor but because he was a thief; as keeper of the money bag, he used to help himself to what was put into it" (Jn 12:4-6).

Judas is no longer enamored with Jesus. I think he has realized that Jesus isn't going to get him where he wants to go—to a life of fame, power and fortune. Turn back to John 6. In John 6, most of Jesus' disciples leave him over his claim that those who follow him must eat his body and drink his blood; in other words, Jesus is a dead Messiah and not some Roman-conquering, power-brokering, fame-and-fortune-seeking messianic figure. In the same context in John 6, Jesus tells his twelve apostles that one of them is a devil. We can infer from John's Gospel as a whole that Jesus is talking about Judas. Returning to John 12, we get the sense that Judas is checking out. Mary's act of devotion prepares Jesus for burial, and within a few days Judas will carry out the ultimate act of betrayal that will lead Jesus to his death. Mary and Judas both make preparations for Jesus' tragic end, but in different ways—one noble, the other ignoble. We must guard against conspiring against the Lord with Judas and must side with Mary.

How might we be conspiring against the Lord? Whenever we use him to fill our pockets with gold (as Judas does), or whenever we use him as a means to an end of caring for the poor (as Judas falsely claims to do), we are conspiring against him. As good as it is to give to the poor—especially as it reflects Jesus' heart and resonates with key aspects of his mission—we should never lose sight of Jesus in the process. Jesus' sharp rebuke to Judas for rebuking Mary is a good reminder to never *use* Jesus for engaging in concern for anything, including caring for the poor. Rather, we should do all things, including ministering to the poor, out of identification with and devotion to Jesus. Jesus' rebuke of Judas is a rebuke to each of us who use Jesus for other things, even noble causes: "Leave her alone. . . . It was intended that she should save this perfume for the day of my burial. You will always have the poor among you, but you will not always have me" (Jn 12:7-8).

Jesus isn't saying that we should never give to the poor. In fact, Jesus makes it quite clear elsewhere that his disciples should give to the poor because his Father has made them partakers of his kingdom (Lk 12:32-33). All things of true merit have been given to his disciples; as a result, they are free to give to those who cannot give to them, just as Jesus gives to each of his followers even though none of us can ever repay him. Jesus is saying that Mary realizes the sacredness of this moment and that she is compelled by gratitude to prepare her Lord for burial. This is the very same Lord who always gives himself graciously and sacrificially for the weak and brokenhearted and poor, as he prepares himself for the supreme sacrifice on their behalf once and for all. Only the poor in spirit and simple in faith can comprehend this, not aspiring and cynical types like Judas. Which type are we?

We can't tell how deep the faith is of those who hail Jesus as their Messiah when he enters Jerusalem. At the very least, their faith separates them from the power brokers whose frustrations—not faith—increase because their plans to squelch the momentum of the Jesus movement are dealt a serious blow by Lazarus's resurrection (Jn 11) and the triumphal entry of Jesus (Jn 12:12-19).

Many people gather at the feast (recorded in Jn 12) to see Jesus and Lazarus. As a result, the leaders conspire to kill Lazarus as well as Jesus: "Meanwhile a large crowd of Jews found out that Jesus was there and came, not only because of him but also to see Lazarus, whom he had raised from the dead. So the chief priests made plans to kill Lazarus as well, for on account of him many of the Jews were going over to Jesus and putting their faith in him" (Jn 12:9-11).

Things only get worse for the power brokers. Not only does Jesus enter Jerusalem, but the heading rightly reads that it is a *triumphal* entry. Not only do the people hail Jesus as the king of Israel, but Jesus adds to the symbolism of the moment by finding a young donkey and sitting on it. The messianic overtones are so incredibly pronounced, and John doesn't want the reader to miss it. So he quotes Zechariah 9:9 (in Jn 12:15), which is a prophecy about the coming Messiah:

> The next day the great crowd that had come for the Feast heard that Jesus was on his way to Jerusalem. They took palm branches and went out to meet him, shouting, "Hosanna!" "Blessed is he who comes in the name of the Lord!" "Blessed is the King of Israel!" Jesus found a young donkey and sat upon it, as it is written, "Do not be afraid, O Daughter of Zion; see, your king is coming, seated on a donkey's colt." (Jn 12:12-15)

Given the impending confrontation, passion and death of the Lord foreshadowed in this chapter, the claim that the entry is triumphant may appear premature and inaccurate to many bystanders and critics. Yet Jesus and John are making a statement—one that bears witness to Jesus' future reign in glory. In fact, we will see that Jesus views his passion and death as facets of his glory. More on that shortly (see "Fifteen Minutes of Fame and the Hour of Glory").

After the triumphal entry, John writes that the crowd that was with Jesus when he raised Lazarus from the dead is continuing to spread the word about Jesus and his mighty deeds. As a result, the Pharisees are brought to the panic point. All their conniving to this moment is getting them nowhere:

> Now the crowd that was with him when he called Lazarus from the tomb and raised him from the dead continued to spread the word. Many people, because they had heard that he had given this miraculous sign, went out to meet him. So the Pharisees said to one another, "See, this is getting us nowhere. Look how the whole world has gone after him!" (Jn 12:17-19)

Do we greet Jesus with expectation and anticipation as he enters our church's city gates? Or do we view him as standing in the way of our own kingdom ambitions, as do these leaders in their concern for their place and the nation's survival? Recall their fears expressed during the emergency meeting of the Sanhedrin soon after the raising of Lazarus from the dead: "'What are we accomplishing?' they asked. 'Here is this man performing many miraculous signs. If we let him go on like this, everyone will believe in him, and then the Romans will come and take away both our place and our nation'" (Jn 11:47-48).

The religious leaders are consumed with concerns for their place and their nation. This is not unlike many church leaders today, who are consumed with fear over their positions and their churches' well-being given all the talk of the collapse of Christianity or Christendom in the West.[36] While I am confident that the true church will survive and thrive, the church as we know it may disappear. Church as big business and spirituality as a shopping mall will likely falter and collapse, as prosperity-gospel preaching no longer proves prosperous in the face of the persecution of the church. How will each of us respond to Jesus as his work leads him and us to Jerusalem and to the cross? How will we respond as he upsets the status quo with God's holy love that breaks through complacent and nominal religiosity?

Of course, we wouldn't dare directly attack, rebel and conspire against Jesus himself for upsetting things. But how do we relate to those who are stirring things up as a result of the movement of God's Spirit that bears witness to Jesus—especially as such movement disrupts and destroys our self-preserving programs of business as usual? We often don't like change; change messes with our comfort zones and stability. We pray that God will show up, but when he does, we don't like it because it confounds our attempts at controlling our—and his—destiny and kingdom ambitions. Jesus has a way of turning things on their heads. When we no longer have a handle on the situation, those of us who are his adversaries frantically grasp after straws—stuck together in the form of a cross.

The claim that the whole world is going after Jesus (Jn 12:17-19) should tell you that the power brokers can no longer sit around and simply conspire against him. Now they have to act, and act decisively. The cross looms large.

Right after the Pharisees say that the whole world is going after Jesus,

John tells us that some Greeks who had come up to worship at the Passover Feast ask Philip if they can see Jesus. Philip and Andrew go and tell Jesus that these Greeks want to see him (Jn 12:20-22). No doubt, Philip and Andrew are excited. Jesus is no longer a local or even a national celebrity. He's global.

Jesus' response may come across as weird and out of place to many readers. We have no immediate indication from the text that he even responds to the request. Later he will respond by saying that he will draw all people to himself, when he is lifted up (on the cross—Jn 12:31-33). But at this moment he appears distant and preoccupied, breaking straight into preaching about a kernel of wheat falling and dying and the hour for being glorified arriving. Rather than taking the Greeks' request to signify that fame and fortune are now at his fingertips, Jesus takes it to signify that his death is imminent. The world has indeed gone after Jesus, as suggested by the Greeks' desire to see him; for Jesus, this means that the time has come to draw *all* people to himself as he is lifted up from the earth (Jn 12:32). Jesus' hour of glory—and not fifteen minutes of fame on *American Idol*—is at hand:

> Now there were some Greeks among those who went up to worship at the Feast. They came to Philip, who was from Bethsaida in Galilee, with a request. "Sir," they said, "we would like to see Jesus." Philip went to tell Andrew; Andrew and Philip in turn told Jesus. Jesus replied, "The hour has come for the Son of Man to be glorified. I tell you the truth, unless a kernel of wheat falls to the ground and dies, it remains only a single seed. But if it dies, it produces many seeds. The man who loves his life will lose it, while the man who hates his life in this world will keep it for eternal life. Whoever serves me must follow me; and where I am, my servant also will be. My Father will honor the one who serves me." (Jn 12:20-26)

No doubt Jesus' press agents—Philip and Andrew—are troubled by what Jesus is saying. They don't want to make these pronouncements public. Just when Jesus should be talking about taking over Jerusalem and going on center stage for the whole world to worship and adore him,

Jesus is singing his swan song. Jesus is the kernel of wheat about to fall to the ground and die. Little do they comprehend that this song accompanies Jesus' victory march: as this kernel of wheat dies, it will produce many seeds. It is the hour of Jesus' glory. The sun is setting, and the hour has come for the great battle to begin. As the darkness closes in, Jesus as the light hides himself to prepare for the battle where he will display his glory. (For the idea of Jesus as the light hiding himself for the great battle at the cross, see Jn 12:30-36; see also v. 46.) The conspirators are about to strike. But when they strike, God will enact judgment on the world. God will enact his judgment by driving out the prince of this world, as Jesus is lifted up in death on the cross: "'Now is the time for judgment on this world; now the prince of this world will be driven out. But I, when I am lifted up from the earth, will draw all men to myself.' He said this to show the kind of death he was going to die" (Jn 12:31-33).

One should get the impression that God is conspiring against the conspirators—from Satan to the Sanhedrin. For all their scheming, God is writing the script, not them. Even though everything appears to be unraveling for Jesus and his mission, God has everything under control. So one should get the sense that things are not going to turn out the way the conspirators expect. For those who might not have this sense yet, consider three things in this passage: Jesus' confidence and purposefulness regarding his mission, his Father's public affirmation and confirmation, and biblical prophecy.

First, consider Jesus' confidence and purposefulness: he is going to the cross ("when I am lifted up from the earth . . . He said this to show the kind of death he was going to die" [Jn 12:32-33]), and nothing is going to keep him from enacting judgment on the world and driving out the prince of this world through the cross (Jn 12:23-26). So although Jesus is troubled in spirit, he is also resolute and confident, full of purpose: "Now my heart is troubled, and what shall I say? 'Father, save me from this hour'? No, it was for this very reason I came to this hour. Father, glorify your name!" (Jn 12:27-28). Such confidence and purpose in his mission should make his opponents step back and reconsider: maybe Jesus knows something about the outcome of the battle that they don't.

Second, consider also the Father's verbal and public affirmation and confirmation of Jesus and his ministry in this passage. You hear the Father's verbal, public vote of confidence of Jesus and his ministry in this exchange: "Now my heart is troubled, and what shall I say? 'Father, save me from this hour'? No, it was for this very reason I came to this hour. Father, glorify your name!' Then a voice came from heaven, 'I have glorified it, and will glorify it again.' The crowd that was there and heard it said it had thundered; others said an angel had spoken to him" (Jn 12:27-29). It's not that Jesus needs the Father's verbal and public vote of confidence at this point. He is so confident that he is doing the Father's will: "Jesus said, 'This voice was for your benefit, not mine'" (Jn 12:30). Rather, the public affirmation is so that everyone else might come to attention and get in step with what God is doing in and through Jesus.

Third, consider biblical prophecy. Besides Jesus' confidence and purpose and the Father's public vote of confidence, Scripture also gives reason for considering that things are going to turn out in Jesus' favor. Biblical prophecy confirms that Jesus is doing his Father's will and that his adversaries are opposing God. John quotes Isaiah 53 and Isaiah 6 in this passage. In fact, all four Gospels quote from Isaiah 6 to convey God's judgment on the hardness of heart displayed by the people and or the leaders in their disbelief and rejection of Jesus (Jn 12:37-41; Mt 13:14-15; Mk 4:12; Lk 8:10). Here's what Isaiah 6 says, as recorded in John 12: "For this reason they could not believe, because, as Isaiah says elsewhere: 'He has blinded their eyes and deadened their hearts, so they can neither see with their eyes, nor understand with their hearts, nor turn—and I would heal them'" (Jn 12:39-40). According to John, Isaiah writes these things because he saw Jesus' glory and spoke about him (Jn 12:41).

Isaiah and John have seen Jesus' glory and speak of him. Others see his glory, but their hardness of heart keeps them from recognizing Jesus as God's Messiah who has come to take away the sins of the world. Still others see Jesus' glory, recognize and believe in him, but refuse to speak openly out of fear of the Pharisees: "Yet at the same time many even among the leaders believed in him. But because of the Pharisees they would not confess their faith for fear they would be put out of the synagogue; for they loved praise from men more than praise from God" (Jn 12:42-43).

What is the real conspiracy against Jesus? Unbelief and fear and false love. Such forces flow from the hardness of heart. One way or another, the hardness of heart is the fundamental problem with the backstabbing Judas, the scheming Sanhedrin, the unbelieving crowds and the people-pleasing leaders who believe in Jesus privately but won't go public because of fear of rejection.

We conspire against God and his purposes for our lives when we refuse to believe in him or refuse to confess him publicly because of wanting to please others. We refuse to believe because we want to be God in place of God (we won't let anyone—even God's Son—take away our place and nation from us [Jn 11:47-48]). Or we refuse to believe because Jesus won't get us where we want to go—to the promised land of the American Dream filled with comforts where all our desires are met (similar to what happens in John 6, in which most of Jesus' followers and the crowds depart). Or we refuse to confess faith in him publicly because we fear others and love people's praises, despising the praise of God (Jn 12:42-43). Which will it be? Whose praise and glory do we seek?

The hour of glory is upon us. It is the pivot point in John's Gospel and the pivot point in our individual lives. It is the moment of decision for each of us. As the seed falls to the ground and dies to bear much fruit, will Jesus bear fruit in our own lives? Only if we believe. Only if we seek after his praise or glory (some translations express the Greek word *doxa* as "glory," others as "praise") rather than our own. Only if we die to ourselves rather than exalt ourselves at Jesus' expense. The religious leaders have refused to receive Jesus because they love their own praise or glory rather than God's glory revealed ultimately in Christ's passion, crucifixion and resurrection. Such love of human glory kills faith, and it is the reason for the widespread cover-up and diabolical conspiracy.

Of course, Jesus' critics and conspirators among the rulers will dismiss any conspiracy theory that would suggest that their motives are based in jealousy, envy, power-brokering and rebellion against God. Critics and conspirators will deny that they reject Jesus because of desires for comfort. The last group of critics and conspirators—those who fear people more than God—would be afraid to admit publicly that they fear their peers, and they would also deny that their refusal to confess faith in Jesus publicly is a form of conspiracy. But if you are not really for Jesus when the going gets tough, you end up being against him. Instead, Jesus' critics and conspirators will deflect attention from themselves and will label Jesus' faithful followers like John as crazy fanatics who concoct wild stories about such conspiracies to excite the masses. These critics are simply trying to cover up for themselves and to hide their real reasons for seeking Jesus' death.

Rather than give their real reasons, the scheming rulers, for example, will say that their basis for seeking Jesus' death is that Jesus is a blasphemer and a rebel. In one sense he is: he denies and rebels against nationalistic and legalistic and consumerist deities out of loving devotion to his Father, who is God over all the nations and passions. Such critics and conspirators will do anything to undermine Jesus and his movement. They'll fix the jury, bully witnesses and try to lock away the evidence in some vault in Jerusalem until the present generation passes from the scene.

Even so, whether or not the rulers succeed in hiding the facts in the present, these power brokers will certainly not win in the end. Judgment is coming to those who do not believe, especially those who have sought to undermine Jesus and his movement. And whereas those who accept Jesus and his word believe also in his Father and come into the light of life, those who reject Jesus and his word also reject the Father. That Word and his Father will judge and condemn the critics and conspirators in the end. The truth will come into the light of day, but the critics and conspirators will remain in eternal darkness:

> Then Jesus cried out, "When a man believes in me, he does not believe in me only, but in the one who sent me. When he looks at me, he sees the one who sent me. I have come into the world as a light, so that no one who believes in me should stay in darkness. As for the person who hears my words but does not keep them, I do not judge him. For I did not come to judge the world, but to save it. There is a judge for the one who rejects me and does not accept my words; that very word which I spoke will condemn him at the last day. For I did not speak of my own accord, but the Father who sent me commanded me what to say and how to say it. I know that his

command leads to eternal life. So whatever I say is just what the Father has told me to say." (Jn 12:44-50)

In the end, we can all blame Judas, making him into a Lee Harvey Oswald who was accused of assassinating John F. Kennedy. But he is simply Satan's and the rulers'—and possibly our own—fall guy. So what do you make of Jesus? Are you conspiring against him, wanting to bring him down by wanting to be God or by pursuing your own comforts or by fearing people rather than seeking to please God? If the answer is yes, and even if you deny it under oath, someday the truth will come out, and your hidden deeds and heart motives will be exposed to the light of day. Judgment will fall.

If you're smart, you'll tell all. Not only that, but you'll change sides and align yourself publicly with Jesus and his mission. You'll take your place on the witness stand and let the truth and your true love be made known to everyone. You'll pour out the perfume of pure love like Mary; you'll pour out true words like John.

You have less time than you think to make the decision. The sealed vault bearing Jesus' body will be blown open in just a few days—not fifty or seventy years later. Even now, the divine conspirator is at work, foiling Satan's and the rulers' plans. In just a little while, everything will be exposed. There'll be no more concealment, no more covert operations. The clock is ticking. The hour is upon us. Whose side are you on?

TRANSITION

The Dark Side of the Force

IT IS NOW GETTING DARK. John foreshadows this time of approaching darkness in John 12. Here we find Jesus predicting his death (Jn 12:20-36) and also saying,

> "You are going to have the light just a little while longer. Walk while you have the light, before darkness overtakes you. The man who walks in the dark does not know where he is going. Put your trust in the light while you have it, so that you may become sons of light." When he had finished speaking, Jesus left and hid himself from them. (Jn 12:35-36)

John moves from Jesus talking of approaching darkness to how God's people continue in their disbelief and rejection of Jesus (Jn 12:37-50). John 12 closes with Jesus talking publicly (Jn 12:44-50). From there, John fast-forwards to the upper room in which the evening meal—the Last Supper—is being served (Jn 13:1-2).[1] John ushers us into the room to witness events surrounding the supper, such as the foot washing and talk of denial and betrayal. Within hours, Jesus—the light of the world—will enter into his passion in the dark of night. He will go there at the hands of Judas, who goes out into utter darkness after Jesus hands him the bread and the devil enters him (Jn 13:26-30). Even so, the light of the world is in his loving, heavenly Father's hands, even in the darkest, hellish depths.

Among other things, it is important for Jesus to assure his followers that what they see in Jesus they will experience with God. This assurance will strengthen them. It will give them hope and confidence and lighten their spiritual countenance in the midst of the darkness.

What about us? Do we understand that Jesus is like the Father? Do we comprehend that Jesus as light is like his Father who is light, and that there is no darkness in Jesus or the Father? Such knowledge will sustain us, especially during dark times.

In our darker moments, we live the Christian life as if it were a *Star Wars* movie. We tend to think—perhaps subconsciously—that good and evil are two sides of the Force (call it "God"), coexisting as equals for all eternity; and we have a hard time not falling prey to the dark side. I recall Yoda's words to Luke Skywalker in *The Empire Strikes Back*: "A Jedi's strength flows from the Force. But beware of the dark side. Anger . . . fear . . . aggression. The dark side are they. Easily they flow, quick to join you in a fight. If once you start down the dark path, forever will it dominate your destiny, consume you it will, as it did Obi-Wan's apprentice."[2]

In these darker moments, we tend to look at God as if God has two sides—the dark side (the Father) and the light side (Jesus). You know what I mean. When left to ourselves at these times, we think: *If only God were like Jesus . . . I like Jesus, but I don't know what to make of the Father. After all, my own dad abused me as a kid.*

It's as if we believe the ancient heresy of Manichean dualism, where light and darkness coexist as equals for all eternity as ultimate reality. From this distorted perspective, we look at God as divided, with a dualism running through his triune being; according to this erroneous point of view, we view the Father as "Anger . . . fear . . . aggression," and Jesus as the exact opposite. But there's no dualism in God, only harmonious distinctiveness. Evil does not arise from God, but is a cancerous absence of the good that attacks it. Evil is the darkness that resists the light, the shadow that emerges and lurks wherever the light of God breaks forth. In contrast, in luminous and harmonious distinctiveness, the Son reflects the radiance and glory of God's holy and creative love and speaks the creaturely lights into being as God's Word: "In the beginning was the Word, and the Word was with God, and the Word was God. He was with God in the beginning" (Jn 1:1-2). The Word—Jesus—is God's very own self-expression from all eternity. What is expressed in Jesus reveals the very heart and being of God. If you want to know what God is like, look no further than Jesus. Don't look around him to God. You won't be able to find God that way. The best way, the ultimate way to know what God is truly like, is to look at Jesus: "No one has ever seen God, but God the One and Only, who is at the Father's side, has made him known" (Jn 1:18).

But still we ask: "What does one make of all that 'anger . . . fear . . . aggression' in the Old Testament?" We "Marcionites"—people who believe there is an Old Testament deity of law and a New Testament deity of grace—like the New Testament God, not the Old Testament one. What we fail to see is that Jesus is holy and has righteous anger, and that God in the Old Testament is full of love in his hatred of sin. God is a holy lover who pursues us no matter how far we wander. And although he gives us over to our dark desires so that we might see the foolishness of our ways and return, he never treats us as our sins deserve. Instead, he always invites us back into the light of his life no matter how far we have strayed from his law. For the law—while good and therefore gracious instruction—was given through Moses; grace and truth in their full revelation, on the other hand, come through Jesus Christ, from whose fullness of grace we have all received one blessing after another (Jn 1:16-17). In fact, as the true light of life, Jesus comes into the world to expose darkness and overwhelm it and to bring everyone into the light. As Jesus himself says, "I am the light of the world. Whoever follows me will never walk in darkness, but will have the light of life" (Jn 8:12; see also Jn 1:5, 9; 3:16-21).

The dark side doesn't exist in God, nor did God create the dark side of the Force. The Word of God, the Word of life and light, is the one through whom the Father created all things, and we know from his life on earth that there is no darkness in him: "Through him all things were made; without him nothing was made that has been made. In him was life, and that life was the light of men. The light shines in the darkness, but the darkness has not understood it" (Jn 1:3-5). I like the alternative translation for the ending of verse 5 in the footnotes of the NIV: "and the darkness has not overcome it." No matter how morally dark the world becomes, no matter how dark our hearts, the darkness will never overcome the light. The light of life will penetrate the darkness no matter how deep its depths.

When they roll the stone over the entrance to the tomb, Jesus is shrouded in darkness. It looks as if Judas's treachery and the rulers' travesty of justice on the night of Jesus' passion, followed by Pilate's vacuous verdict and the darkness of death the next day, have overcome his light.

But God's light is persistent and tenacious. *He* does not flicker and go out. You may try to block him out and close the door on him, but the light of life will find his way through some crack, even if he has to split rocks and roll stones away to overcome and overwhelm the darkness. The light bursts forth in dark places—even in our hearts. For every Judas departing from Jesus to go out into darkness (Jn 13:30), there's a Nicodemus who comes to him at night (Jn 3:2). For every legalistic scribe wanting to throw stones, there's an adulterous woman dragged from her lover's bedroom who pleads for mercy at Jesus' feet (Jn 8:1-11). For every lame man who is healed but who is still crippled by fear of others (Jn 5:1-15), there's a man who was blind but who now sees through the façade of pharisaic false righteousness and beholds the blinding, beckoning light of truth (Jn 9:1-41). The latter person in each pair comes out of darkness into the light of life's embrace.

On which side are you and I—the dark side of death or the light side of life? A Christian's strength flows from the force of God's life-giving light. Beware of the darkness where "anger . . . fear . . . aggression" dwell. "Easily they flow, quick to join you in a fight. If once you start down the dark path, forever will it dominate your destiny, consume you it will," as it did Judas, Annas, Caiaphas and Pilate. But how can you master it? You can't on your own. It's only as the light of God's life-giving grace, truth and love flow through you that you will not be consumed.

The Spirit of truth, whom the Father sent at Jesus' request (Jn 14:16-17, 26), moves around you and me, blowing as the wind, beckoning, luring, wooing, cleansing, enlightening (Jn 3:5-8). The world does not accept the Spirit because it doesn't see or know him. But those who know Jesus know the Spirit. The Spirit lives in them and through the Spirit, the Father and Son dwell in them (Jn 14:15-31). As the Counselor, the Spirit points you and me to Jesus, shines the light of truth on him, sheds light on our path and draws us to him (Jn 14:16-17, 25-26).

When your experience tells you that God doesn't love you, that you're on a bad cosmic karma trip or that the Father is the dark side of the Force, open your eyes and look at Jesus. For if you have seen Jesus, you have seen the Father. Moreover, don't be like Philip, who is not content with seeing Jesus:

Don't you know me, Philip, even after I have been among you such a long time? Anyone who has seen me has seen the Father. How can you say, "Show us the Father"? Don't you believe that I am in the Father, and that the Father is in me? The words I say to you are not just my own. Rather, it is the Father, living in me, who is doing his work. Believe me when I say that I am in the Father and the Father is in me; or at least believe on the evidence of the miracles themselves. (Jn 14:9-11)

Jesus and his Father are light. They are the source of all true light, and there is no darkness in them. What greater miracle is there than the miraculous sign of the Father's love—that the Father so loves you that he would send his only Son for you, to die for you, to rise for you and to raise you to be in his Father's presence forever? What greater miraculous sign of his love could he give you? Know that it was the Father who initiated the Son's journey to this earth to save you, and that the Son fulfilled his Father's will in going to the cross because of his love for the Father, who loves him and us in him (Jn 14:21-23, 30-31; 17:20-26).

I believe all this. Yet sometimes the dark forces of the world, my flesh and the devil crowd out God's Word in my life, especially during seasons of adversity when others have done me wrong. On one such occasion, upon receiving some horrible news, I went to the office of a friend who happens to be a New Testament scholar who has written extensively on John. As I wept in his office, he comforted me with these words: "Sometimes the only way we know that God loves us is because of his Son hanging from the cross for us." Those words, spoken almost two decades ago, have stayed with me and will stay with me my entire life. But it has taken some time for them to sink in. These words didn't take away the "anger . . . fear . . . aggression" at the time, but they have left an impact, and they must continue to sink deep in my heart. God has truly sent his Son to this world for you and for me because he loves us.

When I first received the tragic news mentioned above, "anger . . . fear . . . aggression" welled up in my soul—toward God and toward others. The prince of this world had a hold on me, and I could not break free. In time, however, I have come to realize that God's providential care is often revealed in all its brilliance and warmth in the depths of darkness more than in the light of day. As I think back, I recall what another professor had told me a few years prior to that dark day. He told me, "Paul, you know a lot *about* God and his providential care, but you know very little experientially of God's care for you. In time, circumstances in life will lead you to the point where your head knowledge finally becomes heart knowledge." Through the years, the light has found its way through this and that crevice in the caverns of my heart, exposing darkness and revealing God's love for me. It's still going to take some time for the light to break through, after all the years of "anger . . . fear . . . aggression" that have built up walls in my heart's chambers.

The prince of this world—the devil—would seek to get a hold on you and me. Not unlike the dark-sided Emperor and Darth Vader in *Star Wars*, he uses "anger . . . fear . . . aggression" to gain that hold. But that prince has no hold on our Prince of Peace, whose profound awareness of the Father's love for him upheld him and drove him to the cross and beyond for us (Jn 14:30-31).

Sometimes the only way we know that the Father loves us is by gazing on his Son of life and light hanging in death and darkness on that cursed tree. Beyond "anger . . . fear . . . aggression," it's God's love that sent Jesus to the cross. Beyond "anger . . . fear . . . aggression," it's God's love that raised him from the dead. Beyond "anger . . . fear . . . aggression," it's God's love that rises in your heart as the Spirit draws you to Jesus. Respond to his love, and may it "dominate your destiny."

Jesus as the light of the world now prepares his followers to respond to his Father's and his love, enlightening them and illumining their minds and hearts and path. Even though they do not understand everything Jesus tells them and does for them now, they will later. They will move forward with confidence that Jesus is like the Father. Like them, we must come to know that Jesus is like the Father. Only then will we fully realize that there is no dark side to God and that Jesus truly is the light of the world. The light of Jesus' life and words will lead them and us forward, preparing all of us to pass safely through the dark valley of the shadow of death on our way to the Father's house.

PREPARATIONS

As stated in the introduction to this book, I have titled John 13:1–17:26 "Preparations" because Jesus is preparing his followers for his passion, death and resurrection through which he returns to the Father and through which he prepares a lasting home for them.[1] Before he talks about his return to the Father and before he prepares a place for them, Jesus prepares his followers to be leaders in his kingdom here below by giving them an example to follow—washing their feet (Jn 13:1-17). Such training should make clear to them that they are dealing with a very different Messiah and a very different kingdom order. Jesus also prepares his followers for some possible hindrances to accomplishing his mission—hindrances that are, in fact, anticipated and incorporated into his grand strategy of inaugurating his kingdom: Judas's betrayal (Jn 13:18-30) and Peter's denial (Jn 13:31-38).

At the outset of Jesus' lengthy discourse in chapters 14–16, we find Jesus talking about going to prepare a place for his followers (Jn 14:1-14). No doubt Jesus wants to assure his followers from the start of this discourse—often referred to as the farewell discourse—that he is not saying goodbye forever. In fact, we soon realize that Jesus will return to be with his followers shortly, although in new ways.

What are some of the ways Jesus will manifest himself after departing from his followers to make preparations in his Father's house through his cross and resurrection? For one, the Spirit, whom they have not yet received, will descend and take up residence in their midst (Jn 14:15-17, 25-26; 15:26; 16:5-15). They will also have access to him through one another, as they share life together lovingly and self-sacrificially (Jn 13:12-17; 15:9-17). They will also have access to him through obedience to his Word. Through obedience to his Word in love, Jesus and the Father will come and take up residence in their midst through the Spirit (Jn 14:23; I believe "through the Spirit" is implied from the immediate context). It is vital that Jesus' followers depend on the Spirit who is a counselor of the same kind as Jesus (Jn 14:16-17), on one another as Jesus' intimate friends (Jn 15:15) and also on his Word (Jn 14:15, 21), for persecution awaits them (Jn 15:18-27; 16:1-4).

In view of what awaits them, Jesus warns them (15:18-27; 16:1-4) and prays for them (Jn 17:6-26). Knowing what awaits him, he prays for himself as well (Jn 17:1-5). Jesus does not go into the darkness of this night blindly or haphazardly or in doubt or panic-stricken, but with eyes wide open and with purpose, confidence and providential poise. Looking into the future and looking back, Jesus' followers will find reassurance from the realization that Jesus knows all that awaits him and them and that he holds everything in his hands, just as his Father holds him in his hands. This assurance is important to the author, as he seeks to assure the church in his day that Jesus is providentially leading the way and that their future is secure, even in the face of ongoing persecution.

John's initial readership—and his readership today—are included in Jesus' closing portion of his prayer in John 17 (Jn 17:20-26). Like John's original readers, we also find reassurance from Jesus' teaching and prayer. The close connection between the discourse and the prayer to which it leads naturally and supernaturally, and in which saints through all the ages are included, conveys the sense that we are there with Jesus and his followers that evening and that they are with us now.

We may not face overt persecution in the sense that our homes are taken away or that our blood is shed. But we still face persecution and spiritual warfare as we battle it out with the world system, the flesh and the devil. Whether we face persecution and suffering for the faith overtly or subtly, we should come to the firm realization that Jesus has overcome the world. Jesus shares hard teachings with his followers, not to cause suffering but to grant peace in the midst of suffering: "I have told you these things, so that in me you may have peace. In this world you will have trouble. But take heart! I have overcome the world" (Jn 16:33).

The confident assurance that Jesus has overcome the world and that he is victor helps us sense our victory in the midst of victimization. Jesus' teaching and prayer of preparation are intended to fill us with peace and joy and love. In the midst of chaos, we will find that Jesus is our peace (Jn 16:33). In the midst of sorrow, we will find that Jesus is our joy (Jn 16:20). In the midst of hate, we will find that Jesus' love and the love of the Father are ours for eternity (Jn 17:23-26). Our sufferings and persecution will surely pass, but our eternal joy in the glorious presence of our Lord will last forever. Take heart. Jesus has overcome the world. As a result of this good news of victory through Jesus, we can lay our lives down in loving service, just as Jesus lays down his life for us in holy love as the greatest servant of all.

DOORMATS AND RED CARPET
John 13

I like being called a servant leader—until someone treats me like one. No one likes being treated like a doormat, and that's often what happens to servants.[2] I, for one, don't wear well when I'm stepped on.

A servant leader sets the example for what servanthood looks like. Let's be clear: the leader in question doesn't simply lead servants—the leader is a lead servant. He or she leads others into a lifestyle of service by laying down his or her life for them. That's what we find in John 13. Here Jesus prepares his followers for what is to come.

If Peter had been writing this script, I wonder whether he would have excluded this incident from his Gospel account. For one, Peter doesn't look so good. He refuses Jesus' service at first (Jn 13:8); and besides, he's told in this passage that he's going to deny his Lord in a little while (Jn 13:38). Moreover, Jesus doesn't look so good either. Apart from his position as rabbi in the Passover celebration here in the upper room, there's no indication of how special Jesus really is. No one is rolling out the red carpet for Jesus in this chapter, and he's acting more and more like the world's doormat. For one, he takes off his outer garments, bears a towel and water basin, and kneels to wash his followers' dirty feet. Moreover, while the foot washing is going on in the upper room, the opposition to Jesus outside is increasing dramatically and will ultimately lead to his crucifixion. You would have thought the world would roll out the red carpet for Jesus—and keep it out. After all, he's the Lord God Almighty!

In John 12, the people are rolling out the red carpet for Jesus for his triumphal entry into Jerusalem. By chapter 18, they are already rolling up the carpet to store it for someone supposedly more deserving. Their version of *People* magazine had voted for Jesus as the sexiest man alive—not for one year, but for one week. Now the fan base has moved on with harsh predictability. The people of John 12 and 18 are fickle, while Jesus remains faithful to his calling and to them. We are so like them and so unlike Jesus. In his faithfulness to his calling, Jesus becomes the world's doormat even as he rolls out the red carpet for them and for you and for me. In John 13, as he washes his followers' feet, we see the first real evidence of how radical, humble and sacrificial Jesus' love is.

"It was just before the Passover Feast. Jesus knew that the time had come for him to leave this world and go to the Father. Having loved his own who were in the world, he now showed them the full extent of his love" (Jn 13:1). This is Jesus' farewell dinner. This is when he's supposed to be honored by his adoring followers. Instead of being memorably loved on, he loves on them in an unforgettable way.

> The evening meal was being served, and the devil had already prompted Judas Iscariot, son of Simon, to betray Jesus. Jesus knew that the Father had put all things under his power, and that he had come from God and was returning to God; so he got up from the meal, took off his outer clothing, and wrapped a towel around his waist. After that, he poured water into a basin and began to wash his disciples' feet, drying them with the towel that was wrapped around him. (Jn 13:2-5)

You'd think that Jesus would at least wait until Judas departs to do the dirty deed of betraying him, or at the very least pass him by as he washes the others' feet. After all, he knows what Judas is about to do (Jn 13:10-11, 21-30). This is like adding insult to injury: no doubt Judas finds Jesus' act of humility humiliating. How could he have followed such a loser for so long? Soon he will kiss Jesus on the cheek to betray him, the equivalent of spitting in his face. And yet, knowing all this, Jesus still washes Judas's feet. He washes the other disciples' feet as well—a group of timid, cowardly and not-so-smart nobodies who will abandon him as soon as the going gets tough.

Unlike most people for whom red carpets are rolled out, Jesus rolls out the red carpet for us because of his love for us and not because of our merit or performance. If merit and performance were the criteria, we would get the doormat treatment instead. Many of us already know this story so well that we no longer understand it. We no longer sense the shock and bewilderment and confusion, and no longer experience the sense of gratitude that Jesus' disciples must feel—especially after this evening when they all abandon him. They have no leg to stand on, no boast of costly discipleship; they have only Jesus' favor based on mercy and not merit. Up until the abandonment, Peter will boast of his merit (just as he and the others cannot believe that one of their own would betray Jesus—Jn 13:22): "Peter asked, 'Lord, why can't I follow you now? I will lay down my life for you.' Then Jesus answered, 'Will you really lay down your life for me? I tell you the truth, before the rooster crows, you will disown me three times!'" (Jn 13:37-38).

Jesus knows all this, and yet he rolls out the red carpet for them. Certainly, he performs the foot washing to give them an example to follow. As the text says,

> When he had finished washing their feet, he put on his clothes and returned to his place. "Do you understand what I have done for you?" he asked them. "You call me 'Teacher' and 'Lord,' and rightly so, for that is what I am. Now that I, your Lord and Teacher, have washed your feet, you also should wash one another's feet. I have set you an example that you should do as I have done for you. I tell you the truth, no servant is greater than his master, nor is a mes-

senger greater than the one who sent him. Now that you know these things, you will be blessed if you do them." (Jn 13:12-17)

Now we are to roll out the red carpet for one another, even if that means becoming doormats for our brothers and sisters. If we comprehend that Jesus doesn't ultimately perform the foot washing to get us to perform well like him, but because he loves us, and if we truly know and experience the greatness of his humble love, we will love like he loves and will live into the full extent of his love (Jn 13:1).

◆   ◆   ◆

In our CEO church culture that prizes hierarchy and status and national platform, it's very difficult to imagine the full extent of Jesus' love being lived out in our midst. Often we will find our role models not among the CEOs of corporate Christianity sitting at the head of the table but among those we expect to be at the foot. We need to change places with those at the foot of the table from time to time to get prepared for the day when the roles and the placement of name tags are reversed—when their day of elevation comes.

I know of such a servant who often sits at the foot of the table, and I need to change places with him. His name is Gavin. Gavin is nothing more than ordinary by most standards, except by the standard that really counts—Jesus' example lived out in John 13. Gavin is a lead servant who partners with me in ministry; he leads the way from a position of influence in loving and caring for others in sacrificial love, assisting with mentoring and speaking into people's lives, sacrificing his time and energy. I remember the first time I had the opportunity to see Gavin at work. We were moving to a new home. I hardly knew Gavin at the time, but he volunteered to help us move. After all of our friends returned home to their families, having given sacrificially of their time and energy that day, Gavin stayed with us. Gavin suffers from diabetes, and he had to take occasional breaks to recuperate and replenish his system, but he emphatically insisted on staying until the work was finished. My wife could not believe it; nor could I: "Who is this guy?" We would have never finished the move that evening if Gavin hadn't helped us. In effect, Gavin rolled out the red carpet for us as we moved into our new home. I am forever indebted to Gavin, not simply because of his help that day and night, but also because he continues to love us sacrificially with his time and energy. (One time he helped my kids design and build cars for a pinewood derby after I had failed miserably in doing it myself; my kids even won some races as a result of his help!) Now Gavin is putting in place a system to help student interns, who have served in a ministry of our seminary called New Wine, New Wineskins, stay connected after they move on to the next stage in life. I watch him as he cares for others; they're in good hands as he washes their feet.

Some may think of Gavin simply as a doormat; they probably think the same thing about the Jesus disclosed in John 13. Gavin is just a guy who gets the fact that Jesus has laid down his life for him, rolling out the red carpet on the night of his passion so that Gavin can journey home to the Father's house (Jn 14:1-4). The more we experience Jesus' red carpet treatment, the more we'll lay ourselves down as doormats for others and live out the full extent of Jesus' love: "A new command I give you: Love one another. As I have loved you, so you must love one another. By this all men will know that you are my disciples, if you love one another" (Jn 13:34-35).

CHANGING HE-MEN INTO HALFLINGS
John 13

Jesus prepares his followers for the battle that lies ahead. He changes these he-men into halflings or hobbits as he turns the world upside down, beginning with a family meal (Jn 13:1-4), a foot washing (Jn 13:4-17) and a farewell speech (Jn 14–16). Halfings—or hobbits—are those little people who appear in J. R. R. Tolkien's *Lord of the Rings*, who bear the evil ring of power to the fires of Mordor.

Jesus knows that he's about to be taken into custody for a crime he didn't commit. But instead of having his followers build up a stockpile of ammunition, Jesus chooses to carry on with preparations for the Passover meal he will celebrate with his men just before his arrest. It's all a matter of priorities and strategy.

But Peter fails to grasp the strategy. So when the time comes for Jesus' arrest, Peter cuts off the high priest's servant's ear. In turn, Jesus gives Peter an earful: "Put your sword away! Shall I not drink the cup the Father has given me?" (Jn 18:11).

Jesus must drink this cup, and in this manner. Only Jesus can drink this cup of God's wrath—down to the dregs. Jesus alone can bear this burden to its doom in the fires of Mordor—this burden of evil, which spurns the Creator and turns his creations into objects to be exploited for our own power games and financial gain. This battle can only be won communally, never on evil's commodifying terms.

Jesus does it the hard way, the enduring way, the relational way. Peter and I fail to get it time and time again. We seek to rid the world of evil with our swordsmanship—whether by steel blade or ballpoint pen—and are often frustrated by Jesus and his halfling tactics.

Why does Tolkien choose a halfling—a hobbit—to bear the ring, and not a warrior or a wizard? Because hobbits do not desire to rule the world. And most hobbits do not seek financial gain (except Bilbo's relatives, the Sackville-Bagginses, and we all know a few kin like them). Rather, they seek out fellowship and feasts and celebrations, kind of like Jesus.

Jesus does not use these he-men for his kingdom work only to dispose of them later. To the contrary, he gives *himself* to be disposed of for them, for *they* are his kingdom work. They are his friends, his very own. That's why he feasts with them and washes their feet, transforming them into halflings.

Turning them into halflings so that they can grow into the fullness of their union with him is what it's all about for Jesus. He loves them and has no trouble expressing his love for them. Why else would he wash their feet? "Having loved his own who were in the world, he now showed them the full extent of his love" (Jn 13:1). And he'll serve them again in the end when the fullness of his kingdom comes. (See Lk 12:37: "It will be good for those servants whose master finds them watching when he comes. I tell you the truth, he will dress himself to serve, will have them recline at the table and will come and wait on them.") This is not a typical form of male bonding, not the typical thing one does as leader of the pack. But there's nothing common about this common-looking king.

I suppose it's his appearance as a mere ranger and his halfling ways that deceive us; we dupe ourselves into thinking him a conjurer of cheap tricks. No wonder we think we must take matters into our own hands to save the world. Sometimes we foolishly think we're the ones most able and ultimately responsible for changing the world—like Boromir or Peter. Like Gimli or Peter, we mistakenly think we can destroy the ring by striking it with our axe.

Ultimately, it's Jesus who changes the world, and we bear witness to him. That should free us. The burden of the world is not on our shoulders or around our necks. Jesus alone can bear this burden to its destruction, and he uses every one of his halfling tactics to get the job done. So we had better climb on his shoulders for the duration of the trek. For Jesus has been to Mordor's fires and back again. He alone can lead us there.

How does he lead us there? Through humility and vulnerability. We see humility in the foot washing (Jn 13:1-17), and vulnerability in his washing the denier Peter's (Jn 13:31-38) and the betrayer Judas's feet (Jn 13:18-30). Two marks of great leaders include leaving a good example of service for others to follow and allowing people to get close enough to hurt them. You will never turn he-men into halflings if you wear that tough guy exterior, if you never risk it all for others; you will never get at someone's heart like Peter's by masking yours with bravado. You will never get past the ever-watchful eye of Sauron if you enter by the front gate and not the back way of humility and vulnerability.

True bravery allows others to get inside the walls of one's heart. It always moves beyond the safety of the Shire to secure the Shire's future by getting inside Mordor. Though Jesus loves fellowship with his band, his is the fellowship of the ring. His band's mission is to bear witness to him as he bears the ring through unimagined dangers to its destined end.

And what an unimagined fellowship it is! No homogeneous unit here: an elf, a wizard, a dwarf, some hobbits, a tax collector, a zealot, a doubter, a deceiver, a few of thunder's sons and their fellow fishermen. They don't always get along, to say the least. And none of them have any ambition for being the least. So every night Jesus has to put his sleeping bag smack-dab between Matthew the tax collector's and Simon the Zealot's (so that the zealot doesn't slit the throat of the Roman subject/Jewish traitor). And Jesus always has to get after the likes of Peter, James and John for trying to prove to one another that they're the biggest, the baddest and the best. No wonder he leaves them with the world-changing and he-man-defying call to wash one another's feet.

They fail to realize that it's often the smallest person who makes the biggest difference, for there's more to it than size. One must account for substance. Large love marks the greatest lives, and "Greater love has no one than this, that he lay down his life for his friends" (Jn 15:13). Jesus is the greatest, and so he can love the most and become the least, even demonstrating by becoming the least how great he truly is. Now we are Jesus' friends if we do what he commands and love like he loves (Jn 15:14-17), changing from he-men into halflings, becoming great by becoming less.

One way or another, it comes back to relationships. Most of the pressing problems facing the world today can be reduced to a lack of practical, self-sacrificial, halfling love for others. While many of us have no trouble tackling mountains of problem issues around the world, we stumble over stepping stones of loving the people next to us as we climb over them to make our way there. But loving the people next to us is the first step to getting there.

◆ ◆ ◆

In closing, let me tell you how I am personally trying to take the first step to getting there. I am part of a far-from-homogeneous halfling small group: we are multiethnic, multiclass, multigenerational, multilayered and multigrain. (What can I say? We like diversity.) It's a missional-home or homey-missional or missing-home community (whichever suits your consumer preference) meeting to address pressing race and class issues facing the consumer church and broader consumer culture today.

People think we're crazy. They think we're climbing a mountain whose peak we'll never reach and that we'll probably fall off the cliff at some point along the way. Maybe we are crazy, and maybe we will fall off the cliff one by one—or better yet, all together. But that's just it. It's as much about the process of climbing together over newfound family meals, sharing old family photos along with sharing far-from-fairy tales from the past, sharing our feet for washing and sharing ideas for parting speeches from the shire, as it is about making it all the way to Mount Doom's fires.

In fact, just as Frodo could never have made it to Mordor without his precious Sam and the rest, I would never make it up the mountain of doom that stands within my own heart to cast away the ring if I did not share sacrificial life with these precious halflings so very different from me. For although Frodo was willing to take the ring to Mordor, he readily admitted he did not know the way. He needed the help of this diverse fellowship. And even if he had made it there without Sam and the rest, what good would making it there and back again have been? For the fellowship of the ring is as much about the fellowship as it is about the ring.

The ring of power stands for isolation and oppression, for sacrificing others en masse—the opposite of sacrificial fellowship that includes "the other," including particular others of this and that race and class. What good would it be to conquer the world's pressing problems as an individual in isolation, with no one to celebrate at journey's end? In the end, for all my he-man talk of saving the world from bitter racism and class strife, I would come to the bitter realization that I had never parted with "my precious"—that world- and self-destroying ring. And so I'll readily admit I do not know the way. But Jesus does, and Jesus is the way.

So give me family feasts, foot washings, and farewell speeches with tax collectors, zealots, fishermen and thunder's sons-turned-hobbits, as we leave the Shire all together. It's the only way to turn a he-man world upside down, as Jesus welcomes in his halfling kingdom made up of former he-men turned hobbits.

GRAN TORINO JESUS
John 14

None of Jesus' disciples can see it coming. Nor can we see it coming—unless we have already read the Gospel script. We expect Jesus to be like all the other messianic protagonists in the Hollywood of his day, shooting it up with the power brokers and thugs, like Clint Eastwood in an old spaghetti western.

But Jesus does not play according to the typical messianic character type. He functions more like the atypical Clint Eastwood in *Gran Torino*—or better, Clint Eastwood in *Gran Torino* functions like him, taking a few lines from Jesus in the Gospel script.

The further we get into the Gospel of John, the more we see Jesus acting out the role of Messiah in an atypical manner. First there is the foot washing (Jn 13), and then the farewell discourse and high priestly prayer (Jn 14–17), followed by his passion and the cross (Jn 18–19). John's farewell discourse prepares Jesus' first disciples and us for what is to come. Yet we tend to project Jesus painting Jerusalem Town red with other people's blood, like an ancient version of Clint Eastwood.

Although certain facets of Eastwood's character in *Gran Torino* fit Eastwood's typical character type in other movies, these traits don't fit him in *Gran Torino* in the end. He isn't the outlaw Josey Wales or the Pale Rider or the High Plains Drifter. He isn't Dirty Hairy. He is Walt Kowalski—a cantankerous and disgruntled retired Ford factory worker and Korean War veteran who becomes the unlikely savior of the Hmong community that has "invaded and overrun" his suburban, working-class Detroit neighborhood.[3] No one can quite understand him or his actions—not his kids, not the priest and not even the two Hmong youths who live next door, whom he comes to love and vows to protect.

Now for Jesus. As stated above, no one can see it coming. Although certain facets of Jesus' career fit the messianic character type—the power and miracles and electrifying teaching that win him fame and popularity—what is now transpiring doesn't fit the messianic character type at all. Jesus ends up being, well, Jesus, and not what we would expect him to be. We envision a Messiah being the old blood-and-guts-dripping, teeth-kicking, Roman-and-Sanhedrin-conquering king who takes his throne in Jerusalem and reigns with an iron scepter.

If we think about it, the Pale Rider fits many of our projections of what a Messiah should be. But Jesus ends up looking a lot like Kowalski (apart from Kowalski's foul mouth and cantankerous, disgruntled personality). Or is it the other way around? In either event, Kowalski is not your typical Oldsmobile—or better Gran Torino—version of Eastwood, and Jesus isn't your Oldsmobile version of the Messiah.

Confusing? You bet it is. No wonder Thao—the Hmong teenage boy next door whom Kowalski takes under his wing to make him a man—doesn't understand Kowalski's waiting game of cerebral tactics. Up until that point, Kowalski is prone to shoot first and ask questions later. So you can understand Thao's confusion, rage and questions when he demands to know what Kowalski is going to do to take vengeance against the Hmong street gang who violently raped his sister. The same is true of Jesus' disciples. They don't understand all Jesus' cryptic allusions to his departure from this world (Jn 14:1-4), the Spirit's coming (Jn 14:15-27) and the prince of this world's approach to do battle (Jn 14:30-31). You can understand Jesus' disciples' bewilderment, questions and angst (Jn 14:5, 8, 22).

In the end, both Jesus and Kowalski lay it on the line for their friends. The prince of this world and the Hmong street gang don't know what's coming and are taken captive by surprise. Jesus and Kowalski lay down their lives to deliver the ones they love: Jesus' followers from sin and death, and Thao, his sister and their community from more intimidation and violence. The manner in which Jesus and Kowalski lay their lives down sacrificially and exit the scripts is so noble, though strange. It is so triumphant, though bizarre. I couldn't have written either script.

I'll leave it up to you to figure out how *Gran Torino* ends. I don't want to spoil it for you, if you haven't seen the movie. And I won't jump ahead and tell you more than I already have about what you'll find after John 14. We'll stick to chapter 14 of John's script. And even though John's version of Jesus has already told the disciples he's going to the cross (Jn 12), they're still clueless. I suppose it's because they've seen all those Hollywood versions of messianic figures played by earlier versions of Eastwood. The only other similarity between Jesus and Kowalski that we'll draw attention to at this point is that both men try to assure their followers that their plans will work out for the best in the end.

Jesus tells his followers at the beginning and end of John 14 that they should not let their hearts be troubled about his departure, for it is best that he goes (Jn 14:1, 27). It is important that Jesus prepare his disciples for his departure, giving them reasons that he must go at this time. Why is it best that he goes? First, it is best that Jesus goes because he is going to prepare a place for them in his Father's house, and will come back and take them home: "In my Father's house are many rooms; if it were not so, I would have told you. I am going there to prepare a place for you. And if I go and prepare a place for you, I will come back and take you to be with me that you also may be where I am" (Jn 14:2-3). Jesus doesn't abandon his followers, leaving them to face the music alone. Rather, he goes to make preparations for them in his Father's house by way of his death on the cross and resurrection and ascension.[4] In other words, he goes the distance. And after he finishes making preparations for them through his saving work, he will come back to get them and take them home to be with him forever. This all just goes to show how Jesus' followers *are* his ministry. He doesn't use them to do the ministry; they, and the people to whom they minister, *are* his ministry. How many ministers would want the people to whom they minister to come and live with them forever? This is radical: Jesus is relational to the core of his ministerial being.

Second, it is best that Jesus goes because his followers will do greater things than Jesus: "I tell you the truth, anyone who has faith in me will do what I have been doing. He will do even greater things than these, because I am going to the Father. And I will do whatever you ask in my name, so that the Son may bring glory to the Father. You may ask me for anything in my name, and I will do it" (Jn 14:12-14). Later Jesus says, "You heard me say, 'I am going away and I am coming back to you.' If you loved me, you would be glad that I am going to the Father, for the Father is greater than I" (Jn 14:28). Just as his ministry to his followers is relational to its core, Jesus' greatness is also relational. Jesus is about to complete the work he could do in their presence here on earth through his death and resurrection, and then he will continue his work of preparation for them in his Father's house through his ascension. This involves interceding on their behalf before the Father. Hebrews talks more about Jesus as our great high priest interceding for us before the throne, but we also get a sense of it here. In his work as the ascended Messiah and great high priest, Jesus will perform greater deeds in and through his followers, as he will be in the presence of the Father. Notice that for all his talk about the Father being greater than him, he also says that *he* will do anything for which they ask in *his* name for the glory of his Father. But Jesus doesn't leave it there. While he is going to the Father on their behalf, he will also be asking the Father to send them another counselor—the Spirit of truth—who will come in Jesus' name to be with them forever. This brings us to our third point about why it is good for them that Jesus departs.

Third, it is best that Jesus goes because he will ask the Father to send the Spirit, who will be with them forever, and through whom the Father and Son will come and live with them:

> "If you love me, you will obey what I command. And I will ask the Father, and he will give you another Counselor to be with you forever—the Spirit of truth. The world cannot accept him, because it neither sees him nor knows him. But you know him, for he lives with you and will be in you. I will not leave you as orphans; I will come to you. Before long, the world will not see me anymore, but you will see me. Because I live, you also will live. On that day you will realize that I am in my Father, and you are in me, and I am in you. Whoever has my commands and obeys them, he is the one who loves me. He who loves me will be loved by my Father, and I too will love him and show myself to him." Then Judas (not Judas Iscariot) said, "But, Lord, why do you intend to show yourself to us and not to the world?" Jesus replied, "If anyone loves me, he will obey my teaching. My Father will love him, and we will come to him and make our home with him. He who does not love me will not obey my teaching. These words you hear are not my own; they belong to the Father who sent me. All this I have spoken while still with you. But the Counselor, the Holy Spirit, whom the Father will send in my name, will teach you all things and will remind you of everything I have said to you." (Jn 14:15-26)

Jesus is sending another counselor or advocate, but one of the same kind as he is, not someone completely different from him (Jn 14:16).[5] This counselor or advocate is the Spirit of truth (Jn 14:17). Jesus says that they are already familiar with this counselor whom he is sending to live in them, for he already dwells with them (Jn 14:17). I take this to mean that Jesus and the Spirit are so intimately related that when one is with one of them, the other is present too.[6] The Spirit who is with them now will dwell inside them when Jesus returns to the Father (Jn 14:16-17). Though the Spirit is with them now through the mediation of Jesus, Jesus and his Father will send the Spirit to dwell inside them upon Jesus' return to the Father (Jn 14:16, 26). Then Jesus and the Father will come and dwell with them, making their home with them (Jn 14:23), through the mediation of the Spirit.

Let's meditate on the Spirit's work of mediation a bit more. Jesus doesn't simply leave the keys to the Gran Torino with his followers (thankfully, he doesn't leave the keys to your father's Oldsmobile either). And he doesn't simply leave a lot of good memories with them. Nor does he simply leave them with another counselor or advocate (just think what it would have been like if Walt Kowalski would have sent one of his sons or even Dirty Hairy to take his place: the future would have looked less bright and less redemptive). Jesus leaves them with the same kind of counselor, the same kind of advocate as he, one who will carry on where Jesus leaves off: "But the Counselor, the Holy Spirit, whom the Father will send in my name, will teach you all things and will remind you of everything I have said to you" (Jn 14:26). Jesus and the Spirit speak the same message, the same language. There will be no change of message or approach to life. It is so vital that in the midst of chaos—the night that ushers in Jesus' passion and as he talks of departing—Jesus comforts them and assures them of the triune God's constancy. The Spirit is so secure—just like the Father and Jesus. The Spirit has no need to prove he's in charge when he takes center stage. In fact, the Spirit's aim on center stage is to make sure Jesus remains in the spotlight and to prove to Jesus' followers the constancy of God's holy love and abiding presence. Thus, there is more to the Spirit's mediatory work of counseling and advocacy than the reassuring news that he will call to mind and instruct Jesus' followers in the truth of Jesus.

Through the Spirit, Jesus as the Truth will abide with them, and this through the Spirit's indwelling presence. So not only are the message and language the same; the divine presence will be constant. If anything, God's abiding presence will be more intimate: the Spirit, the same kind of advocate as Jesus, has already been living *with* them, and will now be *in* them. Moreover, Jesus will come to them and will be with them through the Spirit's indwelling presence: "But you know him, for he lives with you and will be in you. I will not leave you as orphans; I will come to you" (Jn 14:17-18). The Spirit's work of mediation complements and confirms and internalizes Jesus' work as the sole mediator between God and humanity (1 Tim 2:5); there is no competition between Jesus and the Spirit.

Such assurance. Such intimacy. Jesus will make his home with his followers along with his Father in this world through the indwelling mediation of the Spirit, and then his followers will come and live with him in his Father's house forever. In no way will Jesus leave and abandon them—or us—as orphans (Jn 14:18). Jesus will always be with his followers. The Spirit comes to remind, instruct and assure them and us in this good news, and to make it possible for Jesus as the ultimate good news to dwell in each of us.

Just as Jesus leaves the keys not to the Gran Torino but to his heart, Jesus doesn't say in his will that the church gets the keys to the house. Rather, he keeps the door to his Father's house open so that the church can move in with him when the time comes. We'll address this theme in the next essay, "Front Porch Light." So let's bring this tale to a close.

Like with all good Eastwood movies, Jesus and Kowalski go it alone in the end. But Kowalski's friends will never be alone, nor will Jesus' friends. Kowalski's friends have his song playing in their memories as the movie closes, and Jesus' friends have a vital sense of his abiding presence through his Word and Spirit as the script continues to unfold.

Jesus goes it alone, but he does it for his followers. Even after he departs, he will be with them—and you—forever. As Jesus pours out his life as an overflow of his communion with the Father so that we can join them someday in the Father's house, the Spirit is poured out from heaven to be present with us and to prepare us for that day when we enter the Father's house through Jesus. Don't let your hearts be troubled.

FRONT PORCH LIGHT
John 14:1-11

Coming home from grade school, I was always comforted by the knowledge that my mom would be there. Sometimes when she welcomed me home, the smell of freshly baked cookies would also greet me at the door.

During my college years, when I would travel several hundred miles home for Christmas break, my mom and dad would say they'd keep the front porch light on for me. Sure enough, that light would be on. And sure enough, they would be up too, waiting for me, no matter how ungodly the hour.

In a most ungodly hour, on the night of his betrayal into his enemies' hands and ensuing passion, Jesus' thoughts take him home to his Father's house. And he tells his friends that when their time comes to leave this place, they will find a home with him in his Father's house. Like them, we who follow him today can be assured that the front porch light will still be burning bright when we get there and that Jesus will have already prepared a room for each of us. Jesus prepares his followers for his departure by comforting them with the news that he goes to prepare a place for them in his Father's house:

> Do not let your hearts be troubled. Trust in God; trust also in me. In my Father's house are many rooms; if it were not so, I would have told you. I am going there to prepare a place for you. And if I go and prepare a place for you, I will come back and take you to be with me that you also may be where I am. You know the way to the place where I am going. (Jn 14:1-4)

Even though Jesus is trying to prepare and comfort them, and even though they will later find these words very reassuring, his disciples are presently at a loss. You could even say they're panicking with Jesus' talk of departing and going back to the Father. They don't want to be left alone, especially on a night like this one. Thomas is perplexed and asks Jesus how he can possibly expect them to know the way, since they don't even know where he is going: "Lord, we don't know where you are going, so how can we know the way?" (Jn 14:5). Back then they didn't have MapQuest or Google Maps. And Thomas is afraid that Jesus' directions (which are less than sketchy) will get him so lost that he'll never arrive. Remember, he's known as "Doubting Thomas."

Jesus replies that he is the way to the Father (make sure you don't miss that exit ramp, Thomas): "I am the way and the truth and the life. No one comes to the Father except through me" (Jn 14:6). Jesus' response might not seem to offer them much by way of clarification and expansion, but it really does. We're not talking about geography here, but relationship. Jesus escorts them—and us—to his Father's house. He will come back "and take you to be with me that you also may be where I am" (Jn 14:3). But Thomas and the rest of them are still completely lost, and so Philip asks Jesus to at least give them a glimpse of the destination—the Father: "Lord, show us the Father and that will be enough for us" (Jn 14:8).

Maybe Philip is simply curious. Or perhaps he isn't content with trusting in Jesus. After all, throughout this Gospel many fail to recognize that Jesus is from above, not from below. And so perhaps he thinks that Jesus is a distant second to the Father and cannot deliver on his promise to take them home.[7] Or maybe Philip isn't comforted by Jesus' promise that Jesus' followers would live with Jesus *in the Father's house*. Perhaps he fears that the Father is very different from Jesus, that the Father is an exceedingly hardcore disciplinarian or a hard-to-please, crotchety and distant deity. But Jesus assures them that he is like the Father: "Anyone who has seen me has seen the Father" (Jn 14:9). There won't be any unpleasant surprises in the end, including when God opens the door.

Some of us don't want to go home on Christmas break because we fear unpleasant surprises that may await us as soon as we open the door. Sometimes my students in seminary ask for prayer just before Christmas break. They face uncertainty and anxiety about going home to be with their families. Some of them fear that parents and siblings will be antagonistic to their newfound faith, or that they will get caught in the middle of yet another family feud.

Some of us don't have homes to go to on Christmas break. My parents are still alive, but I don't look forward to the day when they're gone. While I don't get home very often anymore, at least I know I can go back there, taking my wife and kids with me. But someday, after my parents have passed away, someone else will live in their house and I won't be able to go and be with Mom and Dad back home. Yet I have a home that I go to every night. My wife and kids and dog are my true home now, and so are the roof and walls that house us. What would it be like to go from walking the streets by day to sleeping beneath a bridge by night? What would it be like to have no one to go home to? I can't imagine what homelessness—physical or relational—must be like. Even worse, I can't imagine what it would be like to leave this world and not have a home with the Father, to instead wander aimlessly for an eternity without direction and without community.

For others of us, this place is too much like home. We don't care to go home to be with the Father because we're having too much fun. We just hope that Daddy will send us down some money to keep us happy whenever we wire home for more.

Still, for others of us, the Father's house is the only home we've got. That's the way it was for Jesus' first followers, and that's the way it should be for us. While we should enjoy God's good creation, and while we should make the most of our time here, this is not our final destination. The new heavens and the new earth are our destination, where we will live with God forever in face-to-face and heart-to-heart encounter with God through Jesus in the Spirit. Jesus' first followers' hopes were set fully and firmly on his promises of enduring presence in their lives through the Spirit, and then later in face-to-face encounter with Jesus in the Father's house. Certainly, the security of Jesus' presence in this world and the next would give them hope and assurance in the face of opposition and persecution. When I'm low, discouraged and distraught, facing difficulties or even persecution, there's nothing more reassuring than going home and talking with my wife. Her presence and our conversations at home are a refuge to me, just like my parents were when I was growing up. I could go home and cry in their arms after being bullied or teased by other kids at school, just as my children do now with us. Jesus' presence and promises, including the promise that they would live with him in the Father's house, meant the world to Thomas and Philip and the rest of the disciples. And Jesus' presence and these promises should mean the world to us today.

Knowing that my parents were always there for me—that they would keep the front porch light on and that they would be waiting for me when I got home—meant the world to me. I remember that light burning. I remember them coming to the door when my car pulled up in the driveway. The looks on their faces. The room prepared for me. The late-night dinner with dessert. It doesn't get any better than that. Or does it? It does. Those of you who have never experienced what I'm talking about will one day experience more than what I'm talking about. As beautiful as these experiences were, they are shadows of things to come for you and for me. God's front porch light will be glowing when we arrive. The Father will be there to greet you and me at the door. Jesus has already prepared a room for us through his work at Calvary and the open tomb—and he will be there at his Father's house and will greet us at the door: "Welcome home. We've been expecting you."

THAT DIRTY LITTLE FOUR-LETTER WORD
John 14:15, 21

I grew up singing the song "Trust and Obey." I don't really like the tune, but the title gets at something quite significant. We don't find too many songs today that call for obedience, although we do find bracelets worn in some circles asking, "What would Jesus do?" It's as if *obey* has become a dirty little four-letter word. But trust, coupled with obedience, is an essential mark of Jesus' followers' lives. Here's what Jesus says: "If you love me, you will obey what I command" (Jn 14:15), and "Whoever has my commands and obeys them, he is the one who loves me. He who loves me will be loved by my Father, and I too will love him and show myself to him" (Jn 14:21).

I suppose there's a hidden assumption in some contexts that to call people to *obey* Jesus turns the Christian life into drudgery, taking away from our experience of God. To the contrary, if we don't talk about obedience—and more importantly, if we don't *experience* what it means to obey Jesus—we're taking away from experiencing intimacy with him.

I can understand where some of this type of thinking might arise. Those turned off by the "What would Jesus do?" bracelet may associate the question (rightly or wrongly) with those dutiful Christian types who place *obey* in front of *trust* as a cart before a horse. It's as if those dutiful types are saying, "Whether or not you love Jesus, you should obey him; it's your duty to obey him."

Regardless of what you make of the bracelet, the dutiful kind of Christian living is a bad trip, in my estimation. Dutiful, grit-your-teeth-and-just-do-it Christianity leads to drudgery, and I don't want to live the Christian life from the standpoint of sheer obligation. But that doesn't mean that we should throw out obedience (more on that later). Indeed, how could I live the Christian life out of sheer obligation given all that Jesus has done for me, and given that he is living his life in and through me through the Spirit? In place of mere obligation, I want to live my life from the standpoint of immense gratitude for what Jesus has done for me, and for who he is in my life. In place of the dutiful and drudgery-filled Christian life, I want to experience the devoted Christian life—bound up with responding to Jesus' love for me.[8]

I'm not alone in this desire. Take, for example, the famed evangelist John Wesley, who was always a stickler for rigorous Christian discipleship. The founder of the Methodists was known for his systematic methods, rigorous morals and social action, and for building a movement of committed Christians along such lines. But he did not always have the experience that internalized and energized his evangelical and missional rigor. After training for a career in the church as a young man, he was sent from England to the Americas to reach Native peoples for Christ. Later he left the Americas by boat, a defeated man spiritually and emotionally—a real shipwreck of a missionary. Regarding his failed missions endeavor, he wrote something to the effect: "I was sent to the Americas to save the heathen. But who will save me?!" It was only after he heard Martin Luther's commentary to the Romans being read aloud at Aldersgate Street in London on May 24, 1738, that he came to experience the assurance and affection so necessary to living out the Christian life of radical obedience for which he is known. Wesley penned in his journal the following words concerning his conversion experience at Aldersgate, which today can be found etched on a bronze memorial at the site:

> In the evening I went very unwillingly to a society in Aldersgate Street, where one was reading Luther's preface to the *Epistle to the Romans*. About a quarter before nine, while he was describing the change that God works in the heart through faith in Christ, I felt my heart strangely warmed. I felt I did trust in Christ, Christ alone for salvation; and an assurance was given me that He had taken away *my* sins, even *mine*, and saved *me* from the law of sin and death.[9]

This experience revolutionized Wesley's life and ministry. The good news of Jesus' love and assurance traveled throughout England and the world through Wesley and his Methodist movement. Wesley and his followers proclaimed the gospel in word and deed, called people to repent of their sins and trust in Christ alone for their salvation and fought on behalf of orphans and widows and slaves in their distress. Wesley and his movement faced all kinds of obstacles in their missional endeavors, but nothing could separate them from the love of Christ—absolutely nothing. Some scoffed at Wesley and ridiculed him and his movement. He was not allowed to preach in many churches, and so he often resorted to preaching to the masses in the open air. Some of his followers faced the constant threat of death for their fight against the slave trade.

The trust and assurance of which Wesley speaks leads to radical obedience; such trust is birthed in God's love for us poured out in our hearts and lives through the Spirit of Jesus (see Jn 3:1-21 and Jn 14:15-27 for a discussion of the Spirit's role in relation to God's initiatives in loving the world and the disciples in particular through the sending of his Son; see also Rom 5:5 on the Spirit and the outpouring of love into Jesus' followers' hearts). Our obedient love for God and one another is a response of trusting in God's love for us.

Such trust and assurance do not lead to inaction or a negative reaction to God's Word, but to a profound response of radical obedience. That's what happened in Wesley's life, and that's what happened in Peter's, James's and John's lives as well. With this in mind, I have no trouble with "What would Jesus do?" as long as this question is birthed in a "What would Jesus love?" kind of thinking. The latter reflects a model of spiritual formation that is centered in the heart, whereby we think in terms of heart-to-heart relationship and communication with God. We must make sure that the horse goes before the cart, and that love, birthed in the trust and assurance of God's love for us in Jesus, is what motivates us to obedient action.

Talk is cheap when it isn't coupled with action. And Jesus' words give us all the motivation we need to put our claims of loving him into obedient action. Jesus says that those who obey his commands truly love him. What's more, those who obey him will also be loved by his Father, and

Jesus also will love them and show himself to them (Jn 14:21). In other words, the more we love in obedience, the more Jesus reveals himself to us. What more do we need by way of incentive to obey him? Don't think that God or Jesus only loves us if we obey Jesus' commands. For God in Jesus loves the world unconditionally (Jn 3:16). Rather, we're talking about relational love involving reciprocity. By speaking of reciprocity or mutuality, I am not speaking of a quid pro quo orientation in which we give in order to get from God. Rather, it involves each party engaging the other out of love and affection. From this standpoint, we respond to God's initiative of pursuing intimacy with us. God gives himself to us in the freedom of his love as an unmatchable gift, and we respond to his love and grace in trusting, loving obedience and gratitude.

I love my children regardless of what they do. But intimacy and significant relationship with my children involves profound give-and-take of mutual care and regard for one another in word and action. Ideally speaking, as I give my life for my children (just as God has done in Jesus) and heartily do so out of sacrificial love for them (just as God has done in Jesus), so they, as those secure in that love, will respond in obedience out of love for me (just as Jesus' true followers respond to God's care in Jesus for them).

Jesus tells his disciples that obedience is a sign of intimacy with him. His followers will soon face grave trials in their faith journey, as Jesus will shortly go to the cross. Jesus goes to the cross in love for the Father and for them. They will bear their crosses in love for the Father and for Jesus. Jesus ultimately bears his cross in love because he is assured of the Father's love for him, and they will ultimately bear their crosses in love because they are assured of God's love for them in Jesus.

God called these first followers, and later Wesley and us, to win the world for Christ. But how can we win the world if our own hearts have not been won for Christ, if they have not been strangely warmed by his love? Obedience is a key ingredient of an authentic faith journey. But so, too, is love.

This reminds me of the story of another famous evangelist, the late Dr. Bill Bright, founder of Campus Crusade for Christ. The story as I heard it goes that Dr. Bright was being interviewed by a secular journalist, who was going around asking Christian leaders what Jesus meant to them. All the other Christian leaders interviewed waxed eloquently and theologically about Jesus. But when the journalist asked Bright the question, Bright broke down in tears. Jesus meant everything to him, absolutely everything—far more than could be delineated theologically. Perhaps that is why Dr. Bright's evangelistic efforts were so explosive. Bright gave himself sacrificially to win the world for Christ because he was assured of Jesus' great love for him.

I suppose if you had asked John—the beloved disciple—before the cross and after the cross what Jesus meant to him, you would have gotten completely different answers. John may have actually wept on both occasions, given that he sensed that he was so dearly loved by Jesus. But only after the cross did John realize how costly Jesus' obedient love to the Father and obedience-inspiring love for him truly were. A costly love leads, in turn, to a costly love. And that is why John and his fellow followers gave themselves sacrificially to win the world for Jesus, laying down their lives daily for him.

Jesus' costly love marks our lives for radical obedience. Such love leads us to give our lives radically for one another (obedience to Jesus' commands in his farewell discourse in John's Gospel entails sacrificial love for one another). Such loving obedience to Jesus, reflected in love for one another, will bear witness to the world that God's love is radical and authentic.

As disclosed in the farewell discourse of John 14–16, Jesus is preparing to leave his "short-term" missions trip of thirty-plus years on earth for heaven, and he is preparing to send his followers out on a similar mission trip. Jesus is successfully finishing his tour of duty and is making the necessary preparations to assist his followers with success on their own tours. Obedience to his commands will be central. But obedience apart from love—apart from a love from God for one another—will be fatal to the mission. Without such love-borne obedience, without such assurance, they will end up shipwrecked on their tour of duty. For duty alone will not suffice to help Jesus' followers navigate the treacherous waters of hatred and strife. The world's disobedience, displayed in hatred of Jesus and his followers, will be too much to bear if they don't have the assurance of the love of God and each other (Jn 15:18-27).

I have heard it said that the number one reason that missionaries return home before their terms are over is because they can't get along with other missionaries. It's not because of disease or dysentery. It's not because of doctrinal disagreement. It's because of disunity—a lack of practical love. They'll probably never tell you that it was disunity, but that's often the case. Disobedience is often their little secret because *obey* (as in "love one another"—Jn 15:9-17) is often a dirty little four-letter word. And *obey* is often a dirty little four-letter word because God's love for them is really only a foreign word that never gets translated into their hearts.

As I look out at the faces of my students preparing for Christian service here and abroad, I pray that they might truly experience the assurance of God's love for them. That's the only thing that will secure them for years of Christian service of obedience to Jesus in loving others, including their co-laborers. It's the only thing that will secure them in their missional endeavors to win the world for Jesus when they endure disease and dysentery and doctrinal divisions—not to mention a lack of obedience on the part of their brothers and sisters manifested in disunity, which reflects a lack of practical love. It all starts with Jesus telling his followers at the outset of his farewell discourse: "Do not let your hearts be troubled. Trust in God; trust also in me" (Jn 14:21). We can trust Jesus because he's trustworthy, because he loves us so sacrificially. This assurance frees us up to love others sacrificially. And we need to uphold one another with that same love, expressing mutual care for one another.

As I write this essay, one of my former students and his wife are enduring difficulties overseas. From their own account, they are trying to bear witness to Jesus by calling for the breaking down of divisions between people groups in their community; unfortunately and grievously, they are facing a backlash from some in their community. Perhaps their detractors like affinity groups of homogeneous people more than true community made up of diverse peoples, in which unity is centered in Christ rather than personal preferences. Possibly these detractors are threatened by what biblical unity really looks like. I don't know what's going on inside these detractors' hearts and heads. But I do know that my young missionary friends are finding the work excruciatingly difficult. They're finding it difficult to obey God by continuing to call for the breaking down of divisions. They're finding it hard to love their disagreeable brothers and sisters. If they're not careful, my young friends will find *obey* a dirty little four-letter word. But if they're mindful, they'll see this as an incredible opportunity to join the Wesleys of our time—whose message has gone out to all the world—in experiencing more and more fully Jesus' love for them. It's that other four-letter word—*love*—that keeps *obey* clean and beautiful.

My friends need to see that this Jesus who loves them is giving them the profound privilege of identifying with him on his lifelong missional journey, a journey that Wesley also experienced. For while Jesus returns home from his short-term missions trip soon after the cross and resurrection, he comes right back in love through the Spirit. (Reflect on Jesus' promises to return in the context of the giving of the Spirit in Jn 14:15-31.) Jesus is now there across the ocean with my young missionary friends today, just as he was with Wesley a couple hundred years ago, and with Peter, James and John before that. I pray that my young friends will continue to obey Jesus by loving in the midst of all the disunity—loving even the disagreeable ones—so that they can experience what is entailed by obedience: Jesus showing himself more fully to them today (Jn 14:21). And I also need to obey God by loving my brother and sister and assuring them of Jesus' profound and beautiful love for them in whatever way possible, identifying with them in their plight.

God has never left me alone as an orphan (Jn 14:18), just as he never left Wesley or Peter or James or John alone. This assurance and experience gives me the grounds for assuring my young friends overseas that Jesus will never abandon them to isolated lives of empty obedience. And so I'm writing this essay for them. I would have my young friends know that Jesus' love sustains me, even as I have been ridiculed for calling for breaking down race and class divisions in Christ's body and beyond, even as I've been adjectivally attacked with dirty little four-letter words.

I recall here for my friends one occasion where I was ridiculed by some heavyweight power brokers outside the realm of evangelicalism for my call to break down race and class divisions in the church. While they didn't use dirty little four-letter words, and while I have been attacked at

times within my own movement for the same stances, their barrage hurt
me more than most. I remember sitting in my living room that evening,
weeping and telling God, "It's just too hard to do this stuff [translate:
obey] anymore. I can't handle the pain of rejection anymore—from the
right and now from the left. Why are people so threatened by this message of reconciliation?" The next day, one of the power brokers at that
event came to me and behind closed doors apologized for not standing
up and calling the others to account for their wrongful opposition. His
concern for me at that low moment profoundly manifested to me Jesus'
love. He said something that has stayed with me ever since and that has
encouraged and motivated me to join the Wesleys and the Wilberforces
of this world with renewed energy: "In the 1700 and 1800s, liberals
talked a good talk about justice initiatives on behalf of the slaves but
didn't do anything of substance. (Instead it was the lowly and despised
evangelicals who actually did the real work of freeing the slaves.) So now
a young evangelical is doing something about the race and class divisions
in the church and beyond, and the brilliant and powerful elites attack
him for it." God has used these words to rejuvenate me and assure me of
Jesus' care for me and call on my life.

Believe me. I know I'm no John Wesley or William Wilberforce. I
know I've blown it many times and haven't always stood as a witness in
view of God's Word and work against oppression. I know that I haven't
always loved my enemies well, in part because of fear of what the opposing forces might think or say (and they've said a lot). But I'm as thankful
as I can be that Jesus is giving me the privilege to identify with him and
with these missional forbearers. I'm thrilled to participate on the sacrificial, missional journey of God's assuring and reassuring love that is so
compelling and threatening and world-changing, and which many of Jesus' followers behind closed doors or out in the open have demonstrated
to me. Call me an evangelical—a pariah. Call me foolish or stupid or
closed-minded, unschooled and ordinary, a fundamentalist or a closet
liberal—whatever your preference and point of view might entail. Use
some dirty little four-letter word. But dirty as that word may sound, I
hope to *obey* and to care for you—because of Jesus' beautiful and increasingly profound four-letter *love* for me. And to my young missionary

friends, I say: keep going. Keep marching on to the beat of a different drum. Keep in step with Jesus and obey his gospel word because of his costly, priceless love for you. It's worth it.

Sinners, Obey the Gospel-Word![10]

Sinners, obey the gospel-word!
Haste to the supper of my Lord!
Be wise to know your gracious day;
All things are ready, come away!

Ready the Father is to own
And kiss his late-returning son;
Ready your loving Saviour stands,
And spreads for you his bleeding hands.

Ready the Spirit of his love
Just now the stony to remove,
To apply, and witness with the blood,
And wash and seal the sons of God.

Ready for you the angels wait,
To triumph in your blest estate;
Tuning their harps, they long to praise
The wonders of redeeming grace.

The Father, Son, and Holy Ghost
Is ready, with their shining host:
All heaven is ready to resound,
"The dead's alive! the lost is found!"

Come then, ye sinners, to your Lord,
In Christ to paradise restored;
His proffered benefits embrace,
The plenitude of gospel grace:

A pardon written with his blood,
The favour and the peace of God;
The seeing eye, the feeling sense,
The mystic joys of penitence;

The godly grief, the pleasing smart,
The meltings of a broken heart,
The tears that tell your sins forgiven,
The sighs that waft your souls to heaven;

The guiltless shame, the sweet distress,
The unutterable tenderness,
The genuine, meek humility,
The wonder, "Why such love to me?"

The o'erwhelming power of saving grace,
The sight that veils the seraph's face;
The speechless awe that dares not move,
And all the silent heaven of love.

—Charles Wesley

BURNOUT
John 15:1-8

All too often we hear of burnout in work and ministry due to stressful situations, personal problems and difficulties in life. Pastors and other leaders have to take time off or leave the ministry altogether because of burnout. The economic downturn in the global economy, increasing individualism and the rise of secularism in our culture affect churches severely. Those responsible for sowing, nurturing and cultivating God's people as a field for harvest are facing increasing demands to stay alive and not die on the vine. It is so vital that we who are leaders realize that we are branches and that we must abide in the vine.

As Jesus prepares his disciples for what is to come, he even warns them about the possibility of a form of burnout: "If anyone does not remain in me, he is like a branch that is thrown away and withers; such branches are picked up, thrown into the fire and burned" (Jn 15:6). It would be easy for them to think they have to go it alone, given all Jesus' talk about going away, and as a result to end up experiencing burnout. But notice that Jesus speaks here of their needing to abide in him continually—even after he is gone. He will be with them, and they are to remain in him. Thus, they do not need to experience burnout. Those who don't remain in him will not bear fruit and will be useless in ministry. It is that simple; the reality is that harsh. As Leon Morris states, "These are strong words that emphasize the necessity of remaining in vital contact with Christ if fruitfulness is to continue."[11] Merrill Tenney goes so far as to say, "Jesus left no place among his followers for fruitless disciples."[12]

Jesus' followers will be sorely tested in the days, weeks, months and years ahead. Jesus will be taken from them this very night and be led to his death. And while he will rise from the dead on the third day, return to the right hand of the Father and always be with them through the Spirit, there's no guarantee that they will remain in him—that is, apart from their constant dependence on him and his holding them in his hand.[13] Jesus knows that they will face so many trials that will test their resolve to abide in him. Jesus also knows that we, as fruit-bearing branches that abide in the vine, face trials that test our resolve to abide in him.

Leaders face burnout in ministry today for several reasons. There are so many distractions, so many potential traps that can easily capture our attention, so many special interests competing for our imaginations and so many voices tempting us to find our value in what we do rather than in knowing and being known by Jesus.

The temptations are often very subtle. We easily get caught up in what we are doing *for* Jesus rather than what we are doing *in* him and *being* in him. As one of my friends, Ben Malick, says, it is so easy to view ourselves as human *doings* rather than as human *beings*. Don't get me wrong: Jesus wants us to bear fruit, and a lot of it. But what kind of fruit does he want us to bear? I think answering this question can help us avoid burnout.

Jesus wants us to bear relational fruit. He is so passionate about knowing and being known by his Father and about his followers knowing and being known by God through him. Nothing else is comparable, and so his Father prunes us so that we find our nourishment for life in Jesus—and in him alone.

The finance committee can cut the church budget, but as painful as it is, the committee is not cutting away branches from the vine. Secularism and free-market spirituality can cut into your church's market share among religious consumers, but as painful as they are, these forces are not cutting away branches from the fruit-bearing vine. The Father has a way of pruning us through difficult circumstances so that we reevaluate our priorities and come to see that what really counts is helping people find their relational security in the Father through Jesus. As those working in the vineyard, we do not have to make branches abide in us; we need to provide the ideal conditions for them to abide in Jesus. Nor is it our task to prune branches, but to make clear to those for whom we are responsible that the gardening God is pruning them, and that he has a way of pruning all of us so that we abide in Jesus. I have to guard against trying to make people relationally secure in me, and against trying to find ultimate relational security in them. Branches can never replace the vine.

The older I get, the more difficult life becomes and the more I sense my need for the vine. The weeds, the withering sun and polluted water so easily stunt my spiritual growth. But even worse than these external conditions is my internal condition of wanting to go it alone: I often try to bear fruit on my own, even though I know I desperately need to abide in the vine.

I'm not alone in trying to go it alone. Here's what Jesus says to his first followers: "Remain in me, and I will remain in you. No branch can bear fruit by itself; it must remain in the vine. Neither can you bear fruit unless you remain in me" (Jn 15:4). Jesus wouldn't tell Peter and company that they must abide in him if they are immune to the temptation of somehow trying to live in isolation from him.

God has a way of clipping away at my autonomy, just like he does Peter's and the rest of Jesus' followers. The Father's way of making me depend on Jesus is to make me depend on him in prayer: "If you remain in me and my words remain in you, ask whatever you wish, and it will be given you" (Jn 15:7). If I want to grow and bear fruit, I need to depend on Jesus' word for my nourishment and to move from meditation on his word to petition in prayer. Now that's dependence. That's what it means to hang by a thread—I mean vine.[14]

I'm not saying that every form of burnout in ministry is due to autonomy or going one's own way. But I do believe such independence, such disobedience, is one major reason burnout occurs. I am so thankful that God is showing me how needy I am for him and how I can do nothing apart from him: "I am the vine; you are the branches. If a man remains in me and I in him, he will bear much fruit; apart from me you can do nothing" (Jn 15:5). I am realizing more and more that Jesus isn't saying that I can do some spiritual, life-giving things apart from him; rather, he's saying I can do *nothing* of vital spiritual significance apart from him. If only Israel had understood how its independence from God would lead to its ruin as a vine (Is 5:1-7; see also Ezek 15:1-8). If only I had grasped this truth—that I am a branch in constant need of abiding in Jesus the vine—much earlier in my life. But I am thankful that I am now realizing how needy I am, and I am grateful that God is pruning me so that I abide all the more fully in the vine. Not only am I realizing how much I need Jesus personally; I am realizing how much I need him to bear fruit in my life. Just as Jesus is turning me into someone renewed and transformed in relation to him, Jesus is also doing his relational work through me. It's not how much I do, but how dependent I am on him and his word as I relate to others that makes the biggest impact, bears the most abundant fruit to the glory of God and shows that I am Jesus' disciple (Jn 15:7-8).

The more dependent on the vine we become to bear fruit, the more mature we become. There is ample opportunity to grow in maturity, for there are ample opportunities to depend completely on Jesus. And why wouldn't we want to depend on him? For the maturity of which we speak is bound up with growing in intimacy with God the Father and his Son. John makes clear that the substance and significance of a disciple's life is bound up with abiding in Jesus and Jesus in the believer (Jn 6:56; 14:20, 23; 15:5; 17:23, 26). Such abiding reflects Jesus' abiding in the Father and the Father in him (Jn 10:38; 14:10-11, 20-21; 17:21, 23), and also is connected to our living in the Father and the Son (Jn 17:21) and the Father and Son making their dwelling in us (Jn 14:23).

Jesus is speaking here of union and communion with God in him. The union of which Jesus speaks here is not a matter of right standing (although, biblically speaking, right standing is a facet of our union). Nor is Jesus speaking of stoic grin-and-bear-it duty (which has no biblical basis), but of the obedience that flows from longing for intimacy with the Godhead. Such union does not result from our love for God, for our love is itself created and quickened by God's love. God reveals his love to us through his Word Jesus and his word of promise, creating faith in him, whereby he abides in us. So union involves God's love, which Jesus reveals to us as he makes himself known to us and lives in us: "I have made you known to them, and will continue to make you known in order that the love you have for me may be in them and that I myself may be in them" (Jn 17:26).[15]

As in the case of Jesus' first followers, Jesus and his Father haven't left us to go it alone. They are here with us and in us, and we are to abide in Jesus and his word and in his Father through him. In the face of budget cuts and cuts in market shares, we must depend on Jesus' abiding presence. We must also depend on the Father to prune us so that we can bear relational fruit in the vine. How else will we receive the nourishment we need to bear such fruit? May we sense our need and may we long to depend increasingly on Jesus and his word and his Father. And even if we sometimes don't sense our need and burn out as a result of going our own way, we do know that God can renew us and create a longing for the nourishment of his abiding presence and bear fruit again through us. Abide in Jesus and the intimacy of his love, even though all else burns up around you.

◆ ◆ ◆

In closing, I would like to draw your attention to the story behind the hymn "Abide with Me." A pastor, Henry Lyte, wrote the words to this classic song in 1847 as his life was burning out as a result of tuberculosis. Inspired to write the hymn because of his battle with disease and death, Lyte finished the hymn the Sunday he gave his last sermon in the church he had served so many years in Devonshire, England. Lyte died three weeks later.

The song has left its mark on multitudes of people for generations. It is worth noting that one hundred and fifty years after it was written, "Abide with Me" was sung at the funeral of Nobel Peace Prize–winner Mother Teresa of Calcutta in 1997. Mother Teresa could not have done what she did for so many years in the slums of Calcutta—surrounded by such hopelessness and sickness and poverty—had she not abided in Jesus and his love. Although her body finally burned out and gave way to death, her heart never stopped burning with Jesus' compassion for the least, the lost and the last. How else could she have loved those whom others found unlovable? I for one don't have that kind of love. And yet Jesus calls us to love sacrificially just as he loves us (Jn 15:9-17). It is only as the Father prunes me and causes me to depend all the more on Jesus that I come to love as he loves and to love as Mother Teresa did. Mother Teresa bore much fruit to the glory of God, showing herself to be Jesus' disciple (Jn 15:8). Like her, may we burn with Jesus' love. But let us never burn out without it.

Abide with Me[16]

Abide with me; fast falls the eventide;
The darkness deepens; Lord with me abide.
When other helpers fail and comforts flee,
Help of the helpless, O abide with me.

Swift to its close ebbs out life's little day;
Earth's joys grow dim; its glories pass away;
Change and decay in all around I see;
O Thou who changest not, abide with me.

Not a brief glance I beg, a passing word,
But as Thou dwell'st with Thy disciples, Lord,
Familiar, condescending, patient, free.
Come not to sojourn, but abide with me.

Come not in terrors, as the King of kings,
But kind and good, with healing in Thy wings;
Tears for all woes, a heart for every plea.
Come, Friend of sinners, thus abide with me.

Thou on my head in early youth didst smile,
And though rebellious and perverse meanwhile,
Thou hast not left me, oft as I left Thee.
On to the close, O Lord, abide with me.

I need Thy presence every passing hour.
What but Thy grace can foil the tempter's power?
Who, like Thyself, my guide and stay can be?
Through cloud and sunshine, Lord, abide with me.

I fear no foe, with Thee at hand to bless;
Ills have no weight, and tears no bitterness.
Where is death's sting? Where, grave, thy victory?
I triumph still, if Thou abide with me.

Hold Thou Thy cross before my closing eyes;
Shine through the gloom and point me to the skies.
Heaven's morning breaks, and earth's vain shadows flee;
In life, in death, O Lord, abide with me.

—Henry Lyte

VERTIGO
John 15:1-17

In the surrounding context of John 15, we find that Jesus is leaving shortly for the cross. His followers are beginning to experience spiritual vertigo as they make their way with Jesus toward the Mount of Olives, where he will face his enemies. Having left the upper room (Jn 14:31), and no doubt passing by vines on their way, Jesus tells his followers that they must be like branches that draw life from him as the true vine if they are to bear much fruit while he is gone.

Jesus doesn't tell his followers that they are going to have to suck it up and go their own way when he departs, as if he were totally gone. He tells them that they must draw from him all the nutrients that they will need to survive and thrive, as branches draw from the vine. Jesus will be with them, and they will be in him and will bear much fruit through their union with him (Jn 15:1-8). Jesus also tells them that they must be there for one another and abide in one another's love if they are to abide in his love (Jn 15:9-17).

At the beginning of this discussion, Jesus talks about how his Father prunes the branches that abide in Jesus. The Father prunes branches that bear fruit in Jesus so that they will bear even more fruit: "I am the true vine, and my Father is the gardener. He cuts off every branch in me that bears no fruit, while every branch that does bear fruit he prunes so that it will be even more fruitful" (Jn 15:1-2). If we are to bear fruit in ministry, we must depend on the Father to prune us, as well as abide in Jesus. We cannot go it alone.

I can relate to what Jesus says about his Father pruning his followers so that they can bear even more fruit. God keeps cutting away at me too. At times, it's as if he's cutting me off at the legs, taking away my crutches and making me fall into his arms. Spiritual vertigo.

Against this biblical backdrop, I remember experiencing spiritual vertigo one night when I was speaking to a large group of people I didn't know in a place that was foreign to me. I was hoping to use a YouTube video of U2's song "Vertigo" for my talk. I wanted to illustrate a point about how the apostle Paul experienced vertigo on the Damascus road when Jesus struck him down and made him depend completely on him. The sound guy couldn't get the sound to work, however, and so I was forced to go without my prop. I had to depend on God, instead of Bono, to bring the point home. And in the course of the talk, God did bring the point home. I hate and love those moments—all at the same time.

There was more, though. Not only did the sound for "Vertigo" not work, but the moderator's introduction and the transition to my talk went poorly. The moderator basically said he didn't know much about me, and he failed to list off my capacities, credentials and connections (even though he had mentioned all of them for the person who preceded me!). When I got up to speak, the moderator and the celebrity who had just finished speaking left the room together. I felt as if I were trying to stand on one leg, desperately hopping about in the effort to maintain equilibrium. Nothing worked—I lost my balance. My opening lines fell to the ground with a thud, and I felt like I was falling too.

It's not as if I wanted to be independent of Jesus; in fact, I wanted to honor him—but mostly in my own strength with some help from the Spirit rather than in complete dependence on the Spirit of Jesus and on the Father's pruning work. Such radical dependence is too unnerving, too risky, too destabilizing.

I reached out for Jesus as I fell. But actually he was holding me all along, pulling me away from myself so that I would have to depend completely on him as a fruit-bearing branch depends upon its vine. No crutches, no props—just the vine. Like Bono sings in the song "Vertigo," Jesus' love is also teaching me what it means to kneel, to depend on him, in the midst of wilderness wanderings.

God broke through to people that night during the talk, I was told, as he broke my hold on me. An elderly saint lovingly told me that it was as if someone else were in the room as I spoke, for something supernatural happened. During the talk, I read from 1 Corinthians 1 about the crucified God who turns our kingdom ambitions upside down and calls us to boast in his loving kindness and not in our own capacities— our wisdom or our power or our wealth (1 Cor 1:31 is a quotation from Jer 9:23-24). I then went on to contrast Martin Luther King Jr.'s funeral with John F. Kennedy's, showing slides of King's common coffin on a common cart drawn by pack animals, and Kennedy's ornate casket on Lincoln's magnificent funeral cart drawn by stallions. I left the slides on the screen for people to reflect upon them as I read from King's "Drum Major Instinct" speech, which gets at Jesus' upside-down kingdom of self-emptiness, concern for the least of these and dependence on Jesus for one's eternal destiny and significance. The recording of that speech was played during King's funeral, and the video of the funeral with that audio recording was played at the King memorial museum in Atlanta the day I visited it a few years ago. The words of the speech and the video of King's funeral procession continue to haunt me to this day. I broke down as I read the words that evening about King's vertigo-life, as God broke through to me and to those who were gathered there that evening, turning us upside down.

As I look back on what happened that night, and on what is increasingly happening in my life both day and night, I am reminded of Jesus' words to his followers in John 15 about how his Father is the master gardener, how Jesus is the choice vine and how we are his branches. God keeps cutting away at me—not cutting me out of the vine, but pruning me so that I will depend on him and so that I might bear even more fruit in and through him.

God does not allow me to grow on my own, wildly winding this or that way in search of planting my own vineyard. I could never bear fruit apart from the vine anyway, so why do I keep trying? For "apart from me you can do nothing" (Jn 15:5). Apart from the Father's pruning and Jesus' abiding presence in and through his word (Jn 15:1-2, 7), I can do nothing that really matters for God. I am nothing apart from Jesus, even though I sometimes feel so secure when I am doing things based on my capacities, credentials and connections—that is, until he removes my props and crutches.

I hate it when God takes away my props and my crutches. Whoever said Christianity is a crutch? That person had no idea what true Christianity is like. I wish it were a crutch; I would feel so much more secure. Instead, God keeps pruning me, removing the crutches and props that I depend on so that I will depend only on Jesus. Experiencing vertigo makes me feel so vulnerable that I can only fall into Jesus' arms.

Have you ever played the trust-fall game, in which someone stands behind you and tells you to let go and fall backward because he or she will catch you? I have had such a hard time playing that game. I almost always flinch and try to catch myself as I go down. It's always a relief when the person catches me and doesn't step backward to let me hit the ground. I have often run into a brick wall when I fail to trust in Jesus, but I have never hit the ground when Jesus has pulled away all my props and crutches. I am finding that if I am going to stand strong in Jesus, I am going to have to fall into his arms, for apart from him I can do nothing. The same goes for you. So next time you find yourself depending on props and crutches rather than on him, be prepared to experience vertigo and the strange feeling of falling into love's embrace. Let go. He'll catch you.

As Jesus catches us, he will also cause us to care for one another, just as that elderly saint cared for me the night I experienced spiritual vertigo when I was speaking. That elderly saint in a foreign place encouraged me to continue depending on Jesus, even while everything around me seemed to give way. He abided in Jesus and obeyed his word by caring for me, just as Jesus tells us to care for one another in John 15:9-17.

In this passage, Jesus calls his followers his friends and no longer servants, for he has made known to them all that he has learned from his

Father (Jn 15:15). This is a real relational breakthrough! Now any friend of Jesus is a friend of mine. I shouldn't treat any friend as a servant, though I should serve him or her, and all the more because we are now called Jesus' friends.

As we grow in confidence to depend more fully on Jesus, letting go and trusting that he will catch us, he will also cause us to uphold one another. It is only as we remain in his love and his word remains in us that we love others, and it is only as we love others that we remain in him and his word (Jn 15:7-17). And as we depend more fully, we will come to realize that all we have in this world is Jesus' Father, his Spirit and him, as well as those who, like us, depend on him.

Only as we depend on our triune God's loving care for us and love one another in loving obedience to Jesus will we bear much fruit. We bear fruit as we obey Jesus' word; and we obey his word as we love one another as Jesus loves us (Jn 15:8, 10, 12). And we love one another because Jesus has first and foremost loved us with a selfless, sacrificial love: "Greater love has no one than this, that he lay down his life for his friends" (Jn 15:13). As Jesus' friends, we lay down our lives for one another, just as Jesus has first loved us (Jn 15:12, 14). Of course we will experience spiritual vertigo as we let go of our lives and take hold of Jesus, his word and one another. But after all, falling in love is what life's all about.

ENTITLEMENT
John 15:18-27

A sense of entitlement permeates the American cultural landscape. We talk about our rights and privileges as American citizens and as consumers. Some American Christians talk about what they can expect as "the King's kids"—like a brand-new Cadillac or a bigger home or even a better wife. After all, God wants to expand our territory and bless us with our best life *now*. All we need to do is pick up the phone and give a donation to this or that ministry, or pray the Jabez prayer numerous times a day, or—for those more disciplined—obey God's Word with due diligence. But what happens when things don't turn out the way we expect, when God doesn't meet our demands, when God doesn't match our quid with quo, when God doesn't obey us as we obey him? After all, God owes us; so, God, "Show me the money."

A dear friend who was once an internationally known ministry leader felt entitled to more respect by his board, a better salary from the organization and greater fulfillment in life. His entitlement perspective—subtle as it was from the standpoint of our typical American paradigm—distorted his decision making, and his ministry ended with an extramarital affair. He has since warned me that I should guard against entitlement thinking in my own ministry.

But aren't I entitled to some things in ministry? Well, sure. According to this passage in John 15 and the one immediately preceding it, I am "entitled" to Jesus' abiding presence—and from it follows abundant fruitfulness and effectiveness in ministry, as I abide in his word. Also, in this same context, I am told that I am entitled to my fellow believers' love, just as I am to love them (Jn 15:9-17). The Lord also tells me that I am entitled to experiencing the world's hate: "If the world hates you, keep in mind that it hated me first. If you belonged to the world, it would love you as its own. As it is, you do not belong to the world, but I have chosen you out of the world. That is why the world hates you" (Jn 15:18-19). Entitlement thinking—that prejudicial sense of white-robed, saintly privilege—keeps us from realizing that we are entitled to hardship and persecution as Jesus' followers.

Jesus warns his followers of falling prey to entitlement thinking on the eve of his most severe suffering: "Remember the words I spoke to you: 'No servant is greater than his master.' If they persecuted me, they will persecute you also" (Jn 15:20).[17] Jesus tells them to remember because he is aware that they may forget. Perhaps the disciples think that because they belong to Jesus he will spare them from suffering and persecution. But he tells them that a servant is not greater than his master (translated: they are not greater than him). So they will go through what he endures, and that's a fact. They can bank on it.

We shouldn't go looking for persecution; it will find us. We shouldn't try to be obnoxious, just obedient. The rest will automatically follow, and as with Jesus and his first followers, they will hate you and me without reason (Jn 15:25). The unreasonable reason we will be persecuted is because we belong to Jesus: he has chosen us out of the world (Jn 15:19).

Jesus doesn't want us to experience unpleasant surprises, so he warns us that we will experience unpleasantness and urges us not to forget. I think that some of the disillusionment we experience as Christ-followers today is the result of entitlement thinking, and this entitlement thinking results from forgetting that Jesus has warned us that we will face trials, hardship and persecution. We need to warn one another that disillusionment results from not remembering Jesus' warning, and we need to encourage one another that we are entitled to certain spiritual benefits in the face of the persecution that awaits us: Jesus' abiding presence, abundant fruitfulness in ministry and one another's abounding love (Jn 15:1-17). Perhaps, though, we're not willing to remind one another of the persecution to which we're entitled. Perhaps we're not willing because it's so unpleasant to think about approaching persecution. And perhaps it's even more unpleasant than it should be because we've forgotten that we're also entitled to the spiritual benefits bound up with bearing much fruit in relation to Jesus' abiding presence and one another's love. Or just perhaps we are aware of these benefits but they don't appeal to us.

Whereas Jesus' warning and the reminder of spiritual benefits prepare us to endure hardships, entitlement thinking sets us up for disappointment and disillusionment. Entitlement thinking—the sense that "You owe me"—also prepares us for failures in relationships: our relationship with God and our relationships with one another. I am grateful to the Lord that my friend, who was formerly a ministry leader until he fell into sin, is in close relationship with God and his wife today. In part, it's because he doesn't sense that God—or his wife—owes him anything. Sure, he can count on their love, but that is only as a result of God's covenantal communion with him and his wife's commitment to marital union with him.

It's interesting. Both my friend and his wife were guilty of entitlement thinking concerning his ministry position at the time just prior to his affair, and you could also sense it in their relationship with one another. Each of them thought the other owed them a greater benefits package in marriage. Such entitlement thinking goes something like this: "You do this for me and then I'll do this for you." "I'll do this for you to get this from you." "You do your part, and I'll do my part, and as long as we feel good about the arrangements we'll stick together." I don't sense any of that kind of thinking today when I interact with them, just as I don't sense it in their relationships with God.

How many couples getting married today bring with them a sense of entitlement when they make their wedding vows? Are they really taking note of "For better *or worse*, for richer *or poorer*, *in sickness* and in health"? What went through my mind on my wedding day? And what goes through our minds when we pray the sinner's prayer and vow to follow Christ? Is the vow for good times *and* bad—or is it just for better, richer, healthier seasons in life?

Persecution awaits Jesus' servants, just like hard times await newly-weds. Hardships can either break relationships or make them. Entitlement thinking will surely break them. You owe it to yourself not to make the mistake that so many of Jesus' followers make by putting yourself above Jesus and by pulling out when the going gets tough. And it will get tough.

BIRTH PANGS
John 16

Jesus and his disciples are going through extreme grief given the huge social changes that Jesus is enacting, and to which others are reacting, as he brings salvation to the world (Jn 16:1-5, 22).[18] The due date has come for Jesus to deliver his kingdom in its fullness to the world through the cross and resurrection. Joy will follow the cross, but the birth pangs bound up with Jesus' social and interpersonal revolution are excruciatingly painful.

Jesus seeks to comfort his disciples by acknowledging the pain they are experiencing, making them aware of how painful their ordeal will be and offering them hope that great joy will follow their hardship: "A woman giving birth to a child has pain because her time has come; but when her baby is born she forgets the anguish because of her joy that a child is born into the world. So with you: Now is your time of grief, but I will see you again and you will rejoice, and no one will take away your joy" (Jn 16:21-22).

In the next essay, we will discuss how the Spirit is not a Dr. Phil-like counselor. Here we will discuss how Jesus is not your typical physician who delivers babies into the world. John 16's imagery of birth pangs is simply a metaphor to describe the suffering followed by joy that Jesus' disciples will experience as he enacts their salvation. Nonetheless, we find this image, and the surrounding images associated with childbearing and delivery, helpful in unpacking the contents of this chapter.

I've never gone into labor or experienced firsthand the pain of childbirth, though I have been at the bedside of my wife prior to and during the births of our two children. The closest I've come to experiencing the pain of childbirth was spilling that cup of very hot coffee in my lap in the wee hours of the morning while I sat next to my wife's bed as we waited for the arrival of our firstborn. I won't tell you what I shouted when I jumped, but it wasn't a chorus of hallelujahs. Nor was the jump one of joy. The only other instance of something remotely similar would have been my sigmoidoscopy. (Let me encourage you to choose a colonoscopy instead: the anesthesia I was given prior to my colonoscopy was a heavenly hyper-epidural; I don't remember a thing they said or did during the exam.)

I do remember that until the doctor and nurse came and gave my wife her epidural prior to the birth of our firstborn, she was in so much pain. And while the epidural minimized the pain, it could not take away the exhaustion she experienced over the seemingly unending ordeal. Then there was the anxiety that she and I experienced; we were praying in our hearts that our child would be born with no deformities and with no complications. I tried my best to comfort her, but I don't think she could really register what I was saying. I was also having trouble registering. I was supposed to help her with her breathing exercises, which we had practiced over and over, but I was often lost in thought, watching her from her bedside and holding my breath.

Jesus calmly comforts his disciples and counsels them so well that they won't forget what he says or does for them as he performs surgery on a sinful world. One way in which he counsels and comforts them is by acknowledging and identifying their pain. He doesn't ignore it or tell them, "Just deal with it." He doesn't deny pain and suffering, calling it illusory as some cult groups do. In fact, Jesus shares in their grief. As a doctor, he's got a great bedside manner. Such acknowledgment, identification and participation are extremely reassuring. So, too, is Jesus' revelation of what will occur later—in terms of their persecution, his resurrection and return to them and their victory bound up with him. Such predictions reassure them that Jesus is in control and keep them from stumbling (Jn 16:1, 4). Jesus' revelation of the future indicates that he's not taken by surprise. Moreover, the hope that he nurtures based on his resurrection and return indicate that he is in control and that he has a victor rather than victim mentality.

The best doctors are those who tell you what you need to know, who identify with you in your suffering and yet are not overwhelmed by it. That's Jesus. He doesn't hide necessary information from you. In the case of his first followers, he can't share everything with them on this night, given their grief and present inability to bear it; nonetheless, he shares it with them later through the Spirit (Jn 16:12-15). On this night, he shares with them all they need to know. Jesus is a masterful physician. He doesn't say too little or too much, and he doesn't chuckle or laugh hysterically as he discusses your situation (as one doctor once did in my presence—I now refer to that quack as Dr. Killjoy). On the other hand, Jesus doesn't sob and lose it in your presence, looking to you to hold him together.

As a physician, Jesus has got it all together. He doesn't even make you sign forms so you won't sue him for malpractice. He's too busy saving you to worry about his own well-being. How in the world could Jesus hold it together so? Here he is on his way to the cross, and he has the presence of mind to prepare his followers for his departure and their suffering bound up with his kingdom work! You've heard of mothers having to choose between their lives or the lives of their fetuses. But have you ever heard of a doctor sacrificing him or herself so that a mother and her child could live? While it has likely happened at some point, it certainly happens here this night. The Great Physician sacrifices himself on the night of his betrayal so that we can live. Although we will suffer and perhaps even die because of our faith (Jn 16:1-2), we don't die for our sins. Jesus has already been there and done that for us. In fact, we don't even bring our faith to birth. Jesus does that too. In other words, he's no midwife, who helps us get in touch with ourselves so that we can bring to birth our own salvation. He's not a midwife or simply a doctor; he's the Creator and Savior. No wonder he doesn't lose it when everything gives way. And no wonder he has to go it alone, except for the presence of his Father: "But a time is coming, and has come, when you will be scattered, each to his own home. You will leave me all alone. Yet I am not alone, for my Father is with me. I have told you these things, so that in me you may have peace. In this world you will have trouble. But take heart! I have overcome the world" (Jn 16:32-33).[19]

The disciples are suffering, and their suffering will increase; but their suffering will give way to great joy that no one can take away, a joy that will be complete (Jn 16:20, 22, 24). Through Jesus' death and departure, the Spirit will come (Jn 16:5-15), and Jesus will come again (Jn 16:16, 22) and they will have direct access to the Father through Jesus and the Spirit (Jn 16:23-24).

Jesus has done more than take the Hippocratic Oath to do good and not harm. As the Creator of life and Savior of the world, he has made a covenant with us through his own blood to give us the kind of life that never dies—even if we're killed for the faith. No one can take away the life and joy that Jesus gives us, for he has overcome the world (Jn 16:33).

This is no Rasputin-like faith healer who does you in, or Houdini-like magician who performs a disappearing act and leaves you in your hour of greatest need. Jesus is returning to the Father, but only after he raises himself from the dead to bring you eternal life, and only as the Spirit prepares to come to be with us, and only as the way is opened up for us to have access to the Father through Jesus and only as Jesus comes again to be with us now and forevermore. We will go through suffering, perhaps even extreme suffering; but Jesus undergoes it with us and for us. He also opens up the way for us so that the pains of childbirth we endure in and through him now will not end with a miscarriage of justice. Rather, it will open up to new and righteous and abundant life complete with joy, for Jesus has overcome the world.

DR. PHIL
John 16:7-11

I attended a church once that had its very own Dr. Phil-like counselor. The senior pastor would actually refer to him by that name. Sometimes "Dr. Phil" would give the Sunday morning sermon with the senior pastor, seeking to help people get in touch with themselves and, in turn, with God. While I didn't question the genuineness of their motives, I did question their orientation. The fundamental problem was their starting point: helping people get in touch with themselves.

In John's Gospel, the Holy Spirit is called a counselor. But he's no therapist who helps us get in touch with ourselves. As Counselor, he actually turns us away from going into ourselves, turning us outward toward God. Only as we get in touch with God will we be truly right with ourselves—as righteous in relation to God.

The "get in touch with yourself" orientation doesn't help us get beyond ourselves; the self-centered framework was and is the fundamental problem with Jesus' critics. Even well-meaning people like the pastor and Dr. Phil noted above fall prey to these critics' methods. Jesus' critics have never been personally convicted of their own guilt before God and have never gone to counselors who bring these matters to their attention. Jesus' critics have never thought that they are in need of personal conviction. They have always believed that they are righteous through their own religious efforts. They consider themselves off the hook; however, many of Jesus' critics love to put their hooks into people, burdening them with false condemnation and despair.

Jesus' critics reject the Spirit's work. Not only do they reject the Spirit's counsel that moves people beyond self-righteous validation; they also reject the Spirit's counsel that moves people beyond self-condemnation so that they can enter into righteous relationship with God through Jesus. Here's what Jesus says about the Spirit's work:

> It is for your good that I am going away. Unless I go away, the Counselor will not come to you; but if I go, I will send him to you. When he comes, he will convict the world of guilt in regard to sin and righteousness and judgment: in regard to sin, because men do

not believe in me; in regard to righteousness, because I am going to the Father, where you can see me no longer; and in regard to judgment, because the prince of this world now stands condemned. (Jn 16:7-11)

The heavenly Counselor does not condemn us; in other words, he's no Dr. Guilt Trip who seeks to weigh us down in destructive despair with no way out. In keeping with John 16:8, the Spirit uncovers and reveals our guilt *so that* we will repent and be reconciled to God. This Counselor's aim is redemptive. As he speaks truth into our lives, he seeks to set us free. But we can't be free if we don't believe in Jesus. At its heart, distrust of Jesus is sin (Jn 16:9). Such distrust keeps us from relationship with God, for how can we have a relationship with God if we distrust the very one he has sent to save us from ourselves? The Spirit convicts us of our sin of distrust so that we can find true life with God through Jesus rather than try to find life within ourselves.

In our "I'm okay, you're okay" culture, people struggle with talk of personal sin and the need for repentance. And while people may say they like Jesus, they don't like the kind of Jesus who tells them to repent of their sin and rejection of him as the only way to God. According to them, Jesus is one mediator or guru among many who helps us get in touch with ourselves. From this distorted point of view, Jesus is just like all the other shrinks, and the Spirit serves as the associate of each of them in their counseling practices. But that's not so, according to Jesus. The Spirit's sole ambition is to draw attention to Jesus and to reveal to us that Jesus has been raised from the dead and has ascended to his heavenly Father, of whom he is the one and only Son. This kind of thinking has always eaten at people—in Jesus' day and in our own—for it is fallen humanity's fatal passion to be in control, and to choose this or that therapist to lead us where we want to go.

The Spirit also convicts us in terms of our faulty understanding of righteousness (Jn 16:10). While many thought that Jesus died because he was unrighteous, the Spirit reveals that Jesus' resurrection and ascension to the Father make clear that he alone is truly righteous (Jn 16:10). These events of resurrection and ascension led to the condemnation not of us but of the prince of this world—Satan (Jn 16:11). For the prince of this world was responsible for veiling our eyes in unbelief and sin and for our wrongly thinking that Jesus died a sinner.

People usually don't come right out and say that Jesus died a sinner. But when we don't confess our need for him, but instead assert our autonomy from him through our words, thoughts and actions, we make him out to be a liar. We may even admit we're broken, shipwrecked, torn asunder; but if we don't cry out *for him* in our confession of our brokenness, we deny him. While a former generation may have failed to speak of brokenness, our current generation speaks of it all too often *apart from* consideration of the one who was broken for us on the cross. The Spirit as counselor convicts us of our unbelief and autonomy—not to demean us or to push us away, but to draw us close to Jesus in whom we find meaning and purpose and life.

The Spirit is no Dr. Phil, but he's no Dr. Guilt Trip either. As stated earlier, the point of his conviction is never to demean or condemn us, but to raise us up in new life as he forms our souls and minds and lives in Jesus. Different people have given me counsel over the years: most were good counselors, but a few of them weren't so good. The latter would veil their counsel or rebuke in language of concern, but there was no love in their rebuke, only the sense of power-brokering manipulation. But the former counselors could say anything to me, including firm words of rebuke; their ambition was love, and their tone was caring. Whereas the prince of this world seeks to condemn us, the Spirit and his assistants within the church seek to move us beyond self-justification. This is so important because, among other things, such self-justification leads us down the path of self-condemnation in due course.

One of the areas in which the Spirit moves me beyond self-justification and false redemption is when I seek to find my worth in something other than Jesus—such as my career. Around 3 a.m. on the morning that I am writing this, I woke up and was thinking about my career and my future. Anxiety set in as I wondered about how things would play out for me down the road. Would I make it? Would I prove successful and valuable? In the past, I wasn't aware of how damaging to my spirituality and relationships these anxiety attacks could be. It's as if I'm denying Jesus by faith every time I move in this direction, seeking to validate myself and acquire some sort of secular salvation. It's as if I'm thinking that I must ascend to the Father on my own since I can't see Jesus. And it's as if I've been condemned to live in this destructive pattern of infinite regress, in which I fall further into the pit of my own self-concern and frustration with my state every time I try to ascend on my own.

The Spirit reminds me to face Jesus, assures me that I have ascended in Jesus and causes me to sense his heavenly presence even though I can't see him right now. The Spirit comforts me by confirming that I'm not the one condemned. By contrast, he instructs me that the devil, the prince of this world, is the one condemned, for he has mastered the plan of self-sufficiency and blind ambition to his own ultimate destruction.

This morning, the Spirit gently rebuked me and consoled me, prompting me to find my significance in Jesus, in whom I believe and who has saved me from myself. The Spirit reminds me of this truth on a daily basis, exposing the lie that I daily live; fortunately, I am becoming more aware of his presence and listening better to his counsel. The Spirit does not take me deeper into myself but further *out* of myself, where I find Jesus. What separates the Spirit from Dr. Phil is that the Spirit does not take me into myself in search of better forms of self-preservation and false redemption, with a little Jesus sprinkled on top. What separates the Spirit from Dr. Guilt Trip is that he does not burden me with a sense of self-condemnation in which Jesus smashes me to dust. The Spirit stirs my heart to long for Jesus—in whom I believe, in whom I find my eternal destiny and in whom I find redemption from both self-commendation and self-condemnation. The Spirit is relational, moving me beyond *self*-realization on the one hand and *self*-condemnation on the other. In and through the Spirit, I find my identity and significance *in relation to Jesus*, God's Son.

What about you? While you may find practical insights for living with yourself from Dr. Phil, you won't find relational union with Jesus, who is eternal life. And while you may feel like you are dealing with your brokenness by going to Dr. Guilt Trip, you won't be led into a life of repentance that takes you beyond the vicious cycle of self-condemnation to Jesus, who is eternal life. Neither therapist can help you take the steps you need to take to get you to the faraway place you need to go. The Spirit will tell you that. The Spirit will even carry you there. As Counselor, the Spirit will bring the truth of Jesus home to you, and bring you home to him. Maybe it's time you make an appointment with this Counselor; in fact, he'll see you now.

DEATH ROW
John 17

Those on death row are often asked if they have a last wish or closing word before they go to the execution chamber. Some ask for a last meal or one last cigarette. Jesus has already had his Last Supper, and while he often drinks, there's no indication of him ever smoking. So what does he ask for? What is his dying wish?

Some of you may be asking why I speak of death row here. Although Jesus has not yet been betrayed or falsely tried and found guilty, he has been on death row all his life, even before he was born. The Father sent him into the world to face death to free us from our guilt, solitary confinement, imprisonment and sure death at the hands of the executioner. This is what Jesus is getting at when he prays, "Father, the time has come. Glorify your Son, that your Son may glorify you" (Jn 17:1). Jesus' whole life and public ministry have been moving toward this hour of glory—the cross and resurrection. Through the cross and resurrection, Jesus and his Father will be glorified. This hour of glory is what matters most to him and what he calls out to God about in prayer.

Those who are about to die often share what matters most to them in life. A captain in the Marine Corps stationed in Iraq during the Second Persian Gulf War told me that his men's last written words (which he was responsible to convey to their families) were always "Tell _____ I love them." The same goes for those awaiting execution, as their lives pass before their eyes. While some say they're sorry and others offer parting words of wisdom, still many others ask those standing by to convey their love to those who will mourn their passing.

Jesus pours out his heart to his Father as he awaits the end, as he marches on in the face of death. Through prayer, Jesus makes final preparations for himself (Jn 17:1-5) and for his followers then (Jn 17:6-19) and now (Jn 17:20-26). Jesus' prayerful return to the Father through

Golgotha and the hour of glory paves the way for our own return. For Jesus, everything flows out of his union and communion with the Father, including his communion with his followers and his sense of mission. This time of prayer, on the night in which he enters into his passion and suffering unto death, is the ultimate preparation for all that follows and affects his followers and the world in his day and in our own.

Jesus longs to return to his Father and to be united with him in the glorious love they shared before the world began (Jn 17:5). In this prayer of death row confession, we sense such profound intimacy between the Father and Son. While many of us would cry out to anyone else but God in going to our death—except perhaps for some "Hail Mary" desperation plea—Jesus pours his heart out to the Father with such longing, such fixation and such expectation:

> Father, the time has come. Glorify your Son, that your Son may glorify you. For you granted him authority over all people that he might give eternal life to all those you have given him. Now this is eternal life: that they may know you, the only true God, and Jesus Christ, whom you have sent. I have brought you glory on earth by completing the work you gave me to do. And now, Father, glorify me in your presence with the glory I had with you before the world began. (Jn 17:1-5)

For all the travail of body and soul that Jesus is experiencing in this hour, he also moves forward with great anticipation: Jesus is going home to be with his Father. Such hope bound up with this preparatory prayer strengthens him for the battle that lies ahead in his hour of glory—the cross and resurrection.

As profound as Jesus' intimacy with the Father is, there is still much more to this prayer—and it involves us. Not only does Jesus want to return to his Father to be with him; Jesus also wants his followers to be with him, to experience the Father's love for him, and to know the Father's love for them through union with him. For Jesus knows how much the Father loves them—as much as the Father loves him. As the Lord says:

> May they be brought to complete unity to let the world know that you sent me and have loved them even as you have loved me. Fa-

ther, I want those you have given me to be with me where I am, and to see my glory, the glory you have given me because you loved me before the creation of the world. Righteous Father, though the world does not know you, I know you, and they know that you have sent me. I have made you known to them, and will continue to make you known in order that the love you have for me may be in them and that I myself may be in them. (Jn 17:23-26)

We're also on death row, awaiting execution with Jesus at the hands of the world system. We are to die to ourselves, to the world and to the devil, like the medical missionary who was martyred in Yemen by a Muslim man. When asked why he had done it, the man said that his wife had told him of how she had gone to receive treatment from this medical missionary, and that no one had ever loved her like this Christian woman loved her. Greatly troubled, her husband realized that there was not a power in Islam strong enough to stand against the onslaught of this overwhelming love, and so he decided he had to kill the missionary to stop Jesus' love's advance. The missionary's friends later said that although she had died at the hands of this extremist, she had actually died a long time ago—for she had died to herself in order to live in Jesus' love for others.

Most of us will never be crucified, martyred or imprisoned, awaiting execution on death row. But each of us awaits a thousand deaths—at the simplest level, death to another helping of food or another mixed drink; at a more advanced level, death to making eye contact with the girl across the room while your wife is across town; and at the most advanced level, death to boasting about your accumulation of power or riches or fame or wisdom rather than in the weakness and poverty and infamy and foolishness of God's glorious love lavished on us through his cross-bearing Son. It all comes down to what or whom we love more. We die to the food or drink because we love modesty and sobriety over gluttony and drunkenness. We die to the flirtatious eye because we love our spouse and children more than the passing passion of infatuation. And we die to boasting in our possessions, capacities and accomplishments because, like those soldiers in Iraq, we know that what lasts are those loved ones we leave behind and the living God to whom we must go. The stuff we put stock in, but which never had breath in the first place, rot and decay and die with us in the end anyway.

All these daily deaths bear witness to the one true, noble, life-giving death for all of human history: Jesus' death on the cross. Jesus' death is priceless and pays for all our sins. And for him, union and communion with his Father and with us for all eternity is surely worth it. And so, he sanctifies himself for his first followers and us (Jn 17:19-20), preparing himself for death so that we might be made holy (Jn 17:19), wholly prepared for the day when we will enter into his glory. What would you be willing to die for? Jesus dies for love—love of the Father and us. For him, the cross—as painful and lonesome and shameful as it is—does not compare with the glory that is to be revealed through it. What awaits Jesus and his people beyond the cross is union and communion for all eternity.

Jesus' hope is not yet fulfilled. He's waiting for us to join him, those of us still on death row. Jesus is lonely as he pours out his heart to the Father there in the garden, awaiting his betrayer and the executioner. Yet his heart is filled with hope as he prays in view of his last and greatest wish that we will be with him in glory. What is our last wish? A meal, a cigarette? What would you wish to convey to those closest to you before you depart? What will you pray for, as heaven opens up before you?

Sometimes pain has a way of focusing our thoughts and helping us see more clearly. What goes through the minds of those falsely accused and sentenced as they make their way to Golgotha, the gallows, the guillotine or the electric chair at the green mile's end?

Jesus of Nazareth, Dietrich Bonhoeffer, Sydney Carton and John Coffey: four names. Four different stories, yet so much alike. These stories are bound together through the story of the crucified though glorious Nazarene.

Bonhoeffer dies a traitor's death for siding with victimized Jews; he had taken part in the failed assassination plots to take the life of Germany's true traitor—Hitler. In Charles Dickens's *A Tale of Two Cities* Carton also dies a traitor's death, taking the place of the husband of the woman he adores, who was wrongly sentenced to death for supposedly betraying the people at the time of the French Revolution. And then,

John Coffey, Stephen King's Christ figure in *The Green Mile*, dies a rapist's and murderer's death, wrongly accused of violently raping and killing two girls. As Coffey is led away to the electric chair, he tells the guard (who knows he is innocent) that he looks forward to playing with those same two girls who wait for him in paradise, a place where there is no pain or sorrow or death—just love and joy and abundant life. As Carton is led away to the guillotine, he comforts a young innocent girl, also condemned and about to die, with soothing words and a parting kiss upon her lips before she goes to the guillotine. Carton is next. Before he goes to the guillotine, he repeats the Lord's words recorded in John's Gospel: "I am the Resurrection and the Life, saith the Lord: he that believeth in me, though he were dead, yet shall he live: and whosoever liveth and believeth in me shall never die."[20] Bonhoeffer's closing words to his fellow prisoners at the camp as the Nazis come to take him away to the gallows (and just days before the Allies liberate those imprisoned there) are, "This is the end. . . . For me the beginning of life."[21]

Jesus makes his wish for a new beginning to life, looking forward as he walks his own green mile to Golgotha, as he awaits the betrayer's kiss and the piercing of the soldier's spear, as he goes to hang alone, abandoned. But he does not die alone. In fact, he does not *really* die. None of them really do, for their wish, their prayer and their God sustains them, resurrecting them from the dead through Jesus' own death and resurrection. Their wish is reality. They will be there with them. We who hope to share in his glory will be there with him forever before the Father.

So as you bide your time today on death row, what do you hope to die for so that you can truly live anew? My wish is more than a wish. It is a prayer of hope: to share in Jesus' glory in the loving communion of his intimate union with the Father. Jesus envisions this hoped-for reality in his prayer to the Father : "I have given them the glory that you gave me, that they may be one as we are one" (Jn 17:22). This prayer is not wishful thinking. It envisions ultimate reality, which Jesus has made known to his followers and will continue to make known to them and to the world (Jn 17:23-26). This hope can be your reality too, through faith in Jesus. Jesus' sure hope is that, through faith in him, his followers will experience the same glorious love that he has in his Father's presence for all eternity:

I in them and you in me. May they be brought to complete unity to let the world know that you sent me and have loved them even as you have loved me. Father, I want those you have given me to be with me where I am, and to see my glory, the glory you have given me because you loved me before the creation of the world. Righteous Father, though the world does not know you, I know you, and they know that you have sent me. I have made you known to them, and will continue to make you known in order that the love you have for me may be in them and that I myself may be in them. (Jn 17:23-26)

Instead of filling their heads with wishful thinking, Jesus makes God's love for him and them known over and over again, thereby realizing the triune God's presence in their lives. This hope is sure knowledge. This hope is worth dying for, worth going through the valley of the shadow of death and loneliness for, worth risking all for. This hope is the beatific vision of interpersonal union and communion in and through the glorious and loving presence of Jesus and his Father forever. May this loving hope be your life-giving prayer of faith as you await your end on death row.[22]

TRANSITION
Fifteen Minutes of Fame and the Hour of Glory

IN 1968, ANDY WARHOL PROCLAIMED: "In the future, everyone will be world-famous for fifteen minutes."[1] All you need to do is look at YouTube ("broadcast yourself") to see that Warhol's prediction has been fulfilled. Warhol's prediction was recently adapted to read: "In the future (on the web), everyone will be famous to fifteen people."[2] Warhol was trying to get at the idea that celebrity status is fleeting and based on the whims of the fickle media. Warhol's "superstar" cast, which followed him everywhere he went, was a bunch of nobodies with whom he chose to associate so as to make them famous just to prove his point.

Just like YouTube, reality TV makes fame appear so reachable, attainable. I once asked my hair stylist in the French salon I patronize (Supercuts) about reality TV and why it is so popular. She said that one reason is that it is so comforting—that is, some people are more messed up than her! Reality TV is also so alluring and hopeful—alluring because it is so real and reachable, and hopeful because fame is not the sole commodity of kings, queens and the Kennedys.

We all long for fifteen minutes of fame. Why is that? Our hearts long for glory, for we were wired to experience glory. But we settle for so little—fleeting fame, even when God calls us to so much more. The problem is not *that* we seek after glory—but *where* we seek it. Thus, the famous J. D. Salinger is right and wrong at the same time when he writes (through one of his characters, Franny Glass): "Just because I'm so horribly conditioned to accept everybody else's values, and just because I like applause and people to rave about me, doesn't make it right. I'm ashamed of it. I'm sick of it. I'm sick of not having the courage to be an absolute nobody. I'm sick of myself and everybody else that wants to make some kind of a splash."[3] With Salinger, I would argue that we should not seek after the fame and success and the praise or glory of people. In contrast to Salinger, I believe we should seek after the praise or glory of God. God did not create us to be nobodies, but to be some-bodies in communion with him through participation in Jesus' glorious story. God calls us to perform on the ultimate reality show—to partici-pate in Jesus' hour of glory—even more real, more comforting, more hopeful and appealing and honoring than performing for fifteen minutes of fame.

Before we go further, let me offer a word to the wise. Biblical glory looks very different from what pop culture often imagines fame and glory to be. Whenever I need biblical insight, I ask my eleven-year-old theologian son, Christopher, for help. When I asked him about the rela-tion of fame to glory, he said that fame relates to people and glory relates to God. God alone deserves glory. Kings and queens and presidents don't deserve glory. Glory belongs only to God. Not bad. Not bad at all. We'll return to my son's claim later.

Another thing to note about human fame is that it elevates the funni-est (*Blades of Glory*'s Will Ferrell), the most talented, the most beautiful, the best (*American Idol*), and those who rise up off the backs of others (the Nietzschean "superhuman" inside and outside the church). In con-trast, the apostle Paul says that God elevates the weak, the foolish and those who break their own backs for the sake of others (1 Cor 1). It's as if Paul took a page right out of John's Gospel. John's whole account can be read as Jesus' preparation for and achievement of God's hour of glory. Jesus is in pursuit of God's glory rather than human glory (or fame), and according to God's timetable, not ours. In what follows, we'll look at scenes from John's drama, where he develops this theme. Now it's time for the show.

In John 2, Jesus tells his mother that his hour has not yet come, after she lets him know that they have run out of wine at the wedding (hinting that she would like for him to come to their aid): "'Dear woman, why do you involve me?' Jesus replied, 'My time [hour] has not yet come'" (Jn 2:4).

In John 5, the religious rulers persecute Jesus for healing a lame man on the Sabbath. Jesus claims that their unbelief is the result of their pur-suit of human glory rather than God's:

> I do not accept praise [glory] from men, but I know you. I know that you do not have the love of God in your hearts. I have come in my

Father's name, and you do not accept me; but if someone else comes in his own name, you will accept him. How can you believe if you accept praise [glory] from one another, yet make no effort to obtain the praise [glory] that comes from the only God? (Jn 5:41-44)

In John 7, Jesus avoids Judea because of the rulers' desire to kill him. Jesus' brothers mockingly urge him to make a public appearance in Jerusalem during the Feast of Tabernacles because of his messianic claims. Jesus responds by saying that his hour to be glorified has not yet come:

Therefore Jesus told them, "The right time for me has not yet come; for you any time is right. The world cannot hate you, but it hates me because I testify that what it does is evil. You go to the Feast. I am not yet going up to this Feast, because for me the right time [hour] has not yet come." (Jn 7:6-8)

Later in John 7, Jesus does go to Jerusalem and makes a public appearance. As a result of his message, the rulers try to seize him, but to no avail—his hour has not yet come: "At this they tried to seize him, but no one laid a hand on him, because his time [hour] had not yet come" (Jn 7:30).

In John 8, Jesus says that he seeks after his Father's glory (not his own), and his Father's glorification of him:

Jesus replied, "If I glorify myself, my glory means nothing. My Father, whom you claim as your God, is the one who glorifies me. Though you do not know him, I know him. If I said I did not, I would be a liar like you, but I do know him and keep his word. Your father Abraham rejoiced at the thought of seeing my day; he saw it and was glad." (Jn 8:54-56)

In John 12, we find that Jesus' hour to be glorified has finally come:

Jesus replied, "The hour has come for the Son of Man to be glorified. I tell you the truth, unless a kernel of wheat falls to the ground and dies, it remains only a single seed. But if it dies, it produces many seeds. The man who loves his life will lose it, while the man who hates his life in this world will keep it for eternal life. Whoever serves me must follow me; and where I am, my servant also will be. My Father will honor the one who serves me. Now my heart is troubled, and what shall I say? 'Father, save me from this hour'? No, it was for this very reason I came to this hour. Father, glorify your name!" Then a voice came from heaven, "I have glorified it, and will glorify it again." The crowd that was there and heard it said it had thundered; others said an angel had spoken to him. Jesus said, "This voice was for your benefit, not mine. Now is the time for judgment on this world; now the prince of this world will be driven out. But I, when I am lifted up from the earth, will draw all men to myself." He said this to show the kind of death he was going to die. (Jn 12:23-33)

In John 13, we find Jesus at the Last Supper with his disciples. Again, John tells us that Jesus' hour to be glorified has come: "It was just before the Passover Feast. Jesus knew that the time [hour] had come for him to leave this world and go to the Father. Having loved his own who were in the world, he now showed them the full extent of his love" (Jn 13:1). And how does Jesus reveal his glory in this hour?

The evening meal was being served, and the devil had already prompted Judas Iscariot, son of Simon, to betray Jesus. Jesus knew that the Father had put all things under his power, and that he had come from God and was returning to God; so he got up from the meal, took off his outer clothing, and wrapped a towel around his waist. After that, he poured water into a basin and began to wash his disciples' feet, drying them with the towel that was wrapped around him. (Jn 13:2-5)

In John 17, we come to Jesus' prayer just prior to his betrayal. Notice his focused attention on the hour of glory that has come:

After Jesus said this, he looked toward heaven and prayed: "Father, the time [hour] has come. Glorify your Son, that your Son may glorify you. For you granted him authority over all people that he might give eternal life to all those you have given him. Now this is eternal life: that they may know you, the only true God, and Jesus

Christ, whom you have sent. I have brought you glory on earth by completing the work you gave me to do. And now, Father, glorify me in your presence with the glory I had with you before the world began." (Jn 17:1-5)

Later in the same chapter Jesus prays:

I have given them the glory that you gave me, that they may be one as we are one: I in them and you in me. May they be brought to complete unity to let the world know that you sent me and have loved them even as you have loved me. Father, I want those you have given me to be with me where I am, and to see my glory, the glory you have given me because you loved me before the creation of the world. Righteous Father, though the world does not know you, I know you, and they know that you have sent me. I have made you known to them, and will continue to make you known in order that the love you have for me may be in them and that I myself may be in them. (Jn 17:22-26)

In the first part of the chapter, Jesus focuses on the glory he shares with the Father. After that, he focuses on our participation in this same glory.

We see from these passages that *God's glory is the splendor of his sacrificial and spreading sacred communion*. This glory is bound up with the triune God's sacrificial life of love, by which the Father gives up his Son and the Son gives up himself in the Spirit for the salvation of all. We experience this salvation by faith through the death and resurrected return of God's Son in the Spirit.[4] Any "glory" that does not resonate with and revolve around this glory is *not* truly glorious or sacred. Some views of glory leave God's glory out of the picture (i.e., only humans are glorious), or Christ's sufferings out of the picture (i.e., God does not suffer humiliation in his glory) or us out of the picture (i.e., we do not share in Christ's glory).

Karl Barth's view of glory includes all three facets—God is glorified; God's glory includes Christ's sufferings; and God reconciles us to himself through his work of humble glory, where Christ's suffering spells our exaltation. The following statement reflects the first two facets of God's glory revealed in Christ at the very least:

God shows Himself to be the great and true God in the fact that He
can and will let His grace bear this cost, that He is capable and
willing and ready for this condescension, this act of extravagance,
this far journey. What marks out God above all false gods is that
they are not capable and ready for this. In their otherworldliness
and supernaturalness and otherness, etc., the gods are a reflection
of the human pride which will not unbend, which will not stoop to
that which is beneath it. God is not proud. In His high majesty He
is humble. It is in this high humility that He speaks and acts as the
God who reconciles the world to Himself.[5]

It's not only extraordinary theologians who get at this act of extravagance. Ordinary people living extraordinary lives get at it as well, living
out the far journey close to home: sick kids caring for others, single moms
working for their kids rather than partying to get their kicks, stay-at-
home dads staying home for their kids and corporate people choosing
corporate solidarity with the people rather than the corporate climb.
They do this because they see themselves as participants in God's far
journey through his Son.

My niece Hannah experienced this far journey. Hannah had a way
about her. She drew people to herself. I think it was her electric and em-
pathetic personality. She was so funny and so full of joy, even as she felt
so much pain—her own and that of others. Hannah died of leukemia a
few years ago, after battling it for three rounds over a twelve-year span.
Her funeral service in her home town in Connecticut was something like
Princess Diana's. People were waiting in line up and down the street in
hopes of getting inside the church building for the service. The reception
line to express sympathy to the family was long too, and it was such a
long time before we all left the church building that afternoon. That line
was filled with people whose hearts Hannah had touched, caught and
embraced. She caught and embraced my heart too.

One memory stands out most vividly. The day after Hannah's older
sister's wedding a year earlier, my little girl, Julianne, came down with a
horrible eye infection. The whole family was at a post-wedding party
when my wife and I decided that we had better take Julianne to the emergency room at the local hospital. We were strangers in this country town

on the opposite end of the nation from our home. The town was filled with winding forest roads, and so someone needed to lead us to the hospital a few miles away. Who volunteered to lead us? Hannah. Why Hannah? She had missed so many parties as a child due to spending seasons in hospital beds. Certainly she deserved a break. Certainly she should have been out partying with her friends on this beautiful summer day. Certainly someone else should have led us there. No, it was Hannah. She led the way to the hospital and stayed with us there, while Julianne cried and we worried over what was wrong with her eye. It was a good thing we went to the emergency room when we did; one of the doctors told us that the instantaneous infection was so bad that Julianne might have lost her eye if we had waited even a day. It was a good thing we started medication that very day, and it was a very good thing that Hannah went with us and comforted us while we waited.

I wish I could have been there at the hospital a week later to comfort Hannah when a specialist told her that the cancer had returned to her body. We had already flown home to the other end of the country. And I can no longer fly back to be with Hannah, though I will someday. Hannah is no longer here to comfort us, even though the memories of her presence still do. Hannah knew how to comfort people, in part because she knew such pain. Her electric personality filled up dark emergency rooms with light. She has now entered into her glory—the glory of the Son whom she grew up learning about in Sunday school classes, whose own glory involves suffering for the world.

Hannah never appeared on *American Idol* (though she fervently enjoyed watching it up to the end of her life). And I wouldn't call her funeral service her equivalent of fifteen minutes of fame. Fame is fickle, fleeting and gone. It's often bound up with bright lights and big splash. Fame is easily forgotten because it doesn't capture hearts with love—just TV viewers and egos. Hannah captured many hearts while she lived, and she lives on in our hearts this day.

I've often had difficulty sitting in dark rooms alongside those who are suffering and listening to normal people sharing mundane stories. I like the big lights. I love action. I want my fifteen minutes of fame. I want it all, and I want it now. American idols or not, that's the American way.

But God's way is very different. That's why you'll find Jesus again and again walking down hospital corridors and kneeling in upper rooms, washing feet and wiping runny noses.

Hannah belongs to Jesus' "superstar" cast. That cast looks very different from Warhol's, though. While Jesus' superstars may be nobodies, they're not seeking after celebrity status with Jesus; they're experiencing Jesus' hour of glory with him. And unlike Warhol, Jesus doesn't choose these superstars simply to make a point; he chooses them because he loves them, having died for them to raise them up with him to be with him forever. Hannah is with him now.

I miss Hannah. I also long to live as well as she lived and to play my part as well as she played hers. Each of us is wired to participate in Jesus' hour of glory, not Warhol's fifteen minutes of fame. But only a few of us ever taste this glory. We settle for so little, when God calls us to participate in something so much more profound.

Next time you're watching *American Idol*, enjoy it for all it's worth. Just know that there's more to life than performing on reality TV. Reality TV actually points beyond itself, whether its producers intend it to or not. The divine producer programs every episode of life and calls all of us to perform on the ultimate reality show—the hour of glory. This hour is even more real, more comforting, more hopeful and more appealing than fifteen minutes of fame.

"All the world's a stage," Shakespeare once wrote.[6] But it's a stage for performing God's "hour of glory" production. God is searching for his supporting cast. Whether we know it or not, we've been auditioning for the show. And now the hour has come for each of us to shine, as Jesus enters his glory through the cross and resurrection and beckons us to participate in the divine drama of the triune God. So quickly: put on your makeup and rehearse your lines one last time. The curtain rises: "Lights . . . Camera . . . Action!" The grand adventure. The far journey. This supreme act of extravagance. Encore!

HUMILIATION/ GLORIFICATION

John 18:1–20:23

We now come to the hour of glory, as Jesus goes to the cross and through death to the resurrection. John 18:1–20:23 presents Jesus' passion, death and resurrection, which together with his ascension constitute the hour of glory. As stated in the introduction, rather than labeling the sequence of events as "Humiliation *and* Glorification," I am categorizing this material as "Humiliation/Glorification." The reason is that Jesus' humiliation is part of his glory. John would have us perceive glory as a dialectical and multifaceted reality. He portrays Jesus' death as glorious and divinely purposed, and reveals his death and resurrection as one diverse reality.

The foot-washing scene in John 13 foreshadows this supreme act of humility and glory (Jn 13:1-17). Upon the conclusion of Jesus' farewell discourse and high priestly prayer in the garden (Jn 14–17), the events of his passion begin. The passion begins with Jesus' unjust arrest in which Judas betrays him (Jn 18:1-11) and then continues with his trials before the Jewish leaders and Pilate (Jn 18:19–19:16), including the Roman soldiers' cruel treatment of him (Jn 19:1-3). To add further insult to injury, during the trial before the Jewish rulers, Peter denies Jesus (Jn 18:12-26). The passion climaxes in Jesus' crucifixion, death and burial (Jn 19:16-42). It culminates in his resurrection, followed by post-resurrection appearances to Mary Magdalene and his disciples (Jn 20:1-23). As we noted in the previous essay, the hour of glory theme runs throughout the whole Gospel. The idea that Jesus' hour had not yet come appears in one form or another at various points throughout the narrative. This indicates to the reader then and now that God does not play by our rules, that Jesus does not seek to be the kind of messianic king that the world wants, that he turns the tables on our false ambitions for him and that glory providentially comes to him and his Father—and to us, as John 17 indicates—through Jesus' suffering on the cross.

It is not wrong to seek glory. God has wired us for glory. It is just a matter of where we seek it—on our own, apart from Jesus and the cross, or in and through him and for him. Do we seek to be included in Jesus' hour of glory? If so, it will mean taking up our own crosses. But carrying crosses is not simply about denial, and it should never lead to a sense of morbidity. We must understand that we go through Jesus' cross to attain the resurrection. And so Jesus' cross is ultimately about affirmation: it involves dying to ourselves that we might truly live in and through him and his ultimate hour of glory.

Jesus' hour of glory is the only true hour of glory. All other hours of glory are false and fading. This hour remains forever. And so a lot is at stake here. It's show time. Are we ready? Do we have our game face on, like Peter? Will we succeed, or falter and fall like Peter does? Will we deny Jesus, or possibly even betray him? Or will we respond favorably to him?

I am sorry to be the bearer of bad news, but apart from Jesus, we can't even respond favorably to him. The good news, however, is that even in those moments when we are unfaithful and in those seasons when we are inconsistent, Jesus will remain faithful. The real difference between Peter and Judas is that Judas goes to the wrong priest after it is all said and done. He should have thrown himself on the mercies of God, just like Peter. Peter comes to realize by the end of John's Gospel that no matter how much spiritual bravado and idealism one has, one can never have enough of it. We just cannot perform well on the grand stage of God's drama. We choke. Jesus alone is ready for this hour, and he alone is able to save the day. He is ready to save us.

In the end, after bidding farewell to his followers, Jesus goes it alone. He has to go it alone. We are not able. We are not willing. Only Jesus can handle the pressure. Only Jesus can take away our sins. All we can do is throw ourselves on his mercy. Only then will we find shelter from the storm and enter into his glory through the cross and resurrection.

GIMME SHELTER
John 18:1-27

If you or I were Jesus, we would likely be looking for shelter from the storm rather than entering into it. Fortunately and providentially for us, Jesus isn't us. Jesus doesn't hide from Judas and the weapon-wielding mob he leads. Judas knows the place where Jesus is going. In fact, I believe Jesus wants Judas to find him. So as soon as Jesus is finished praying to the Father, he goes to a place that is familiar to Judas: an olive grove. Jesus had gone to this olive grove many times before with Judas and the rest of the apostles (Jn 18:1-3). When Judas and his mob come to arrest Jesus, Jesus goes out to meet them (Jn 18:4). (John tells us that Jesus knows everything that is going to happen to him. It is important that the reader knows that Jesus is not taken by surprise—he is in total control.) Jesus asks them the leading question rather than engage in delay tactics: "Who is it you want?" (Jn 18:4). When they speak, Jesus does not deny who he is but tells them plainly that he is the one they seek (Jn 18:5-6). And when he speaks, saying "I AM he," they fall over (Jn 18:6; capitalization added). As the great I AM, Jesus is not the one who should be seeking shelter from the approaching storm (and so he doesn't). *They* should be.

We find here that Jesus is in total control of the situation. He's the one who initiates the encounter and gives himself up to his enemies. He also tells them to let his followers go (Jn 18:8). Jesus dictates the terms and conditions for his arrest. If they don't abide by his terms, he will not give himself over to them.

I am sure Jesus must be frustrated with Judas and his mob. They are taking up too much time, falling over and freezing up in the presence of

Jesus and completely in a stupor. They are keeping him from drinking the cup of God's wrath and entering fully into his hour of glory through the cross (Jn 18:11). So Jesus has to ask them again, "Who is it you want?" (Jn 18:7) When they tell him once again that they seek Jesus of Nazareth, Jesus again tells them that he is the one they seek. And then he adds, "'I told you that I am he,' Jesus answered. 'If you are looking for me, then let these men go'" (Jn 18:8). I am sure it is only later that John and the other disciples realize that this occurs so that Jesus can fulfill his words and his mission: "This happened so that the words he had spoken would be fulfilled: 'I have not lost one of those you gave me'" (Jn 18:9; 6:39). As the author of the script and divine agent of the drama, Jesus is in total control.

Not only is Jesus frustrated with Judas and his mob; Jesus is frustrated with Peter. Peter is also slowing up the proceedings by drawing a sword and wildly swinging and cutting off the high priest's servant's ear (Jn 18:10). Elsewhere in the Gospels, we are told that Jesus heals the servant's ear before departing with Judas and his weapon-wielding mob (Lk 22:51), which bind the weaponless Jesus and bear him away to his trial before Annas and Caiaphas the high priest (Jn 18:12-14, 24). Here Jesus commands Peter, "Put your sword away! Shall I not drink the cup the Father has given me?" (Jn 18:11) Jesus is driven by his passion to drink from the cup of God's wrath and enter into his glory, and so he enters the raging storm.

Certainly, Jesus' followers go in search of shelter as soon as Jesus is taken into custody. Their utopian age has come to an end, and they are completely lost. If we were to put the discussion in more modern terms, we might say that their Woodstock festival flower children dreams have given way to the nightmare of Altamont.

People often contrast the Woodstock and Altamont rock-and-roll festivals. While the 1969 festivals were only four months apart, you may think they were light years away. For many, Woodstock symbolizes the rise and rule of the hippie generation, while Altamont symbolizes its sudden demise. There was a lot of love going around at Woodstock, whereas at Altamont things spiraled out of control into violent chaos.

It's interesting to compare Joni Mitchell's "Woodstock" played by

Crosby, Stills, Nash & Young with the Rolling Stones' "Gimme Shelter." "Gimme Shelter" was the opening track of the Stones' 1969 album, *Let It Bleed* (actually spelled "Gimmie Shelter" on the album), and also the title of the 1970 documentary of the Stones' 1969 tour that ended at Altamont. "Woodstock" conveys the sense of hope and progress on issues of war and peace, while "Gimme Shelter" conveys the haunting and ominous sense that murder, rape and destruction are but "a shot away."

Even though the Rolling Stones' song ends with words of hope that love is only a kiss away, I don't find that the tune matches those particular words. The melody conveys such a foreboding and ill-omened quality throughout, as if the Stones sensed that unforeseen events would betray the hippie movement; after all, the era in which the hippie movement emerged was so violent, as Mick Jagger pointed out in a 1995 interview with *Rolling Stone* magazine. Just think of the Vietnam War and the assassinations of John F. Kennedy, Bobby Kennedy and Martin Luther King Jr. Jagger himself noted in the interview that the song and the album as a whole are very apocalyptic.[1] I would add that all along the road, as with any movement going somewhere, denial and betrayal and apocalypse are but a kiss away.

What does all of this have to do with John's Gospel? Normally one doesn't associate Jesus with Jagger, especially given Jagger's "sympathy for the devil." Here's the connection: things were going so well for Jesus and his band and their groupies on their concert tour only a few months earlier, but as they stay in Jerusalem awaiting the approaching Passover celebration, they can sense that something is very wrong. And yet Jesus' band has no idea that betrayal and denial and death are but a Judas kiss and cock-crowing away.

Peter is no longer strutting around like Mick Jagger after Judas's kiss in the garden (nor is Jagger strutting about like Jagger as things begin to get ugly at Altamont). Peter is on the run. All his hippie hope is taken from him, as he watches all his flower-children dreams fade away. Peter is desperately looking for shelter after denying Jesus a third time, as the rooster crows like a Keith Richards guitar riff. "'You are not one of his disciples, are you?' the girl at the door asked Peter. He replied, 'I am not.' . . . As Simon Peter stood warming himself, he was asked, 'You are not one of his disciples, are you?' He denied it, saying, 'I am not.' One of the high priest's servants, a relative of the man whose ear Peter had cut off, challenged him, 'Didn't I see you with him in the olive grove?' Again Peter denied it, and at that moment a rooster began to crow" (Jn 18:17, 25-27).

The record keeps playing in Peter's head long after the music stops: "You are." "I am not." "You are." "I am not." "You are." "I am not. I am not. I am not. . . . Who am I then?"

By denying Jesus, Peter is denying the DNA of his own being. Peter has nowhere to go. Though he will go into hiding (Jn 20:19) and though he will go back to fishing (Jn 21:1-3), he won't get any shelter. Disillusionment with the movement and disillusionment with himself has set in. On account of his disillusionment, he is in danger of becoming one of those hippies who—though he speaks out against capitalism and corporate America during the sit-ins on the mount and on the plain—ends up making it big as a bourgeois capitalist ten years later. Who knows? "Like a rolling stone" with no sense of direction (rather than as the rock on which the church is built!), Peter is in danger of ending up in a Victoria's Secret television commercial, just like Bob Dylan. Cock-a-doodle-do?

Denial of one's own DNA, disillusionment, no sense of direction, with no way home. No more Woodstock. Only Altamont. It doesn't get any worse than this. When this storm hits, there's no shelter to be found—no matter how big and cozy your mansion on the hill. You can't get any shelter when you're hiding from yourself. For you will always end up face to face with you, looking at yourself in the mirror, gazing into your own soul.

I'm a lot like Peter: high on idealism and momentum bound up with the Jesus movement, but low on tolerance for hardship and disillusionment when things don't go as planned. So are a lot of other young-at-heart Christ-followers. So what happens when things don't go as planned, when the movement loses steam and when things spiral out of control? Do we give up, or at the very least sit back and coast without passion on the road to nominal Christianity? A lot of old-of-heart Christ-followers (an oxymoron, if there ever were one) will say, "I used to have your passion, your idealism. This is just a phase in your life. In time, it too shall pass." It's as if they're saying, "I am not. I am not. I am not." They say this type of thing now because they got disillusioned along the way, as the journey became increasingly difficult. A person who loses his or her passion and idealism will become old and cold. There's no way we can finish strong when we lose heart. No matter how difficult the journey gets, I sure hope you and I don't fall off the path and lose our youthful passion and idealism, like those who are disillusioned.

That isn't the only type of person we encounter who may lead us to stumble and fall, never to get up again. When I was young, older young-of-heart Christ-followers would strike fear into me by warning me against not finishing the race. "Don't be an also-ran" (someone who starts the race well, but who doesn't finish). Such warnings, such set-me-up-for-failure-and-guilt trips, always caused me to stumble and kept me from focusing on the finish line and the hope of making it home. No matter how hard I tried to take heed to their warnings, every once in a while I would stumble and fall in the middle of nowhere and in a storm; there was no place within my soul to find shelter from the pouring rain of disillusionment with myself. I thought to myself during those times: "Should I even bother getting up? Should I just lay here and die, soaked to the bone, forever eulogized on the road from Woodstock to Altamont as someone who gave up the hippie ghost?"

The same kind of question continues to plague me whenever I stumble and fall: "Why bother getting up?" But there are other questions, far more constructive questions, that also require answers: "How does one run the race well? Where does my hope lie in the midst of disillusionment with myself for falling off the path? Where will I find shelter from the storm that rages within me whenever I stumble and fall?"

The secret to running the race well is not with Victoria. My reason for getting up and my hope for staying up are not with Dylan or Jagger or Peter or the priests or Pilate or myself. My shelter is not in some movement, no matter how great the manifesto. Placing my hope in any such individual or institution or ideology will only lead to disaster in the end. But left to myself, I would align myself with them.

Left to ourselves, we would have too much "sympathy for the devil" as he dances about on the cosmic stage the night of Jesus' betrayal and ensuing passion. Like the panicking apostles, we would consciously or semiconsciously seek to save ourselves rather than cast our lots with Jesus. Like the priests and Pilate, we would maneuver to protect our positions of power and privilege and comfort. Like them, we would throw in our lots with the devil rather than associate ourselves with the scapegoat Jesus. Providentially rather than fortunately or luckily, Jesus does not leave us to ourselves.

The reason for getting up again, the secret and the hope for staying up and the true shelter from the storm is standing in the high priest's courtyard—even now. Retrace the steps of that night or nights when you, Peter and I try to keep our faith a secret, when our hope is gone and when we cannot find shelter from our frozen souls while warming ourselves by the fire. As we stand there denying Jesus, Jesus stands there affirming us, even as he does not deny himself or his DNA.

Our reason for getting up again, our secret and our hope for staying up and our shelter stands between our first and second and third denials. After recounting the first denial, John writes:

> Meanwhile, the high priest questioned Jesus about his disciples and his teaching. "I have spoken openly to the world," Jesus replied. "I always taught in synagogues or at the temple, where all the Jews come together. I said nothing in secret. Why question me? Ask those who heard me. Surely they know what I said." When Jesus said this, one of the officials nearby struck him in the face. "Is this the way you answer the high priest?" he demanded. "If I said something wrong," Jesus replied, "testify as to what is wrong. But if I spoke the truth, why did you strike me?" Then Annas sent him, still bound, to Caiaphas the high priest. (Jn 18:19-24)

In contrast to Peter and us, Jesus speaks openly in public, not secretly behind closed doors. Unlike Peter and us, Jesus remains faithful to us and to himself and to his spiritual DNA—even when we are faithless, even as we weep bitter tears bound up with our betrayal of him, even when we are unjust.

After the third denial, Luke tells us that Jesus turns and looks straight into Peter's eyes, as the rooster crows: "Peter replied, 'Man, I don't know what you're talking about!' Just as he was speaking, the rooster crowed. The Lord turned and looked straight at Peter. Then Peter remembered the word the Lord had spoken to him: 'Before the rooster crows today, you will disown me three times.' And he went outside and wept bitterly" (Lk 22:60-62). Jesus' look is not one that kills Peter's soul, but one that ultimately tears through Peter's fleshly confidence in himself in order to heal and secure him in relation to Jesus. Jesus' look pierces Peter's soul and rips from him confidence in his boastful claims and flesh. Later, after Jesus rises from the dead, Peter will throw himself on Jesus' faithfulness to him in spite of his own unfaithfulness. Until then, Peter is left to cry bitter tears in secrecy, without shelter and without hope.

As pious as it may sound, it's only after we're stripped of our piety, only after we're robbed of our spiritual bravado and religious pat answers, only after we weep bitter tears of desperation and only as we come to throw ourselves on Jesus that we find shelter from the storm. Our religious and rock-and-roll icons will surely fail us, and so will we. No manifesto can sustain us, not even a Christian creed. Beyond Peter's nauseating boasts, beyond the late-night trial and the fire in the high priest's courtyard, beyond the nostalgia surrounding Woodstock and the nightmare of Altamont, you will find that Jesus alone is faithful. You will find that he's just a prayer, just a brokenhearted kiss away.

THE INCONVENIENT TRUTH
John 18–19

The trial moves from proceedings before Annas and the high priest Caiaphas to the palace of the Roman governor Pilate. As in the case of the Jewish authorities, the Truth is staring Pontius Pilate in the face, but like Annas and Caiaphas, Pilate can't see him—the eternal Word made flesh (Jn 1:1, 14), the way, the truth and the life (Jn 14:6-7). Or perhaps Pilate doesn't want to see him. "What is truth?" Pilate says to Jesus (Jn 18:38). Then Pilate turns and walks away. But no matter how far he walks away, Pilate can't escape Jesus—the eternal Truth. He'll be staring Pilate in the face long after this trial is over. And while Pilate thinks Jesus is on trial, actually it is the other way round. The world system and its prince now stand condemned (Jn 16:11).

I am assuming Pilate has read Plato's philosophy in which Plato talks of the eternal Word. Actually, Pilate sounds like one of Socrates' dialogue partners who discount absolute truth. With this in mind, I wonder if the skeptically minded Pilate has ever watched *Hero*, starring Dustin Hoffman and Andy Garcia. It sure sounds like it. In the movie, the character Bernie LaPlante played by Hoffman says,

> You remember when I said how I was gonna explain about life, buddy? Well the thing about life is, it gets weird. People are always talking ya about truth. Everybody always knows what the truth is, like it was toilet paper or somethin', and they got a supply in the closet. But what you learn, as you get older, is there ain't no truth. All there is is bull—, pardon my vulgarity here. Layers of it. One layer of bull— on top of another. And what you do in life like when you get older is, you pick the layer of bull— that you prefer and that's your bull, so to speak.[2]

Pilate has already picked his layer of bull for his truth, and that truth is his own self-preservation. But Jesus doesn't deal in toilet paper, and he isn't politically correct like Pilate, Annas and Caiaphas. They are all about self-preservation. (See Jn 11:45-53 regarding the Jewish religious leaders' desire to preserve their position of rule and their nation.) While these political and religious leaders may have started out their careers desiring to follow truth and justice wherever they would lead, at some point they decided that such idealism would lead them to their own dead ends if they were to take it all the way to its logical conclusion—like God-inspired idealism will lead Jesus to his death shortly. After a while, talk of truth and justice becomes a joke to opportunistic, disillusioned, cynical and hardened people like Pilate. Such talk becomes a well-worn coin, like a dead metaphor, as Nietzsche would call it. Might makes right, and power is knowledge—and not the other way around.

Pilate wants to release Jesus because he senses something is wrong, and possibly that this little trial is going to come back to haunt him at some point. Besides sensing that the Jewish leaders want Jesus dead out of envy, not truth and justice (Mk 15:10), he is warned by his wife (according to one of the other Gospel accounts) that he should have nothing to do with Jesus' condemnation. She bases her advice on an ominous dream she has just had about him that day (Mt 27:19). It's all about self-preservation and self-promotion. In the end, Pilate gives Jesus up to be crucified—washing his hands of the whole bloody mess—not because he's convinced that Jesus is guilty, but because he knows that he would be found guilty of siding with a king other than Caesar (Jn 19:12-16).

Jesus is politically incorrect—the ultimate inconvenient truth. Convenient truths are one thing. Like cheap toilet paper, they don't really cost you anything. In fact, convenient truths gain for you good standing and get you ahead in life, like knowing that two times two always equals four, and that it is always good to get your ducks in a row. But Jesus has a way of messing with the math tables and moving the ducks all around and getting your neck out of joint so that you end up wanting to slap him for saying the right thing at the wrong time (and by the way, there is never a good time to say many of the things that he says: Jn 18:19-24). Then Jesus has a way of keeping quiet when it would be in his best interest from your point of view—and Pilate's—for him to speak (Jn 19:8-11). But you wouldn't want to hear the things he'd have to say. Jesus isn't politically correct; he's the ultimate inconvenient truth.

Pilate is generally viewed as unbending, brutal and ruthless—known for having mixed Galileans' blood with their sacrifices (Lk 13:1). The only probable reason that Pilate seems so pliable and indecisive here is that he has already caused so much upheaval among the Jewish people that it has won for him the emperor's displeasure; as a result, Pilate wants to keep things as peaceful as possible. Moreover, Pilate is faced with the dilemma of knowing that Jesus is innocent. So either he wins for himself more upheaval and outrage at the hands of the Jewish rulers and the people under them and further displeasure with Rome, or he condemns an innocent man to death, which will make a mockery of Roman justice, especially in view of his intuition that this man Jesus may be a divine visitor.[3] Jesus is inconvenient—especially at a time when things have a tendency to get explosive anyway in Jerusalem; after all, it's the Passover.

Pilate may not think of Jesus, at first appearance, as all that inconvenient. No doubt, he's had to deal with messiah figures before. But Pilate's got a bunch of Jewish religious leaders up in arms (Jn 18-19). And he has to give up Barabbas—who had taken part in a rebellion (Jn 18:38-40)— in exchange for satisfying the leaders and keeping Rome from getting involved. I'm sure Pilate doesn't want the knife-bearing Barabbas on the streets again. And I'm not sure he wants to go home that night: he's going to have to deal with his wife, who has warned him about Jesus (Mt 27:19). He's going to have to deal with his nagging conscience (what little is left of it) while lying awake in bed—after all, he has knowingly cruci-fied an innocent man. Even more importantly, he has to deal with his emerging fear of Jesus, given claims about him as well as Jesus' own claims and presence (Jn 18:33-37; 19:7-12).

No doubt Pilate has faced down messiah figures before, watching them wilt in his presence as he sentences them to crucifixion for rebel-lion. But Pilate has never faced anyone like Jesus. Pilate is the one begin-ning to panic and wilt here, as if he's the one who's been caught and taken in for questioning. Jesus' stare, silent treatment and providential poise would wilt anybody, even Caesar. As the questioning goes on, we find that Pilate is dumbfounded and terrified that Jesus is not afraid. The tables have been turned on Pilate, and Jesus is standing in judgment over him. Regardless of Jesus' immediate fate, Jesus' eternal destiny as the Son of God and Son of Man who will return to God's right hand is never in question. And that's why Pilate's questions of interrogation give way to questions of self-doubt and self-incrimination, as he himself is on the hot seat. By the time Pilate enacts judgment, the right-minded reader for the jury will conclude that Pilate is really the one who is guilty, and that talk of Roman "justice" at this trial is a bunch of bull:

> The Jews insisted, "We have a law, and according to that law he must die, because he claimed to be the Son of God." When Pilate heard this, he was even more afraid, and he went back inside the palace. "Where do you come from?" he asked Jesus, but Jesus gave him no answer. "Do you refuse to speak to me?" Pilate said. "Don't you realize I have power either to free you or to crucify you?" Jesus answered, "You would have no power over me if it were not given to you from above. Therefore the one who handed me over to you is guilty of a greater sin." From then on, Pilate tried to set Jesus

free, but the Jews kept shouting, "If you let this man go, you are no friend of Caesar. Anyone who claims to be a king opposes Caesar." When Pilate heard this, he brought Jesus out and sat down on the judge's seat at a place known as the Stone Pavement (which in Aramaic is Gabbatha). It was the day of Preparation of Passover Week, about the sixth hour. "Here is your king," Pilate said to the Jews. But they shouted, "Take him away! Take him away! Crucify him!" "Shall I crucify your king?" Pilate asked. "We have no king but Caesar," the chief priests answered. Finally Pilate handed him over to them to be crucified. (Jn 19:7-16)

It all adds up in the end—but not according to the math tables and legal codes Pilate learned at school. No wonder that although he knows Jesus is innocent and no mere mortal, Pilate still blows it by writing down "Caesar" instead of "Jesus" as his answer for whom to fear when "the Jews" warn him of disloyalty to the emperor (Jn 19:12-16). Perhaps Pilate reasons that he can delay his own demise by putting away Jesus now and facing the consequences later. The first wave of consequences will come more quickly than he realizes, however. Without jumping too far ahead, we can say that Pilate will soon have to deal with Jesus' disciples, who, within a few weeks, emerge as a redemptive force to be reckoned with and who will proclaim Jesus' resurrection and impending return. Questions about truth no longer appear academic or insignificant. Jesus is the most significant, most inconvenient truth of all. Go ahead and crucify or stone or drown or shoot Jesus and his witnesses. It doesn't matter. His kingdom is not of this world (Jn 18:36). That doesn't mean that Jesus is politically irrelevant but that he is politically inconvenient, for his kingdom intersects and undercuts and calls into question and into judgment this world's system, which is passing away. From where I sit and write, the Roman Empire is long gone. Jesus' kingdom, however, has only just begun.

What is perhaps most inconvenient about Jesus is that his truth does not fit into neat, rational, moral and power-brokering boxes. Jesus isn't a control freak. He doesn't put down his opposition by crucifying or stoning them, just as you can't put him down by crucifying or stoning him; his kingdom is of a different world and order. Instead of using the power of life-taking brute force, Jesus employs the power of life-giving love—which messes with our systems and programs and schedules. Such truth comes knocking at the most inconvenient times—just as we are building our very own retributive Roman and legalistic Jewish empires.[4] Jesus' kingdom of life-giving love is the truth of which he speaks and which he embodies. This is why Jesus still can take time to give over his mother to John as her son and Mary as John's mother out of compassion for her (Jn 19:25-27). This is why Jesus can make room for late-coming disciples Joseph of Arimathea and Nicodemus in his kingdom after he dies, as they risk their own well-being to bury Jesus (Jn 19:38-42). It is why he can make room for a thief in paradise at the last minute even though the thief will have no time to right his wrongs (Lk 23:39-43), and it is why he can forgive and later restore Simon Peter (Jn 21:15-19), who is nowhere to be found since his third denial (Jn 18:27). Because Jesus' kingdom is of another world and order—an eternal one—he can take time and make space for losers like them and us. No wonder the retribution-driven Romans and legalistic Jews cannot tolerate Jesus. He doesn't fit their boxes and, in effect, undermines their systems with his loving grace and mercy. He's *the* inconvenient truth whom Judas exchanges for thirty pieces of silver (Mt 26:14-15). He's the truth whom others of us exchange for a few well-worn coins of Nietzschean dead metaphors of tolerable religion (intolerable to Nietzsche and to me), while soldiers cast lots for his clothing (Jn 19:23-24). How inconvenient for them in the long run—especially Pilate and the Jewish rulers (Jn 19:11)—that they have chosen so poorly.

Poor conniving, weaseling, flip-flopping Pilate. He writes "JESUS OF NAZARETH, THE KING OF THE JEWS" on a sign and posts it above Jesus on the cross—bearing witness to this intolerable truth for the first time (Jn 19:19-22). Perhaps the sign is made of toilet paper—simply a spiteful, mocking jab at the Jewish religious leaders. Perhaps not. Regardless of the motive, though, Pilate is bearing witness to ultimate truth, perhaps for the first time in his life. Above the din of the flesh-ripping, body-beating and clothes-tearing soldiers, and above the agonizing gasps of Jesus as he slowly dies upon the cross, one can hear Pilate's conversation with Jesus echo through the chambers of Pilate's palace and in our souls:

Pilate then went back inside the palace, summoned Jesus and asked him, "Are you the king of the Jews?" "Is that your own idea," Jesus asked, "or did others talk to you about me?" "Am I a Jew?" Pilate replied. "It was your people and your chief priests who handed you over to me. What is it you have done?" Jesus said, "My kingdom is not of this world. If it were, my servants would fight to prevent my arrest by the Jews. But now my kingdom is from another place." "You are a king, then!" said Pilate. Jesus answered, "You are right in saying I am a king. In fact, for this reason I was born, and for this I came into the world, to testify to the truth. Everyone on the side of truth listens to me." (Jn 18:33-37)

The truth is resounding in our ears and staring us in the face, just as with Pilate. What side are you and I on? The side of truth? Some sources say that Pilate later becomes a Christ-follower. Whether or not this is true (and I doubt it), the real question before us is this: will we confess Jesus of Nazareth as the King of the Jews, as the king of our lives, as the one whose kingdom is not of this world's system of retribution and legalism but of grace, mercy and love? Will we confess him as the ultimate inconvenient truth? It's time to choose. Truth's judgment on the world has come. There's no time to waste.

HURT
John 18–19

Jesus, as the gracious and loving Truth, comes into this world to reveal to us our hurt, to locate the source of our pain and to heal us at the cross. He does not come to condemn us. And yet we often live the lie. We often act as if Jesus has postponed his hour of glory and has left us to take care of unfinished business. We fail to realize that the only work left for us to do is to live into the work that Jesus has finished for us rather than force others to die for our sins or to die for them ourselves.

We often deny Jesus' final words on the cross: "It is finished" (Jn 19:30). Some of us deny that we're hurt or how we're hurt. Others of us deny the source of our pain—that we hurt one another, even Jesus. And some of us, perhaps all of us, deny wanting Jesus to heal us. Even so, we need Jesus to heal us. Will we let him heal us and live into his finished work for us, or will we take matters into our own hands, cutting and hurting ourselves in the process?

◆　◆　◆

My friend walked into a room and found her covered with blood. A girl in his youth group had cut herself, and blood was everywhere. Why did she do it? Some will claim that she was trying to gain attention. Perhaps. But why was she trying to gain attention in the first place, and why would she have used such extreme measures to gain attention? Besides the possibility of crying out for others to love her, perhaps she was trying to get at the hole in her heart through the hole in her skin. Maybe she was trying to locate the source of her pain. When everything in her life was pain, maybe she couldn't locate its source. If she could locate it, she could work to heal herself.

It is healing to locate pain in a body wracked with it, and to get at the pain's source, so that one can somehow try and manage it. It can be healing to know one still hurts, that one is still alive in the midst of the overwhelming, numbing tragedy of life, in which pain is the only thing left that's real. Broken homes. The barrage of evening news tragedies. Death all around—from wars to natural disasters to the loss of life within one's soul and the death of innocence as one grows older, sometimes wiser and often more cynical.

We try to deal with our pain one way or another. Some people amuse themselves to death while watching sappy sitcoms and soap operas.' We use the TV or other forms of technological amusement to distract us from despair; it's like dangling keys on a ring in front of a baby to keep it from crying. Other people cut themselves in their attempts to cope with life's raw pain. Perhaps they're trying to locate the pain, arrive at the truth or come to terms with reality. Perhaps. And then again, perhaps not.

Nine Inch Nails' song "Hurt" begins with Trent Reznor singing of having hurt himself to see if he can feel anymore. He sings of concentrating on his pain, which he takes to be the only reality. According to Reznor, all of life gives way to suffering, death and utter futility. To

Reznor, our experience shouts at us, telling us that the only thing that's real is pain. It's the only thing that tells us we're alive because everything else in our lives is numb, illusory, broken and dead. *I feel pain; therefore I am.*

For all the realism in the song, the video version isn't realistic enough, or at least not personal enough. The video definitely reveals hurt, but it is primarily the world's hurt—dying and decaying animals and holocausts, not the holocaust of one's own life's death and decay. Johnny Cash's video version of his remake of the song "Hurt" is quite different. His video matches the song's words of personal brokenness better than Nine Inch Nails' own video version does.[5]

Cash sees his own brokenness and need, and realizes that all his accomplishments are empty. You sense his loneliness: he laments that everyone he knows goes away in the end (including his wife, June Carter, and his mother). You sense his disillusionment: he tells his listeners/viewers that they can have his entire kingdom, which is nothing more than dirt (his award-winning songs and superstar career). You even sense the guilt he feels over hurting others; in fact, he goes so far as to predict that he will let people down and hurt them (whoever they may be).

While Nine Inch Nails' video version includes talk of letting people down and making them hurt, the question is why? Is it because the system has abused and hurt us so that we inevitably (though somehow innocently) hurt others? Cash shows no trace of having a victim's mentality. He takes responsibility. In fact, he appears in the video to take responsibility for Jesus' hurt—his deadly life of fame and fortune nailed Jesus to the cross of death. Whether famous or not, infamous or not, we also had a hand in nailing Jesus to the cross.

Cash seems to get at three truths: we are hurt, we hurt one another and we hurt Jesus with our Peter-like denials and a Judas kiss. What do we do when faced with these hard truths? Do we play the victim card, blaming it on our environment and upbringing? If we fail to take responsibility, we lose our human dignity, becoming no different from mindless, heartless machines and Pavlov's dog that simply reacts to external stimuli.

While some of us play the victim card and blame others, some of us try dying for our own sins. Some of us try to make atonement for ourselves, piercing our own hands or sides and placing crowns of thorns upon our own heads. But the guilty can never clear their own names by dying for themselves. A key difference between Peter the denier and Judas the betrayer is that Judas goes to the wrong priest to confess his sins and so ends up taking his own life. Like Judas, will you end up dying for your own sins? It doesn't have to be this way. It was never meant to be this way. Jesus has taken responsibility for our hurt, even the pain we have inflicted on him:

"Then the detachment of soldiers with its commander and the Jewish officials arrested Jesus. They bound him . . ." (Jn 18:12). *I* arrested him and bound him tight.

"When Jesus said this, one of the officials nearby struck him in the face" (Jn 18:22). *I* struck him in the face.

"One of the high priest's servants, a relative of the man whose ear Peter had cut off, challenged him, 'Didn't I see you with him in the olive grove?' Again Peter denied it, and at that moment a rooster began to crow" (Jn 18:26-27). *I* denied him a third time as the rooster crowed.

"Then Pilate took Jesus and had him flogged. The soldiers twisted together a crown of thorns and put it on his head. They clothed him in a purple robe and went up to him again and again, saying, 'Hail, king of the Jews!' And they struck him in the face" (Jn 19:1-3). *I* flogged him, twisted together a crown of thorns and put it on his head. *I* dressed him in a purple robe, bowed before him, mocked him and hailed him as king as *I* struck him in the face repeatedly.

"'Here is your king,' Pilate said to the Jews. But they shouted, 'Take him away! Take him away! Crucify him!' 'Shall I crucify your king?' Pilate asked. 'We have no king but Caesar,' the chief priests answered. Finally Pilate handed him over to them to be crucified" (Jn 19:14-16). *I* cried out with all the rest of them, calling for his death.

"So the soldiers took charge of Jesus. Carrying his own cross, he went out to the place of the Skull (which in Aramaic is called Golgotha). Here they crucified him, and with him two others—one on each side and Jesus in the middle" (Jn 19:16-18). *I* hung him there between two thieves.

"When the soldiers crucified Jesus, they took his clothes, dividing them into four shares, one for each of them, with the undergarment remaining.

This garment was seamless, woven in one piece from top to bottom. 'Let's not tear it,' they said to one another. 'Let's decide by lot who will get it.' This happened that the scripture might be fulfilled which said, 'They divided my garments among them and cast lots for my clothing.' So this is what the soldiers did" (Jn 19:23-24). *I cast lots for his clothes.*

"Near the cross of Jesus stood his mother, his mother's sister, Mary the wife of Clopas, and Mary Magdalene" (Jn 19:25). *I made them suffer.*

"When he had received the drink, Jesus said, 'It is finished.' With that, he bowed his head and gave up his spirit" (Jn 19:30). *I killed him. And so did you.*

We can never play the innocent victim card given what we've done to Jesus and to a host of others. We've oppressed and obliterated, maligned and manipulated, hit and hated. As Rowan Williams says, "I am, willy-nilly, involved in 'structural violence,' in economic, political, religious and private systems of relationship which diminish the other (and I must repeat once more that the victim in one system is liable to be the oppressor in another: the polarity runs through each individual)."[6]

Since we can never play the innocent victim, we can never atone for our own sins. Jesus is the only truly innocent victim. He never victimizes us or anyone else, although we have victimized him and countless others. And while he is the only truly innocent victim, he never plays the victim card. He is the innocent victim who brings victory to us in the midst of our victimization of him. Only the innocent victim can bring an end to the cycle of vengeance and retribution and death through forgiveness, death and resurrection. That is why Jesus can say, "It is finished," and that is why we can hope for the transformation of our lives and relationships. Jesus has come to heal and cleanse us through his cross and resurrection—his anticipated hour of glory. His healing and cleansing work on our behalf is complete. It is finished.

But for many of us, it isn't finished. Some of us may even cut ourselves because we sense we're guilty, but we don't know why. We can't locate the source of our wrongdoing. Everything about us seems so wrong. So we keep cutting away, hoping the release of blood will relieve us of our guilt. But like Lady Macbeth in Shakespeare's tragedy, we can't ever wipe the bloodguilt from our hands.

And even if we don't feel guilty, we still hurt from the wrongs committed against us. Some may think: "Jesus suffered for me, but I'm the one who's suffering now." We fail to imagine that Jesus' wounds are fresh each time we sin, and each time we're sinned against, even though his saving work was finished long ago. He is here for us in his pain and suffering and life-giving power; his is the death of one who has risen never to die again, and who is ever-present—the suffering though victorious Lamb and Lion who takes and takes and takes away the sin of the world.

Stephen King gets at this idea of Jesus' ever-present suffering and saving presence in *The Green Mile*. In the movie, the Christ figure, John Coffey, appears on the scene to suffer for and with and in the place of others. But Coffey doesn't simply suffer in their place or feel their pain; he mysteriously absorbs the pain and guilt and shame of all, even absorbing the horrific shock of young innocent lives destroyed by rape and murder as well as the deadly charge in the electric chair for the killer's crime, which he did not commit.

On the cross, Jesus becomes the victim and the victimizer. He becomes sin—he becomes genocide, pedophilia, rape; he becomes envy, rivalry, greed; he becomes white lies, unfaithfulness, lost innocence—so that we can become God's righteousness (2 Cor 5:21).

Jesus walks the green mile to the electric chair, to Columbine, to Auschwitz, to the room covered with blood where the cut girl sits crying. He takes the shock and the electric charge. He takes the bullet to the head and heart. He takes the hit of gas in the Holocaust's chamber while hanging in Nuremberg Trials' gallows. He takes the girl's razor to his flesh—torn brow, palms and side, blood and water flowing (Jn 19:34).

It is finished.[7]

◆ ◆ ◆

I am so grateful that it is finished and that Jesus didn't postpone the hour of glory when he would complete the work he came to do. We no longer need to cut and victimize and die a thousand deaths on a daily basis. His humiliation is our glorification. We can now live anew.

GROUND ZERO
John 20:1-23

It is fitting that all life starts anew early in the morning on the first day of the week, for it is then that Jesus rises from the dead. "Early on the first day of the week, while it was still dark, Mary Magdalene went to the tomb and saw that the stone had been removed from the entrance" (Jn 20:1).

Events of great importance don't usually take place early in the morning in a garden on a Sunday. But early on this Sunday morning, the most significant event in human history takes place: Jesus rises from the dead. The impact of the explosion as he rises from the dead in that garden tomb can be felt throughout the world to the end of the age. At Golgotha, we find the climax of Jesus' hour or appointed time of glory, and here in the garden tomb we find the hour's culmination. As we join Mary and the others at the empty tomb (Jn 20:1-9), we find ourselves at ground zero—the place where Jesus destroys the forces of evil and inaugurates his reign.

The term *ground zero* finds its origins in the Manhattan Project (the development of the first atomic bomb during World War II) and the nuclear bombings of Hiroshima and Nagasaki in Japan. I have been to ground zero in Hiroshima, and it is an ominous site—even after all these years. The Genbaku Dome, left largely intact after the blast, stands as a haunting reminder to the tragedy, especially as the new Hiroshima is built around it. I visited the site on a warm, sunny summer day with a group of Japanese tourists, including my Japanese wife and her mother. Yet I recall how cold and alone I felt as a solitary American figure, as I meditated upon the nuclear nightmare that, decades earlier, had shaken the ground where I stood.

The words *ground zero* will also be forever linked to the horrific tragedy that occurred in New York City on September 11, 2001. I have not visited that site yet, but I vividly recall the shock and horror I felt as I watched the video footage of the airplanes rip through the Twin Towers, and the fiery eruption of steel, flesh and blood that burst into the air and fell to the streets below. The terrorists diabolically schemed and chose sites of supreme symbolic importance as their targets of destruction: the two towers of the World Trade Center (economic might), and with them the Pentagon (military might) and the White House or Capitol building (political might). Fortunately, they never hit their third target.

Terrorist masterminds also tried to sabotage and destroy God's kingdom purposes. They chose Jesus as their supreme target, crucifying him outside the city between two thieves. They intended it to be of supreme symbolic importance. And while they hit their target, they didn't realize that they were in God's sights the whole time. God was orchestrating his counterterrorism campaign through Jesus' atoning martyrdom; providentially (not luckily or fortunately), Jesus rose from the dead. God wreaked havoc on the terrorists at ground zero as he built his kingdom through the crucified and resurrected Jesus.

The demonic culprits, and their Roman and Pharisaical accomplices, intended to convey to Jesus' disciples and to everyone else that this is the fate of anyone who stands in the way of their empire's expansion. Because of their inflated sense of self-importance and pride, they failed to realize that their own empire was nothing more than a terrorist cell from the standpoint of God's eternal kingdom. God's eternal purposes for his kingdom's advance through his Son would not be hindered; instead, through Jesus' passion and death, God's purposes would be propelled forward, faster than the speed of light.

God is so in control and he is so fast that he can take his time as he advances. He and his angelic forces don't race to the tomb and bear Jesus away before the enemy forces can react. The time is taken to remove the burial clothes, to fold the cloth that had been around his head and to lay the cloth down separately from the linen (Jn 20:6-7). Two angels meet the grieving Mary at the tomb (they are seated inside the tomb where Jesus' body had been, one at the head and the other at the foot). Jesus himself appears to Mary at the site of the resurrection blast, but only after she goes and gets the stupefied Peter and John and they return home from the grave (Jn 20:1-2, 10-15). Everything happens according to God's timetable, as he turns the tables on his enemies, taking his own sweet, shalom-filled time.

Jesus has already won the war. Not only is he so secure that he can take his time in continuing his mission; he's so secure that he's not about revenge but about making right and transforming the world. He does not invade a country militarily, launch missile strikes after rising from the dead or impose economic sanctions. Instead, we find him in the garden, talking with Mary Magdalene, comforting, assuring and encouraging her (Jn 20:15-17). We find him appearing to his bewildered and defeated disciples, unhindered by locked doors, comforting, assuring and encouraging them as well (Jn 20:19, 26). His message to his followers is "Peace be with you!" (Jn 20:26), not "Let's get even."

Whatever one makes of America's response to the events of September 11 (which is outside the scope of my present concern), Jesus does not do battle the way nations or individuals often do battle—by retribution rather than redemption. Instead he builds his community, centering his people in his loving embrace through his victorious cross and resurrection and extending his love to the defeated world that opposed (and still opposes) him.

The war, not simply this or that battle, has already been won. So we don't need to do battle the way the world does battle. We can move forward with confidence that skirmishes and roadside battles belong to the Lord; as a result, we can respond in love, and not hate, with forgiveness in light of Jesus' forgiveness. Sure, Jesus still needs to return to the Father where he will reign from on high. Yes, there is work for us to do here below. True, the enemy still reacts, striking at Jesus' forces. But no matter how hard the terrorists try to take away freedom, there is no taking away Jesus' people's freedom to forgive, which is bound up with Jesus' forgiveness and the security of his eternal embrace. So why do we often hide in fear behind locked doors, like Jesus' first followers did (Jn 20:19, 26)?

Perhaps it's because we don't realize the war has already been won. Perhaps we think Jesus only won an important battle and that the war's outcome is ultimately in our hands. Or perhaps we think the real war is being fought elsewhere than at Golgotha and in the garden with the empty tomb.

After the September 11 attacks, American church leaders understandably sought to comfort their congregations. People were in a state of shock, insecure and anxious about the future. It was certainly pastorally correct to comfort them—as long as it wasn't politically correct. Yet I know of at least one church leader who comforted his congregation with words to the effect of: "Don't be afraid; the terrorists will never take away our freedom as Americans." That was the thrust of his Sunday morning message. While there is a vital role for civic engagement and public righteousness, the church's public role first and foremost is to bear witness to Jesus' cross and resurrection from the dead—for his church, and through his church for the world, and not to promote national self-interest and security. Pastoral words of comfort should be, "Don't be afraid; the terrorists will never take away our freedom as the church." That much we can count on, and that is to be our main preoccupation and occupation as God's people. We don't know the ultimate future of this or that country, no matter how great or small; but we do know the ultimate destiny of the church. While this or that church building may rise and fall, the church as God's people will forever stand based on the resurrection of Jesus Christ from the dead and his return to the Father's side.

Jesus' resurrection is not a private affair that only concerns religious people like Mary at garden parties outside empty tombs. Rather, it affects national and international security: his resurrection as well as his ascent bears upon the whole world order, and the world's destiny has been secured by him and through faith in him. He has overcome the world (Jn 16:33) to save the world (Jn 3:16). His work is already complete, and he has placed limits on all rule and foiled the ultimate ambitions of terrorists with their plots. That's why he can take his time in the garden, meeting first with the weeping Mary. He has won the war to end all wars; at his return and consummation of his kingdom, all wars will cease.

The site of his resurrection and first appearance has supreme symbolic importance. Although the pillars Peter, James and John will take the good news of Jesus' resurrection to the temple courts and Solomon's colonnade, and Ph.D. Paul will take it to Mars Hill and Caesar's courts, the explosive message emanates from here: the garden with the empty tomb. Here the resurrected Lord makes known to Mary that he is back and tells her to tell the others that he is returning to his Father and their Father (Jn 20:17). No need for a public showing of pomp and power and declarations that he will show the terrorists who is boss. The empty tomb in this garden says it all. He has risen; the war is won.

Eventually, Jesus' first followers will emerge from secrecy and come out from behind locked doors. In fact, they won't simply emerge onto alleyways and side streets; they'll explode onto the public square, as the Book of Acts makes clear. Sure, persecution, imprisonment and death await them; Jesus has already told them so (Jn 15:18-25; Jn 16:1-4). But their own resurrection to life from the dead awaits as well. With Jesus' ascent to the Father and the descent of the Spirit upon them, they will rise up and move out in the face of clear and present dangers. While they will have trouble in this world, they will go forward with confidence and in peace, knowing that Jesus has overcome the world (Jn 16:33).

Jesus does not give to his people the peace that the world gives (Jn 14:27); he gives his Spirit to us. His peace, bound up with the Spirit who will be with us forever, is eternal (Jn 14:16, 26-27). So do not let your hearts be troubled; do not be afraid (Jn 14:27). The Spirit of peace who testifies in the face of persecution will make it possible for us to testify— even with our lives, just as Jesus' first followers testified (Jn 15:18-27) and just as Jesus testified.

Jesus is sending us out. Unlock the doors. Move out from the empty tomb at ground zero. We can go forward in peace even in the face of danger because his peace is on us, his Spirit is in us as Jesus breathes upon us, and the forgiveness of sins is ours to give (Jn 20:19-23). "Peace be with you!" (Jn 20:26).

In our best moments, we think and live this way. But all too often our minds are filled with anxious thoughts and doubts, our hearts are restless, and all this talk appears as empty slogans and propaganda. But deep down inside we know it's true. The resurrected Jesus will meet us at our own ground zero time and time again, rescuing us repeatedly from the burning wreck of our former lives to which we often return. So, why do we keep playing those tapes—observing the fatal impact of our fiery passion over and over and over again?

It's because we seldom take the time to meet the Lord at his empty tomb. We lock the door and sit in the dark isolation of our fears and self-preservation rather than go with Mary to meet Jesus in the garden. And yet Jesus won't be locked out. He appears and stands before us now in our mind's eye, calling us to reflect upon his victory, showing us the marks in his hands and side, placing our finger and our hand there, leading us to believe over and over and over again in his signs reported in John's eyewitness news (Jn 20:24-31). Out of the darkness, Jesus' light of his victorious presence appears, penetrating locked doors and extinguishing the night. His words reverberate against the room's walls, drowning out the din of all ground zeros: "Peace be with you!"

TRANSITION
Non-Members Only

JOHN MAKES CLEAR FROM THE OUTSET of his Gospel account that God brings outsiders into his family. In fact, God's Son becomes an outsider so as to make outsiders insiders. Jesus comes to the world, and the world rejects him. He comes to his own people, the Jewish nation—themselves outsiders among the nations, yet chosen by God—and they reject him too. The world does not recognize the Word of creation (Jn 1:10), and his own people do not receive him (Jn 1:11). When Jesus dies on the cross, he even dies outside the city gates. Yet to those who receive him—Jews and Gentiles alike—he gives the right to enter God's family. As John says, "He was in the world, and though the world was made through him, the world did not recognize him. He came to that which was his own, but his own did not receive him. Yet to all who received him, to those who believed in his name, he gave the right to become children of God—children born not of natural descent, nor of human decision or a husband's will, but born of God" (Jn 1:10-13). This text makes clear that one's insider or members-only status won't work with God. God hates presumption and a sense of entitlement. God delights in broken hearts and total dependence and trust; they are the keys that God uses to unlock the door (that we ourselves have locked) to enter into his family.

No wonder Jesus chooses the motley crew he does. Like Israel before them, this band is nothing to brag about to friends and family. There are no celebrities among Jesus' disciples, just fishermen, a tax collector, a zealot and a few other misfits. While John the Baptist may qualify as a celebrity in terms of his public recognition (Jn 1), he never gets into the clubs because he never meets the dress code or performs according to proper social norms and etiquette. Then there is the woman at the well (Jn 4). While she is well-known to her village, they're only a bunch of Samaritans, and she herself is more infamous than famous. As a former prostitute, Mary Magdalene is in a similar situation; people in the red-light district know her but would never roll out the red carpet for her (Jn 20). The man born blind whom Jesus heals no doubt gets kicked out of the synagogue—the equivalent of being kicked out of society—for confessing Jesus publicly (Jn 9). Not counting the unnamed royal official whose son Jesus heals (Jn 4), Nicodemus and Joseph of Arimathea are the only named leaders among the people who publicly confess some form of allegiance to Jesus by asking Pilate for his body so as to bury him properly (Jn 19:38-42). And yet earlier in John's Gospel, Nicodemus's peer group—the Jewish ruling council—treats him as an outsider when Nicodemus defends Jesus (Jn 7). And although there are numerous unnamed leaders from among the Jewish people who come to believe in Jesus (Jn 12:42), they will not confess him publicly for fear of the Pharisees: "Because of the Pharisees they would not confess their faith for fear they would be put out of the synagogue; for they loved praise from men more than praise from God" (Jn 12:42-43).[1]

In light of this, it is rather strange that nonbelievers often find Christians acting like insiders. If we are insiders, it is only by faith and as outsiders who welcome everyone else to come inside by faith in Jesus. This reminds me of a situation that occurred several years ago when I was speaking at a secular university. I had been asked by the professor of a paranormal psychology class at this university to give a guest lecture on evangelical Christianity. It was right after President Bush had won reelection, and many people in the greater Portland area believed evangelical Christians were largely responsible for reelecting him and were taking over America with him. As an outsider within the evangelical fold, my colleagues at the seminary where I teach jokingly told me that it was appropriate that I represent the tradition in a paranormal psychology class, since they considered me a bit paranormal.

I had received permission from the psychology professor to address psychological and philosophical critiques of religion even as I spoke about evangelicalism. During the course of my talk, a young lady sitting halfway up the large theater classroom talked incessantly to the two students next to her. As soon as I was finished and the professor asked if the class had questions, she immediately raised her hand and asked, "Do you think you're better than me?" I wanted to ask, "What did I say that you didn't listen to that would make you ask that question?" but I decided against it. Instead I simply asked, "What did I say that would make you wonder?" She replied, "You Christians think you're better than the rest of us because you talk about having a relationship with God, that you have insider status and that we are outside."

I now understood that she had been so rude to me during my talk because she felt Christians had been very rude and uncaring toward her. There was more there than met the eye or than was expressed in her words. And so I said to the young woman, "God wants to have a personal relationship with you through his Son, Jesus Christ. You, too, can experience God's embrace and communion with him. Would you like to invite him into your life?" She didn't know what to say, and so she said nothing in return. I told her that she should feel comfortable to interact with me at a later time, but she did not accept my invitation. Hopefully, she accepted God's.

Other students asked me important questions about science and homosexuality and about evangelicals supposedly seeking to take over America. Perhaps the most powerful question came from a young woman, arms covered with tattoos, sitting way up high at the back of the classroom. She turned to two of my students, who had accompanied me to the class, and said, "I think that girl who asked the question earlier completely misunderstood what this guy was saying. Is it really that easy? Is trusting in Jesus all that is required to enter into a relationship with God?" Indeed, it is.

No matter where you come from—left of center, right of center, elite circles or low end of the totem pole circles, tattoos or no tattoos, psychology student or theology professor—you are outside. Yet all of you can become insiders by depending on God's outsider—Jesus. No matter who you are or what you have done, God invites you to enter his family, born not of natural descent or human decision or a husband's will but by divine descent and acceptance (Jn 1:12-13).

The real question is not, "Do you think you're better than me?" or "Do you think I'm better than you?" That can serve as a cover to keep you from asking a more significant question: "Do you think you're better than God?" God is inviting you into a relationship through faith in his Son. Will you invite his Son into your life or force him to remain outside?

INVITATION

Lastly, we come to the section titled "Invitation" (Jn 20:24–21:25).[1] John tells us in John 20:30-31 that this book is no mere theological treatise, biography or history lesson. Rather, it is meant to serve as an invitation to people to believe in Jesus as the Christ and Son of God, based on the claims and arguments and facts presented, and to grow in their faith in him. John calls on his readers to respond to Jesus' claim on their lives, for Jesus is the Christ, the one and only Son of God, who entered the world to reveal himself through his miraculous signs, especially the chief sign of his death and resurrection, so that we might believe. There is no place for abstract reflection in John's book, for it is a Gospel. As such, it is an invitation to believe and grow in faith in Jesus as the Christ, the Son of God, as reflected in the following verses: "Jesus did many other miraculous signs in the presence of his disciples, which are not recorded in this book. But these are written that you may believe that Jesus is the Christ, the Son of God, and that by believing you may have life in his name" (Jn 20:30-31).[2]

John does not offer his readers a way out or an opportunity to sit back and ruminate indefinitely in a time zone of indecision about eternal life in the distant future. Jesus' claim on John's first readers' lives is a matter of eternal life and of spiritual death in the present, just as it was for those who interacted directly with Jesus during his public ministry. John wants his readers to experience eternal life *now*. As George Ladd states, "While eternal life is eschatological, the central emphasis of the Fourth Gospel is not to show people the way of life in the Age to Come but to bring to them a present experience of this future life."[3] John would have us know that Jesus' claim is also on our lives *today*. There can be no response for us of "No comment" or "Try again later" (as in the next life). There can only be an either-or response to Jesus here and now: a yes or no. Either Jesus becomes *our* Christ, the Son of God in whom we believe to find eternal life in the here and now and become children of God, or we remain in death. The sine qua non (indispensable means) to experience eternal life and become children of God now is faith in Jesus. It is that simple, and it is that singular. So how will we respond to John's invitation to receive Jesus and believe in his name?[4]

Whether we are doubters like Thomas (Jn 20:24-25), deniers like Peter (Jn 18:15-27) or ever-adoring disciples like John or like other people found throughout John's Gospel and the whole New Testament, there is a place for us in Jesus' story as one of his followers. Like he does with Thomas, Jesus will lead us from doubt to deep devotion (Jn 20:26-28). Like he does with Peter, Jesus will lead us into the riches of restoration (Jn 21:15-22). Like he does with John, Jesus will overwhelm us time and time again (Jn 21:24-25). As with Nicodemus who buries Jesus (Jn 19:38-42) and Mary Magdalene who experiences the risen Jesus at the tomb (Jn 20:11-18), Jesus will blow us away with his love, raise us to new life and make us new.

This section opens with Jesus speaking into Thomas's doubt and having Thomas put his finger in his hand and his hand in his side. It points to the way in which Jesus speaks into our lives and tells John's readership that those who believe in him without seeing him are truly blessed (Jn 20:29). John would have us know that Jesus will draw us to himself, leading us from doubt into faith, that Jesus will restore and renew us, embracing us with his cleansing forgiveness that washes away the guilt of our denial, and that Jesus will engulf us in our devotion time and time again, leading us to drink from him over and over again as we meditate on John's Gospel.

Jesus' love alone fulfills us, blowing us away. No matter where we start, John would have us finish our reading in awe and wonder, with the thrilling sense that we have met Jesus anew and that he is worthy of our worship and deserves to be Lord in our lives. He is love and life and grace and truth, and through faith in him we enter into the fullness of life.

DOUBTING THOMAS
John 20:24-29

I love Caravaggio's painting *The Incredulity of Saint Thomas*. But I don't like the title. I don't think Thomas was incredulous, if we mean by that cynical. Of course Thomas doubted, but he doubted as one who was devoted to the real Jesus and didn't want to be taken in by some figment of his imagination or poser. What I love about the painting is how Jesus is perceived. I find him compassionate, seeking to assure Thomas that he has indeed been raised from the dead. The Lord is depicted as taking Thomas's hand and placing it in his side. Jesus is not put off by Thomas's wariness. He knows that Thomas is devoted to him, and he welcomes the opportunity to lead Thomas deeper into faith.

Perhaps more than any of the other disciples, Thomas gets a bum rap. Of course Judas and his defenders old and new may argue otherwise. Everyone is entitled to their own opinion. But Thomas is not content to base his convictions on mere opinion. He wants to make sure that the confession by the other disciples that the Lord had been raised from the dead is fact and not wishful thinking. That is why he says, "Unless I see the nail marks in his hands and put my finger where the nails were, and put my hand into his side, I will not believe it" (Jn 20:25).

Wishy-washy faith is based on wishful thinking. The kind of faith that pushes disciples to lay their lives on the line for their Lord is not. After all, Thomas has previously told his fellow disciples that they should all die with Jesus (who had told them that they should return to Judea—a real trouble spot for Jesus—where their friend Lazarus lay dead; see Jn 11:7-8, 14-16). Thomas doesn't take his faith claims lightly. Otherwise, he may have been content with wishful thinking, for wishful thinking doesn't cost you anything. Thomas's faith is costly, and so he has to make sure it is based on fact, not fiction.

Thomas is no cynic. Even in his doubt, he should be perceived as devoted. Elisabeth Elliot has been quoted as saying that during difficult, faith-crushing times, Christians move from denial to doubt to devotion. Thomas isn't necessarily denying Jesus' resurrection, just suspending belief until he can believe it for himself, not basing his faith on what his fellow disciples say they saw. Thomas isn't present when Jesus first appears to the disciples to show them his wounds, and he wants to see and experience the resurrection for himself, just as they have done (Jn 20:24).

It is only right that Thomas longs to experience what his fellow disciples have experienced. But actually, Thomas wants to experience more than what they have experienced. Not only does Thomas want to see the nail and spear marks, but also he wants to put his finger in Jesus' nail-punctured palms and his hand in his spear-pierced side. Thomas won't be disappointed. When Jesus appears again to the disciples, he says to Thomas: "Put your finger here; see my hands. Reach out your hand and put it into my side. Stop doubting and believe" (Jn 20:27). As stated above, Jesus is not put off by Thomas's wariness. The Lord does indeed offer a blessing to those who will follow later who believe without seeing—"Because you have seen me, you have believed; blessed are those who have not seen and yet have believed" (Jn 20:29). This is nearly everyone in the history of the church, save those individuals like Saul/Paul to whom the Lord appears in person on the Damascus Road. Even so, the Lord does not curse Thomas. The Lord simply wants to move Thomas from a zone of doubt to a place of total devotion, which is where he knows Thomas wants to be—and where he will soon be: "My Lord and my God!" (Jn 20:28).

The Lord knows that Thomas rejects easy "believe-ism," the kind of faith that costs Jesus everything and his followers nothing in return. For Thomas, faith is not wishful thinking and cannot be based on hearsay and folklore. Thomas is not like many in the American church who believe in the bodily resurrected Jesus because they *need* him to be true, right or wrong. Thomas believes in the bodily resurrected Jesus because he *believes* him to be true. Those who use Jesus as a crutch won't lay it on the line for Jesus; their faith is crippled, so they can't move. In contrast, followers like Thomas will take the good news of Jesus anywhere and everywhere—to places like India, which is where Thomas actually goes, and in an age without airplanes and automobiles.

Jesus welcomes Thomas's honesty and passion for the truth. The Lord does not refuse Thomas's desire to put his finger in his punctured palms and his hand in his pierced side. In fact, he invites Thomas to do so. If Caravaggio's portrayal is correct, Jesus actually takes Thomas by the hand and places Thomas's hand in his side. Jesus doesn't hide from the truth. How can he when he *is* the Truth?

When people raise questions, we should never hide from the truth. How can we expect them to move from denial to doubt to devotion? One of my children asks tough questions about God based on tough experiences he has gone through. The worst thing I can do is ridicule my child or dismiss such questions as unworthy of consideration. If I do, my child may grow up believing, but such faith will only be based on what other disciples—like me—have seen and experienced. Such faith will only be skin-deep. Each follower in his or her own way must put a finger in the palm and a hand in the side. I'm not threatened by my child's questions—because the Lord is not threatened by the questions of Thomases.

I'm so much like the doubting though devoted Thomas. While I have not suspended belief until I have had the opportunity to put my finger and hand in Jesus' literal wounds, I have hung God on a cross more than a time or two, echoing Jesus' cry of dereliction: "My God, my God, why have you forsaken me?" During each trying time, Jesus has taken my hand and put it in his side. I have kept my hand inside his wound and have not yet taken it out in the case of one particular, painful experience for which I still don't have answers. But I do have the comfort of knowing that the Lord lives my question with me until he raises me to new life where sorrow will be no more.

Jesus heartily invites each of us to enter into his wounds, his cry of dereliction and his depths of despair and find God and new life. In some ways, life lived in his wounds is messier. (Imagine what it's like to put your hand in a living person's wounded side; I had a hard enough time dissecting dead, no-longer-bleeding animals in biology class in high school.)

In some ways, it's easier to live on the surface of Jesus' wounds, holding back from taking the plunge. During one despairing season before God, I said to a mentor and friend that I would not question God because I loved him. My friend said in response that if I loved God I would wrestle with God. Wrestling with God is such a painful experience, leading to a pierced side in the case of Jesus and to a dislocated hip in the case of Jacob (Gen 32:25). It has led to such emotional upheaval in my life that I have felt my insides being torn apart from the tight grips and the sudden jerks. But wrestling *with* God is far better than wrestling to free yourself *from* God. So go ahead. Thrust your hand in Jesus' side. Keep it there as long as you need. Jesus will not reject you. In fact, he will hold your hand there. For he knows that only then can you stop doubting and truly believe.

GONE FISHING
John 21:1-23

Peter wore a sign around his soul that read, "Gone fishing. Be back later—maybe." You could read the words when you looked into his eyes. Peter had gone fishing with the rest of the apostles, and in his case, in more ways than one. Peter had checked out. Sure, he had been at the empty tomb. And true, Jesus had appeared to him and the others. But there was this nagging sense that it would never be quite the same again—Peter had screwed up so badly.

All Peter's empty promises and claims: "'Lord, why can't I follow you now? I will lay down my life for you.' Then Jesus answered, 'Will you really lay down your life for me? I tell you the truth, before the rooster crows, you will disown me three times!'" (Jn 13:37-38).

All his bravado: "Peter declared, 'Even if all fall away, I will not.' 'I tell you the truth,' Jesus answered, 'today—yes, tonight—before the rooster crows twice you yourself will disown me three times.' But Peter insisted emphatically, 'Even if I have to die with you, I will never disown you.' And all the others said the same" (Mk 14:29-31).

The bad news is that Peter does disown Jesus. The good news is that Jesus never disowns Peter. But Peter doesn't really know this—yet. While Jesus has risen from the dead, there is still a lingering feeling that Peter has not risen from his failures. Perhaps this is one reason why Peter goes fishing: that's what he did until Jesus called him to fish for people (Lk 5:10). Now that Peter thinks his occupation of fishing for people for Jesus is over because of his failures, Peter returns to his former occupation. The other disciples join Peter (Jn 21:3). And just as on the day he called Peter to himself, when Jesus stood on the shore and told Peter to take him out in the boat, Jesus now calls to Peter and the rest of the disciples from the shore. And just like before, Jesus tells them to try fishing again, even though they have been unsuccessful. And just like before, they pull in an unbelievable catch of fish, and Peter and the others are amazed and astonished. But unlike before, Peter swims to the shore to get to Jesus; the last time Jesus miraculously provided such a large catch of fish, Peter begged Jesus to get away from him because of his own sinfulness. (Compare Lk 5:1-10 with Jn 21:1-9.) One way or another, Jesus has a way of getting his hooks into people.

After the meal, Jesus takes Peter for a walk. Peter may now be thinking, "This is it. He's going to give me the pink slip, or worse." Jesus asks Peter three questions. You would expect the questions to be something like "Why did you fail me?" Instead, they are: "Do you truly love me more than these?" (Jn 21:15); "Do you truly love me?" (Jn 21:16); "Do you love me?" (Jn 21:17).

We don't really know to whom or to what Jesus is comparing Peter's love in verse 15 when he says, "Do you truly love me more than these?" Is Jesus comparing Peter's love for him with Peter's love for the fishing tackle? Is Jesus comparing Peter's love for him with Peter's love for the other disciples? Or is Jesus comparing Peter's love for him with the other disciples' love for him? We really don't know which it is, but we do know that Jesus really wants Peter to come to terms with him.

After the third question along these lines, Peter is grieved (Jn 21:17). I believe Peter's grief is the result of his having denied the Lord three times and the fact that now the Lord has asked him for the *third* time, "Do you love me?" Peter throws himself on the Lord: "Lord, you know all things; you know that I love you" (Jn 21:17).[5]

Jesus has Peter where he wants him, and where Peter needs to be—at his mercy. Not in some "no quarter" or "no mercy" sense, but in a sense that will not allow for Peter's spiritual bravado. And just as there is no room for Peter commending himself to Jesus, there is no room for Peter condemning himself either. No commending or condemning of himself will be tolerated, only clinging to Jesus. That's the way it always has to be with each of us before Jesus. We will find that whenever we as Jesus' followers try to commend or condemn ourselves before the Lord, the Lord will bring us to total dependence on him, in order to raise us to renewed life with renewed purpose and a renewed call: "Feed my lambs" (Jn 21:15); "Take care of my sheep" (Jn 21:16); "Feed my sheep" (Jn 21:17).

All too often, we either commend or condemn ourselves, and often in quick succession, just like Peter. When we commend or condemn ourselves, we are not living according to Jesus' call on our lives. On my own, I have no right to feed lambs or take care of sheep. But based on Jesus' call, I have no right to say "no" either. Peter and all the rest of us stand based on Jesus' call on our lives, and Peter and all the rest of us are lost without it.

In addition to commending or condemning ourselves, we tend to compare ourselves with others. Peter had a way of comparing himself with the other disciples. We see an instance of this in John 21. When Jesus foretells the kind of death Peter will suffer, Peter reacts by wanting to know what will happen to the disciple who has been following them while they talk:

> "I tell you the truth, when you were younger you dressed yourself and went where you wanted; but when you are old you will stretch out your hands, and someone else will dress you and lead you where you do not want to go." Jesus said this to indicate the kind of death by which Peter would glorify God. Then he said to him, "Follow me!" Peter turned and saw that the disciple whom Jesus loved was following them. (This was the one who had leaned back against Jesus at the supper and had said, "Lord, who is going to betray you?") When Peter saw him, he asked, "Lord, what about him?" (Jn 21:18-21)

Jesus' response is classic. Jesus answered, "'If I want him to remain alive until I return, what is that to you? You must follow me.' Because of this, the rumor spread among the brothers that this disciple [John] would not die. But Jesus did not say that he would not die; he only said, 'If I want him to remain alive until I return, what is that to you?'" (Jn 21:22-23). Jesus responds to us in a similar manner whenever we compare ourselves or our life situations with others: "What is that to you? You just concern yourself with our own relationship and follow me."

There's a pattern here: whenever we're commending or condemning or comparing ourselves, we're taking our eyes off of Jesus and his personal call on our own lives. I can relate to Peter. Perhaps you can too. In fact, we should be able to connect with him; there's a little bit of Peter in all of us, and in some of us, quite a bit. I'm quite a bit like Peter. Let me tell you how.

I had walked away from the Lord during my high school years and then returned to the Lord during my college years. Going away to college was really significant in that I was away from my old stomping grounds and the relationships that dragged me down; I could start afresh. I really grew in my relationship with Jesus during my college years, but when I returned to my home town after college graduation, the painful memories of what I was like before college haunted me and almost ruined me. I had sensed a renewed call on my life to serve the Lord during my college years, but given how the things of the past bombarded my psyche and soul back home after college, I felt that I was unworthy and could not serve Jesus in any meaningful way. I had gone from idolizing the late Jim Morrison (lead singer of *The Doors*) during high school to being inspired by the late Jim Elliot (leading missionary and martyr for the faith) during college. I went from being a rock-and-roll-star wannabe to being a holy-roller wannabe. In each case, however, it was way too much about me and all too little about the Lord. A pastor counseled and encouraged me to look to the Lord and to what the Lord was calling me, rather than to my past. His counsel and encouragement served to liberate me from parts of me, even though the struggle within me continues to this day. Since that time I have struggled more with comparing myself with others, especially with those who seem to have it made more than I do. "What about him, Lord?" "And what about that guy over there, the person behind me, or the woman up front?" The answer in each case: "What is that to you? You must follow me."

At some point, Peter comes to compare himself with Jesus rather than with John in terms of his fate. Some sources from tradition tell us that Peter is crucified, perhaps even crucified upside down at his own insistence (possibly because he did not feel worthy to be put to death in the same way as his Lord). Whether or not Peter is crucified upside down, it is true that he is always one for the dramatic.[6] Indeed, Peter's devotion to Jesus is dramatic. Despite Peter's ups and downs throughout his ministry, he keeps circling around Jesus. Jesus keeps a firm hold on the line of his call on Peter's life; his hook is lodged in Peter's heart.

Whether it's Peter, you or me, we often ask the Lord, "What about him, Lord?" "What about her?" "Why does she get so much recognition, and why do so many people flock to hear her speak?" "Why does everything go so smoothly for him in his ministry?" "Why do I have to suffer so much, and why do I have to bear such a heavy cross? Her burden is way too light." Jesus responds the same way at every turn: "What about me, Peter? Look to me, not to yourself and not to others. What I want for others doesn't concern you. You must follow me."

I am finding that I don't have the time or the energy to compare myself with the apostle Johns and Judiths. And besides, comparing myself with them takes my attention off of Jesus, who, in his incomparable mercy and grace, called me when I wasn't worth calling. He keeps calling, even though I still don't measure up. He keeps throwing the line out into the water. He keeps pulling me to shore, even though I keep floundering, just like Peter.

Jesus keeps putting his hooks in us, calling us, beckoning you and me to follow him. It's his call on our lives that really counts. Quit checking out or putting up the sign that reads, "Gone fishing. Be back later—maybe." Quit commending and condemning yourself, and quit comparing yourself with others. Listen to the voice of Jesus. Jesus calls to you now: "You must follow me."

BESTSELLER
John 21:24-25

This is the disciple who testifies to these things and who wrote them down. We know that his testimony is true. Jesus did many other things as well. If every one of them were written down, I suppose that even the whole world would not have room for the books that would be written.[7] (Jn 21:24-25)

Some write books for a living. Others live lives of whom others write. Jesus never wrote a book, but he lived such a life that no matter how many books would be written about him and his deeds, there would never be enough. There would not be enough room in bookstores and libraries for them all.

He's like a *New York Times* perennial bestseller, the subject of endless fascination and debate. There are books like *Jesus Through the Centuries*, *The Politics of Jesus*, *Jesus: God and Man*, *The Challenge of Jesus* and *The Life of Jesus*. There is the Jesus Seminar and there are blogs with names like Jesus Creed. There are blockbuster movies like *Jesus of Nazareth*, *The Lion, the Witch and the Wardrobe*, *The Da Vinci Code* and *Jesus Christ Superstar*. Billions of people are enamored with Jesus and the tales, myths and legends surrounding him. Why? What is it about Jesus?

I think the answer to this question lies in the fact that Jesus was *and is* larger than life. No matter which angle you come at him from, you can never gain mastery of him as your subject matter. How can you, when he is the Word of life (Jn 1:1-4)? As the Word of *life*, he's inexhaustible. As the *Word* of life, he's the ultimate expression of life. The realization that Jesus is the Word of life should keep us from the grand illusion that we'll ever gain mastery of him. Our real aim in reading and writing about Jesus should be for him to gain mastery of us.

That's how it was with John, the author of this Gospel (Jn 21:24). Jesus had gained mastery of him and his imagination—so much so that everything else paled in comparison, including John's family and profession. John himself had a typically meaningful life before Jesus showed up on the scene. By all accounts, he and his brother James were heirs to the family fishing business. Jesus called John, James and other disciples like Andrew and Peter away from their families and livelihoods like fishing to follow after him and fish for people. This offer was so appealing to John and James that they dropped their nets in the boat, left their father and the hired men and followed Jesus (Mk 1:16-20). I would assume that Jesus had had previous encounters with John, James and the others.

Those encounters must have made deep impressions on them; otherwise, they wouldn't have responded in this manner.

Sometimes those who make radical decisions like this later regret saying goodbye to their previous lives. But it doesn't appear that John lived with regret for having followed Jesus to the end. Conservative accounts of the Gospel of John claim that John wrote his Gospel toward the close of the first century A.D. Given the hardships he and his fellow followers endured, it would be understandable if John, at his age, were to look back with a sense of disillusionment and despair at having followed Jesus since he was a young man. For example, Peter, who with Jesus is the focus of much of John 21, likely died in the early 60s—crucified upside down in Rome under Nero. John's brother James was martyred soon after the first church was founded (Acts 12:2). It is likely that all the other apostles were gone, leaving John as the only remaining apostle.

John did not lead a charmed life—the exact opposite of some founding leaders of ministries, who entered the ministry to do good and ended up doing quite well, as Joe Aldrich liked to say of some. Many conservative accounts also claim that John wrote the book of Revelation as well. In the book of Revelation, we are told that John was imprisoned in exile on the island of Patmos as an elderly man. Here's what he says: "I, John, your brother and companion in the suffering and kingdom and patient endurance that are ours in Jesus, was on the island of Patmos because of the word of God and the testimony of Jesus" (Rev 1:9).

It would have been so easy for John, as an elderly man with this set of experiences, to wonder how life might have been if he had never dropped those nets to follow Jesus. But then again, we're not accounting for all his experiences. Another work attributed to John, 1 John (also likely written in his later years), opens with words of wonderment about the Word of life:

> That which was from the beginning, which we have heard, which we have seen with our eyes, which we have looked at and our hands have touched—this we proclaim concerning the Word of life. The life appeared; we have seen it and testify to it, and we proclaim to you the eternal life, which was with the Father and has appeared to us. We proclaim to you what we have seen and heard, so that you also may have fellowship with us. And our fellowship is with the

Father and with his Son, Jesus Christ. We write this to make our joy complete. (1 Jn 1:1-4)

The way in which John speaks here, with all of his sensible images, leaves me thinking that John's numerous hardships in life couldn't compare with the love and joy and purpose he found in Jesus. No wonder John's description of Jesus' story begins and ends with first-person testimony (Jn 1:14, 16; 21:24-25).[8] Not satisfied with simply reporting truth about Jesus, though this is important to him (as emphasized here in Jn 21:24),[9] John is so enamored with Jesus that he can't help but move from objective reporting to personal engagement, longing for us to join him in tasting and seeing that Jesus is good.[10] Far from being disillusioned, John is taken by the fullness of Jesus' grace and truth and so confesses that the whole world would not include sufficient space to contain all the things that could be written about Jesus. John's sense of wonder before Jesus in the midst of his sufferings is beautiful to me. And I think it was strikingly beautiful to many of John's first readers, making his works the equivalents of *New York Times* perennial bestsellers.[11]

We have got to understand that it's not John's creative genius or raw passion that ultimately makes his works great. It's John's subject matter, and how he allows his subject to flow freely through his pen to parchment. Wise move, John, given who your subject was—and is.

Some of us may have one or two or three experiences in life worth recounting for others. But Jesus' whole life was like a highlight reel film—even his mundane activities. John chose just some of the highlights to share with us. And what were some of these highlights? Turning water into wine and feeding five thousand plus, tutoring the scholar Nicodemus in his afterschool program, reaching out to the despised Samaritan woman at the well, healing lame and blind men, forgiving an adulterous woman and the denying Peter, raising Lazarus from the dead, dying for the sins of the world and rising from the dead. Not bad. Not bad at all for a life's work.

But there's more. It's not just what Jesus did. It's how he did it and why he did it. All of these aspects bear witness to who he was and is. Jesus did everything out of compassion birthed in divine love, even when he was judging sin. As Jesus says in John 3:16-17: "For God so loved the world that he gave his one and only Son, that whoever believes in him shall not perish but have eternal life. For God did not send his Son into the world to condemn the world, but to save the world through him." Such compassion turns a "son of thunder," as John was nicknamed, into a beloved disciple and an apostle of love.

The reason that Jesus is the ultimate bestselling life is because he gave all of himself freely, radically, sacrificially, lovingly. It's not his unsurpassable wisdom and all-powerful acts as the Word who created this mysterious universe that make Jesus incomparable. It's that he's the infinite Word made flesh and blood, poured out for you and me in holy love. As a wise sage once said, "People don't care how much we know until they know how much we care."[12]

Jesus knew a lot—he knew everything. And he could do anything too. But it was his all-wise and all-powerful care that makes us want to know him. And unlike other historical personages, you *can* really know him. You don't have to settle for secondhand accounts found in libraries and bookstores. For Jesus is not dead, but alive; God's love raised Jesus from the dead. And so he lives *for you* forevermore. Through faith in God's Word disclosed in John's Gospel through the Spirit, you can know Jesus, really know him, and your life can become a book in which his love is written on your heart—a new bestseller.

A FINAL WORD ABOUT GOD'S WORD MADE FLESH—BLOWN AWAY

Have you ever blown it? I mean *really* blown it? Think back to that U2 song "When Love Comes to Town": have you ever left a woman standing in her wedding gown? (Or going beyond the song, were you ever unfaithful to your husband or wife or a close friend?) And have you ever rolled the dice for Jesus' clothes—not pursuing him, not loving him, not caring for him, only taking from him and using him? Perhaps you feel like you have even torn into Jesus' hands with nails and his side with a spear. Even so, have you ever sensed that God has given you a second chance, and have you ever been blown away by the gracious truth of God's undying love revealed in his Word made flesh?

I blew it big time. I had been raised in a strong Christian home. But during my high school days, I became disillusioned with the church and "churchianity." I was looking for something radical and found a kindred spirit in none other than Jim Morrison, lead singer of the rock group The Doors. I immersed myself in Morrison's life and lyrics. Like him, I wanted to break on through to the other side. Well, I got my chance in the autumn of 1982, the year I graduated from high school. Some friends and I were on our way to a ZZ Top concert. I had told another friend beforehand that I would not be coming home that evening, that this would be the end. By the time the concert started, I was gone—blown away by alcohol and drugs. The next thing I remember was waking up in the early morning hours in an emergency room of a hospital with tubes in my arms, looking up into my parents' and young brother's faces. The deeply sorrowful looks on their faces broke my hard heart, a heart that had enjoyed causing them pain. I realized how lost I was, and how badly I had blown my life. God was giving me another chance, and I was determined to take it and make the most of it. Looking back, it was as if I had died and had been raised again to new life—blown away by the power of Jesus' resurrecting grace and love.

As previously noted, Peter had also blown it—big time. Peter had been a big talker, filled with spiritual bravado. He had claimed that he would follow Jesus to the end, no matter what happened, no matter if all the others abandoned Jesus. That was before Peter denied Jesus three times. Just think of the sorrowful look on Jesus' face when he turned to look at Peter after Peter denied him the third time. It broke Peter's heart.

And even though a few days later Peter finds out the amazingly good news that Jesus has risen from the dead, he believes that Jesus' call on his life is over. And so Peter goes fishing for fish, not people. But then Jesus appears to him again. While Peter and his friends are out fishing, Jesus appears and calls out to them from the shore. When they realize it is the Lord, Peter puts on his clothes, dives into the water and swims to shore. When he and the others arrive on shore, they find that the Lord has prepared a meal for them. After the meal, Jesus takes Peter aside to talk to him (Jn 21:15-19).

The Lord asks Peter three times: "Do you love me?" The whole point of asking him three times is not lost on Peter—he had denied the Lord three times. But the Lord is not reminding him in order to push Peter down, but in order to lift him up—to call him back again. It's as if the Lord is saying, "Well then, since you really do love me, stop fishing for fish and start feeding my sheep." Indeed, the Lord does say, "Feed my sheep" (Jn 21:17)! Peter realizes then and there the amazing news that Jesus' resurrection means that Jesus has blown away the failures of Peter's life, making it possible for him to live anew and follow him.

Jesus does the same with each of us. Just as his grace and love for us drove him to the cross, so, too, his grace and love for us raised him from the dead. And if he had not been raised from the dead, we would still be dead in our sins, as Paul says (1 Cor 15:17). Jesus can give those of us who have blown it—no matter what we have done or left undone—new and renewed life because he has been raised to new life.

I don't know about you, but Peter's story is my story too. Even though I had been raised to new life after that hospital room nightmare, I still thought that I was out of commission. Several months later, though, God spoke to me at a friend's wake. I still remember the wake of my best friend from childhood as if it were yesterday. My friend had been out partying with the gang (I might have been with them that night had the hospital room resurrection not occurred). They had climbed up a water tower to spray-paint graffiti on it. On their way down, my friend slipped and fell, breaking his neck as he fell to the ground. He died on the way to the hospital. When I arrived at the wake, I could hear his mother weeping and wailing. They should have closed the casket, for his head and neck were so bloated. My old friends were talking to themselves about going out that night and partying, getting blown on alcohol and drugs, for that is the way he would have wanted it. I realized at that time the significance of Jesus' words: "The thief comes only to steal and kill and destroy; I have come that they may have life, and have it to the full" (Jn 10:10). God burdened my heart to reach lost people right then and there. Even my friend's mother asked me at the wake if I was going to enter "the ministry." I had never even entertained the thought. In fact, I said no at the time. But that is where I would go, burdened by the needs of the lost and broken like my friends. Not only did God give me a second lease on life; God gave me a renewed sense of purpose, just like he had done with Peter. And he'll do the same with each of us.

Now perhaps some of you have never really blown it, but life has blown up in your faces. Mary Magdalene had blown it, and her life has also blown up in her face. Mary Magdalene's life has blown up in her face with Jesus' death. Jesus was the first man to treat her like a woman and not a plaything. Mary had been a prostitute and demon-possessed. I believe she's the lady of the night who washes Jesus' feet with her tears in another Gospel account. But now all that is gone. The only man who treated her as special, as someone created in the image of God, is gone.

At least she could go to the place where he lay. But when she gets there, she finds that the stone has been rolled away and the body is gone. Not only is he dead, but they have taken his body away. There is nothing to hold on to. Her life has blown up in her face with the loss of this profound love. She is so afraid, so all alone (Jn 20:11-18).

As with Peter, the resurrected Jesus asks Mary some questions: "'Woman,' he said, 'why are you crying? Who is it you are looking for?'" (Jn 20:15). Thinking that he is the gardener, she asks him about the body. Then the Lord calls her by name: "Mary." At this point she realizes it is the Lord and cries out, "'Rabboni!' (which means Teacher)" (Jn 20:16). No doubt she holds on tightly to him, never intending to let him go again. But Jesus lifts her up and sends her to tell the others the good news that he is risen from the dead. Notice how he elevates her. She's the first to see the empty tomb and the first to see the risen Lord. Jesus sends Mary Magdalene to go tell the apostles that he is alive: "Go . . . to my brothers and tell them, 'I am returning to my Father and your Father, to my God and your God'" (Jn 20:17). Once again, Jesus affirms Mary's dignity, takes away her fears and fills her heart with God's pure love for her. Jesus assures Mary that through his death, resurrection and ascension, he is making a way home for her and his other followers. She now has a place in his Father's house and will no longer have to walk the streets. Jesus' Father is now her Father, and his God is now her God; she is his precious child.

Bridgetown Ministries in Portland, Oregon, ministers to people on society's fringe—washing the feet of homeless people, cutting their hair and giving them food. They also give roses to dancers going into the downtown clubs and to the prostitutes on the streets. Girls in junior high school go up to these women and hand them each a red rose. The rose indicates that they are still women, created and loved by God. The girls tell these women: "Here's a red rose just for you. Just as this rose is beautiful, the Lord sees you as beautiful too." These women, like Mary Magdalene, have been looking for love in all the wrong places, or have been forced to do so or have had their lives blow up in their faces. They can see in this rose a God who loves them.

What about those of you who, like Mary and Martha who lost their brother Lazarus in John 11, have lost loved ones in the Lord? Or what about those of you who are dying or those who fear death and lost love?

Paul tells us that we will see our lost loved ones in the Lord again. He writes that we do not grieve the way the world does, because just as God raised Jesus, so too he will raise our lost loved ones in Jesus with us to be with him forever (1 Thess 4:13-18). They are in Jesus' presence now, and will be raised together with us—and all because Jesus has risen from the dead. Though some of you may be near the end of your lives, with bodies breaking down, know that Jesus in whom you hope will raise you to new life, just as he raised Lazarus and just as he himself broke through death to be raised to new life. He is "the resurrection and the life" (Jn 11:25). As the old Gaither tune goes, "Because Christ lives, I can face tomorrow. Because he lives, all fear is gone. Because I know he holds the future, life is worth the living just because he lives." Death no longer has a victory, and the grave has no real sting (1 Cor 15:55). For Jesus has blown them both away and will resurrect our lives as he blows away feared death and lost love and as he and his Father welcome us home, wrapping us in their embrace.

Perhaps you haven't ever really blown it or had life blow up in your face. Perhaps, though, you have sought to blow Jesus off or blow him away. Nicodemus no doubt tried to blow off his evening encounter with Jesus (Jn 3:1-21). But the wind of the Spirit was blowing in his direction ever since, and he could not resist truth's gale-like wind force for long. So, later in John's Gospel, he is willing to identify with Jesus and stand up to his peers who are accusing Jesus unfairly, because he now loves the praise of God more than he loved the praises of people (Jn 7:50-52; see also Jn 2:24-3:1; 5:41-44). Nicodemus even goes to Pilate with Joseph of Arimathea to ask for Jesus' body to bury him (Jn 19:38-42). Jesus has so rocked this old Pharisee's world and given him new life that he is willing to face persecution—perhaps even death—by identifying with Jesus even after he is dead and gone. The harder the heart, the more striking the crack when that heart begins to break.

That's the way it is with Saul too—another Pharisee. John does not mention Saul, but many other books of the New Testament do. As John says in John 21, the whole world could not contain all that Jesus did during his time on earth. Jesus has done and has said a lot more than what can be found in John's Gospel. Consider the story of Jesus revealing himself to Saul, the hard-hearted Pharisee, as reported in the Acts of the Apostles.

Saul sees himself as strong and looks at Jesus and his followers as weak and wicked. Saul despises Jesus and his followers because the Old Testament says that anyone who is hung on a tree is cursed (Deut 21:23; Gal 3:13). No way could the Christian claim that Jesus was the Jewish Messiah be true. Jesus had hung on a tree—the cross. He was cursed, unrighteous and weak. Saul's "God" is blessed, righteous and strong. So, too, is Saul. And so Saul makes it his business to go Easter egg hunting—hunting down these "poached egg" followers of Jesus to imprison and put them to death (Acts 9:1-9). He even stands guard over the cloaks of those who stone Stephen, the first martyr of the church (Acts 7:57-58).

Saul has a false sense of security. He trusts in his own righteousness and in a high and mighty God. Saul cannot stomach Jesus or his followers because of the cross. Saul is not content with blowing Jesus off. He has to blow Jesus and his followers away.

But now Jesus blows Saul away. He does it not to curse him but to break Saul and make him his own. Jesus humbles Saul, blinds his eyes and forces him to depend upon others for a change. How helpless he is. As with Peter and Mary, here Jesus questions Saul: "Saul, Saul, why do you persecute me?" (Acts 9:4) Paul responds with a question: "Who are you, Lord?" The answer hits him in the heart and right between the eyes: "'I am Jesus, whom you are persecuting,' he replied. 'Now get up and go into the city, and you will be told what you must do'" (Acts 9:5-6). Jesus blows away Saul's false security to make Saul secure in relationship with him. Saul will never be the same again, now that he has met the risen Jesus face to face. And so he says in Galatians 2:20, "I have been crucified with Christ and I no longer live, but Christ lives in me. The life I live in the body, I live by faith in the Son of God, who loved me and gave himself for me."

Saul has been so strong, so righteous, so secure in himself. Jesus removes all the hate and hardness of heart that has held Saul back from coming to Jesus. He replaces that hate with holy love. Saul crumbles and falls, rising again as Paul—a new creature in Christ Jesus.

At a benefit dinner for New Wine, New Wineskins, Donald Miller shared the story of a radio show host named Joel, who made it his life's ambition to ridicule Christians on the air. Unfortunately, Don didn't know this before he agreed to do the show. Don watched in horror as Joel turned the tables on a Christian kid named Kyle, who had written a book about Christianity and politics. Kyle broke down in tears on the air. At the commercial break, Joel turned toward Don and said, "You're next." Don said that he wanted to tell Joel that he wasn't Don Miller, the author of *Blue Like Jazz*, but Don Miller, author of a cookbook on tips for barbecuing. But that wouldn't fly. Well, the show was back on the air, and Joel started out by demanding that Don defend Christianity to him. Don said, "I can't defend Christianity to you, Joel, because I have no idea what that means to people when they hear it." Then Joel said, "Well then, tell me about Jesus." Don replied, "I don't know that I can defend him, but I can tell you that I love him. Joel, you'll never understand Christianity until you understand that this Creator of the universe loves Joel. Jesus loves Joel." Joel's eyes started to well up with tears as Don said these words. Live on the air, Joel asked Don if he could take Don out for dinner (rather than trying to eat him for dinner). Over dinner, Joel explained how he had been in love with a woman who had broken off their relationship because of God's call on her life. As a result, Joel became bitter toward God. And then and there over dinner, God's love was breaking through that hardness and bitterness, just like Jesus had broken through to Saul's heart, setting him free of his false security and self-righteous pride.

Do you know what Joel knows now? Do you know that Jesus loves you, really loves you? Do you know that his love that conquered the grave can conquer the pain and the hardness of your own heart? Do you know that he is alive, that he is here with you now by his Spirit, that he is returning, that God the Father revealed in Jesus loves you too and that he wants to have a relationship with you through his Son? While many will blow him off because of hardness of heart and love of human glory, don't settle for their fifteen minutes of fame. God's glorious love is coming your way. Now you can be the disciple whom Jesus loves. This is your story—the day love comes to your heart's doorstep, the day love comes to town.

AFTERWORD

I'm Paul Metzger's pastor at Imago Dei Community in Portland, Oregon. He approached me to write an afterword for this book because he sees in my preaching what he has envisioned for the Resonate series: biblical, theological, cultural and personal engagement of the Scriptures. That's certainly what I see in Paul and his writing, so I was happy to add my voice.

The Gospel of John is, to be honest, a most bizarre story—almost fantastical at points. God taking on flesh and blood, redefining life and glory, rescuing the world from death by dying. It's a bit much, honestly. And it begs the question: how are we to respond?

The appropriate response to instruction is different than revelation. Instruction is all about gaining information and skills; the appropriate response is to put this new information, these new skills, into play in the game of life. Revelation, on the other hand—particularly the type of revelation in John's Gospel—requires a different response. Revelation shakes core beliefs, changes how we see the world and catches us up into what may feel like a mythical reality: being related with the Creator God who is Jesus.

The claim that Jesus is making on us is not one of myth to take or leave but one of truth that is functioning as the metanarrative for all of life and creation—not a story among stories but *the* story, which becomes the context by which all other stories are understood, interpreted through and evaluated by, including our own story. *This* is our appropriate response to revelation.

The divine revelation of Jesus Christ in the Gospel of John lays claims that can't be reduced to instruction about morality or spirituality; instead it asks for an active response to a relationship offered. If we hear it with fresh ears, as we just have in Paul's book, we should be woken up. Many of us who have stumbled into church or faith and wondered if this was all there is are invited to hope again. Religious instruction is *not* all there is. The message of John's Gospel causes something to come into being, something that perhaps was not there before. That something is *faith*.

Here we are at the end of John's Gospel revealing in us and to us Jesus Christ, Creator and Lord. And what is the dominant force of this metanarrative? It is without a doubt the love of God. After hearing this firsthand witness of the beloved disciple, John, we are struck with this question: what is to be our response?

The response John calls us to is most clearly to *believe* and to *be loved*.

Belief goes beyond acknowledgment to the core of our view of the world. The belief called for in John's Gospel is a transforming and sending belief, taking us out of the chaos of our personal cosmos—suffering under decay without God—and sending us to the center of God's world, created, sustained and redeemed by the Creator Jesus. So *believe*. Believe that your personal world is not private or hidden but is factored into the grand story of God's world. Your story comes with significance and meaning. Jesus takes all of it into account here in John's Gospel. You can let go of all that weighs you down under the godless burden of individualism. It's God's world. He's got it. The pain, dissapointment, joys and hope—lots of hope—it's all his.

Out of this belief life springs forth like new shoots coming out from the garden. It's God's life in us: eternal, Spirit-birthed, abundant. You need to look for it, anticipate it, pay attention to it and cultivate it. God's life is there in you, the gift of resurrection in the midst of faith. Believe Jesus.

Believe, the beloved disciple tells us, and *be loved*. Painting a picture of Jesus more glorious than a Rembrandt, John shows us what love is in Jesus: the servanthood of love, the sacrifice of love, the eternal, risen witness of love that we are invited to drink deeply from. The well is deeper than you can consume.

Being loved is often the first thing that many disciples forget as they begin following Jesus. John clearly didn't want you to do that. Perhaps that is why we are left near the end with the restoration of Peter, to remind us that it is never too late to love again.

John may not understand our present predicament: so many work so hard at religion or irreligion, all because they fail to be loved by Jesus. The church stands often reeling under the burden of the elder brother in Jesus' parable of the prodigal son—morality absent relationship; meanwhile the world stands reeling under the burden of trying to fill up their hungry lives with physical sensuality.

In both cases what is starving are hearts that were made for the love of God. Morality-based religion and sensual immorality will never satisfy because they miss the mark—they miss the heart.

John knew this. The beloved disciple was shaped by the all-satisfying love of Jesus. He knew what it was to be loved. My friend Paul writes insightfully about this notion of belovedness in John's Gospel:

> I suppose if you had asked John . . . before the cross and after the cross what Jesus meant to him, you would have gotten completely different answers. John may have actually wept on both occasions, given that he sensed that he was so dearly loved by Jesus. But only after the cross did John realize how costly Jesus' obedient love to the Father and obedience-inspiring love for him truly were. A costly love leads, in turn, to a costly love.

That God loves us is not necessarily new information, Paul recognizes; but the degree, the depth, the *cost* of God's love is new to us every morning. It's not deduced or discovered; it's revealed, and it demands a response. John, Jesus' beloved disciple, calls on you and me today to respond to this revelation, to believe and be loved; for we are the beloved of Jesus.

Rick McKinley
Cannon Beach, Oregon
July 2010

NOTES

Introduction

[1]In speaking of God's love revealed in Jesus in this way, I have in mind the likely Old Testament backdrop to this expression—Ex 33–34. This passage also serves as a backdrop to Jn 1:14-18 as a whole. In Ex 33, Moses begs the Lord God (Yahweh) to reveal his glory to him (Ex 33:18). In response to Moses' petition to the Lord God to reveal his *glory*, the Lord tells Moses that he will reveal his *goodness* to him and will proclaim his name in his presence. He also tells Moses that he will have mercy on whom he will have mercy and compassion on whom he will have compassion. He then adds that Moses cannot see his face but only his back; for no one can see the Lord God's face and live (Ex 33:19-20). Only Jesus has seen God face to face. As the one and only, who is in the bosom of the Father, the Word incarnate has exegeted him—*exāgāsato*, from which we get our word "exegete" (Jn 1:18). He is the enfleshed, name-bearing, name-sharing Son of God, who is the great I AM (see also Jn 8:58). Later, in the same Old Testament passage noted here, when the Lord God reveals his glory to Moses at the writing on the new stone tablets, the Lord God tells Moses that he is compassionate and gracious, slow to anger and abounding in love and faithfulness. This God maintains love to multitudes and forgives our wickedness and rebellion and sin, while not allowing the guilty to go unpunished (Ex 34:1-7). Greater than the glorious goodness, greater than the gracious and truthful word of the law given to Moses, Jesus as the living Word incarnate reveals the fullness of God's glorious goodness, his gracious and truthful love. This is what I have in mind when speaking of Jesus revealing God's love as steadfast and true. A. T. Hanson also sees this expression "full of grace and truth" hearkening back to Ex 33–34. See Hanson, *Grace and Truth: A Study in the Doctrine of the Incarnation* (London: SPCK, 1975), p. 5.

[2]See Robert H. Gundry's and D. A. Carson's discussions of authorship in their respective works: Gundry, *A Survey of the New Testament*, 3rd ed. (Grand Rapids: Zondervan, 1994), pp. 252-54; Carson, *The Gospel According to John* (Grand Rapids: Eerdmans, 1991), pp. 68-81.

[3]See the following discussions: Gundry, *A Survey of the New Testament*, pp. 252-254, 292; Carson, *Gospel According to John*, pp. 82-87.

[4]Such confirmation of the faith also assists Christ-followers in their apologetic and evangelistic witness as they share and invite people to respond in faith to Jesus. For different

perspectives on the purpose of John's Gospel, see Carson's consideration of various perspectives on the purpose of John's Gospel in Carson, *Gospel According to John*, pp. 87-95. See also Stephen S. Kim's treatment of various works and options concerning purpose in Kim, *The Miracles of Jesus in the Gospel of John* (Eugene, Ore.: Wipf & Stock, 2010), n. 42 on pp. 19-21. Carson sees John's purpose as being evangelistic, whereas Kim sees it as largely edificatory. In contrast to Carson, Kim points out that the farewell discourse of chaps. 14–16 is directed to the disciples, and so would not be evangelistic in its thrust. I agree with Kim's assessment that the farewell discourse suggests that John would be writing for believers here. But I also maintain that Jn 20:30-31 involves the evangelistic as well as edificatory purpose as primary. Thus, I see John's purpose being twofold. While sharing Carson's and Kim's concern to distinguish between purpose and plausible effect, I believe the purpose includes both elements as primary: evangelistic and edificatory. For consideration of these and other features, look to other recent discussions on John's Gospel: Andreas J. Köstenberger, *Encountering John: The Gospel in Historical, Literary, and Theological Perspective*, Encountering Biblical Studies (Grand Rapids: Baker, 1999); Köstenberger, *John*, Baker Exegetical Commentary on the New Testament (Grand Rapids: Baker Academic, 2004); Stephen S. Smalley, *John: Evangelist & Interpreter*, 2nd ed., New Testament Profiles (Downers Grove, Ill.: InterVarsity Press, 1998); and Marianne M. Thompson, "John, Gospel of," in *Dictionary of Jesus and the Gospels*, ed. Joel B. Green, Scot McKnight and I. Howard Marshall (Downers Grove, Ill.: InterVarsity Press, 1992), pp. 368-83.

[5]See D. A. Carson's discussion in his Matthew commentary. Carson, "Matthew," in *Matthew, Mark, Luke*, The Expositor's Bible Commentary 8 (Grand Rapids: Zondervan, 1984), pp. 38-39.

[6]It is worth mentioning the uniqueness of John as a Gospel in relation to the other three canonical Gospels: Matthew, Mark and Luke. While some argue that John was unfamiliar with the Synoptic Gospels, I find that hard to believe given the close connections within the apostolic community. I believe John chose the material he did to supplement the Synoptic Gospels (Matthew, Mark and Luke) and also to present miraculous signs of Jesus in conjunction with his teachings so that people would believe and have eternal life through Jesus' name, and for believers to grow in their faith. So what are some of these distinctive features, when compared with the Synoptic Gospels? The reader does not find the extensive use of parables or pronounced discussion of the kingdom of God in John's Gospel, in contradistinction to the Synoptics. John presents the kingdom and eschatology and eternal life more in vertical terms, whereas the Synoptics present the kingdom and eschatology and eternal life more in horizontal terms. George Ladd puts it this way: "While eternal life is eschatological, the central emphasis of the Fourth Gospel is not to show people the way of life in the Age to Come but to bring to them a present experience of this future life." George Eldon Ladd, *A Theology of the New Testament*, ed. Donald A. Hagner, rev. ed. (Grand Rapids: Eerdmans, 1993), p. 293.

The kingdom of God is present in and through the person of Jesus in the Spirit, and we participate in that kingdom or eternal life through faith in Jesus, which is the work of the Spirit: "No one can enter the kingdom of God unless he is born of water and the

Spirit" (Jn 3:5); "For God so loved the world that he gave his one and only Son, that whoever believes in him shall not perish but have eternal life" (Jn 3:16). Also, John presents Jesus' deity more overtly and directly from the outset, whereas the Synoptics present Jesus' deity more gradually and indirectly through the historical story line of the unfolding of the kingdom. Having said that, there is one vital sense in which John presents Jesus' deity indirectly, and that is through his attention to the veil of creaturely flesh: Jesus tabernacles with us in the flesh, and it is through this indirect means along with the cross that his glory is revealed (Jn 1:14; 3:14; 12:23-25, 32-33). This particular emphasis on cruciform or upside-down glory also illustrates John's pronounced use of irony: Jesus' glory is revealed ultimately through the cross. Let's sum up these emphases in John's Gospel noted to this point: as God's Son descends and enters into this world and ascends by way of the cross in glory, and as the Spirit descends upon us and transforms us from the inside out, we are born again or from above to eternal life and enter the kingdom of God presently. Moving on, John reveals that Jesus' public ministry is actually much longer than what one would gather from simply reading the Synoptics. Whereas the Synoptic Gospels only refer to the Passover when Jesus died, John refers to three Passover celebrations, possibly even four, and sets forth Jesus as the fulfillment of the Scriptures not so much through quotations of biblical prophecy and related material but through Old Testament feasts, significant types and key figures. Based on John's Gospel, it is likely the case that Jesus' public ministry lasted three to three and one-half years. Along with this point on the Passover, John gives greater attention to Jesus' Judean ministry, while the Synoptics give greater consideration to Jesus' Galilean ministry.

For further discussion on similarities and differences between John and the Synoptics, see the following: Gundry, *A Survey of the New Testament*, p. 254; A. T. Robinson, *A Harmony of the Gospels* (New York: Harper & Row, 1950), pp. 267-70; Ladd, *A Theology of the New Testament*, p. 344. Beyond items noted in many introductions, John also presents trinitarian, affective and participational themes in a way that are not developed in the Synoptics. John's Gospel does not include a detailed discussion of the Last Supper (only the events surrounding it; see Jn 13), but Jn 6 reflects consideration of Jesus as the Pascal Lamb through whom we find life as we partake of him—his flesh and blood—through faith in him. John 17, sometimes referred to as the true Lord's Prayer—along with the farewell discourse (Jn 14–16), presents our relation to Jesus in his communion with the Father in the Spirit in intimate, interpersonal and participational language. The emphasis by N. T. Wright and others on the political nature of Jesus' kingdom purposes, bound up with Jesus being the fulfillment or replacement of the old as developed in relation to the Synoptics, requires supplementation in light of John's Gospel, in which allegiance to Jesus involves loving his glory and praise rather than that of humans. John's political agenda and covenantal framework is grounded in an alignment of our hearts with Jesus' heart. John calls us to participate in the politics of Jesus' cruciform love that confronts, overturns and replaces the false glory of humanity and that replaces and fulfills God's purposes for Israel (see the "Fifteen Minutes of Fame and the Hour of Glory" essay in this volume). Concerning the point on N. T. Wright, see, for example, his chapter "The Challenge of the Symbols," in *The Challenge of Jesus: Redis-*

covering Who Jesus Was and Is (Downers Grove, Ill.: InterVarsity Press, 1999), pp. 54-73.

[7]Note that Raymond E. Brown develops the "Book of Signs" and "Book of Glory" structure and C. H. Dodd develops the "Book of Signs" and "Book of the Passion" outline in their respective commentaries on John's Gospel: Brown, *The Gospel According to John (I-XII): Introduction, Translation, and Notes*, The Anchor Bible 29 (New York: Doubleday, 1966), pp. cxxxviii-cxxxix; C. H. Dodd, *The Interpretation of the Fourth Gospel* (Cambridge: Cambridge University Press, 1953), p. 289. See Carson's critique of this general approach in his own commentary, *The Gospel According to John*, pp. 103-4.

[8]Whenever I sense that John uses "the Jews" in a given passage to convey opposition to Jesus, I have placed quotation marks around the expression to suggest irony. I believe John is not at all anti-Semitic. Rather, he is ironically conveying that his Christian community, not those who seek to centralize Jewish authority and oppose Jesus and exclude the church, is the true inheritor of the Jewish faith and tradition (since Jesus is the fulfillment of the Hebrew Scriptures). See my discussion on this theme in an extended note on Jn 8. I owe my use of quotation marks to Craig S. Keener, who recommends their use to convey John's intended sense of irony. Keener, *The Gospel of John: A Commentary* (Peabody, Mass.: Hendrickson, 2003), pp. 1:227-28.

[9]This "hour" of glory is often translated as "time" in the NIV.

Chapter 1: Incarnation and Reception

[1]*Crash*, directed by Paul Haggis (Santa Monica, Calif.: Lions Gate Films, 2004).

[2]See D. A. Carson, *The Gospel According to John* (Grand Rapids: Eerdmans, 1991), pp. 114-115; and Robert H. Gundry, *A Survey of the New Testament*, 3rd ed. (Grand Rapids: Zondervan, 1994), pp. 262-63.

[3]Václav Havel, "The Power of the Powerless," in *Living in Truth: 22 Essays Published on the Occasion of the Award of the Erasmus Prize to Václav Havel*, ed. Jan Vladislav (London: Faber & Faber, 1986), pp. 42-43.

[4]Both aspects of the darkness's relationship to the light—not understanding and not being able to overcome—are present in John's Gospel. These aspects noted here in the text and footnote to verse 5 in the NIV appear warranted and may reflect John's multifaceted and multilayered approach to working with his material.

[5]John Calvin, *Institutes of the Christian Religion*, ed. John T. McNeill, trans. Ford Lewis Battles (Philadelphia: Westminster Press, 1960), 1:121.

[6]Eugene H. Peterson, *The Message: The Bible in Contemporary Language* (Colorado Springs: NavPress, 2007), p. 209.

[7]The NIV translates the Greek word *anti* in *charin anti charitos* as conveying "one blessing after another." Carson translates the entire phrase of *charin anti charitos* in verse 16 as "grace instead of grace" in keeping with one of the most common renderings of *anti* as "instead of." While the law of Moses is gracious, it is replaced or surpassed by the superlative grace realized in Jesus Christ. See Carson's discussion of this phrase in *Gospel According to John*, pp. 131-34. A form of the word *plerōma* is used here in verse 16 and conveys that there is no limit to Jesus' grace. I like how F. F. Bruce speaks of it: "This

plenitude of divine glory and goodness which resides in Christ (cf. Col 1:19; 2:9) is an ocean from which all his people may draw without ever diminishing its content." F. F. Bruce, *The Gospel of John: Introduction, Exposition and Notes* (Grand Rapids: Eerdmans, 1983), p. 43. I agree with Gerald Borchert that John's use of *plerōma* (the only occurrence of it in his Gospel) "has virtually nothing to do" with the late Gnostic idea of a "thirty-figure" godhead. Gerald L. Borchert, *John 1-11,* The New American Commentary 25A (Nashville: Broadman & Holman, 1996), p. 123. I maintain that the only reference to Gnosticism would be by way of contrast. Moving on, I am wary of seeing John's Gospel as an overriding apologetic against Gnosticism. While he is writing in an age shaped increasingly by Gnostic leanings and may have Gnosticism in mind at points in his Gospel, I believe John's major concern is showing that Jesus replaces and fulfills the revelation given to Moses as God's all-surpassing gracious and truthful love. Certainly, John's affirmation of Jesus' full deity on the one hand and his full humanity on the other hand would challenge Gnostic teachings.

[8]Gail R. O'Day does a wonderful job of succinctly setting forth the Old Testament imagery bound up with Jn 1:14 and the following verses in the prologue. The Word who becomes flesh and blood is the fulfillment of God's promise to dwell with his people (Ezek 37:27). John draws from the same Greek wording that is used to convey God's tabernacling at the tent of meeting with Moses and the people (I am referring here to the Greek translation of the Old Testament—*skēnoō* is the verb and *skēnos* is the noun). The text literally signifies that Jesus "pitched his tent" in our midst. Along with drawing from Old Testament imagery of God as gloriously tabernacling in his people's midst, John also talks of the law and Moses and grace and truth. "'Full of grace and truth' echoes the Hebrew word pair 'steadfast love' and 'truth' (. . . *hesed* . . . and *emet*; e.g., Ex 34:6) that speaks of God's covenantal love and faithfulness." See O'Day, "The Gospel of John: Introduction, Commentary and Reflections," in *Luke-John,* The New Interpreter's Bible 9, ed. Leander E. Keck (Nashville: Abingdon, 1995), pp. 522-23. Glory (*doxa*) is a key theme in John's Gospel and hearkens back to the Old Testament sense of glory as God's "manifest presence" that is now disclosed in Jesus, the Word made flesh. See also Bruce's discussion of the connection here to the phraseology in Ex 34 in *The Gospel of John,* p. 42.

[9]Jesus' relationship to Moses figures prominently in John's Gospel. While affirming Moses and the law, John wishes to convey to the reader that Jesus is the ultimate revelation of God's grace and truth.

[10]Harper Lee, *To Kill a Mockingbird* (1960; reprint, New York: HarperCollins, 1988), p. 33.

Transition

[1]Russian Orthodox theologian Vladimir Lossky states that the early church's formulations regarding Jesus were intended to preserve the teaching of "the possibility of attaining to the fullness of the mystical union" with God in him. For if Jesus is not fully divine and fully human, mystical union with God is lost. Lossky goes so far as to say that all of Eastern theology has as its end consideration and attainment of union with God. Vladi-

mir Lossky, *The Mystical Theology of the Eastern Church* (Crestwood, N.Y.: St. Vladimir's Seminary Press, 1976), pp. 9-10. While the Western church often frames union and communion very differently, theologians like Augustine, Luther and Calvin would share this emphasis on union and communion being more than rational and also more than positional. Union with the Father, Son and Spirit involves interpersonal communion (rather than the union of natures) and mutual indwelling, as John makes clear. For a Reformation text on this subject, see Martin Luther, "The Freedom of a Christian," in *Martin Luther's Basic Theological Writings*, ed. Timothy F. Lull (Minneapolis: Fortress, 1989), pp. 595-629.

[2]See Royce G. Gruenler's study of John's trinitarian framework: *The Trinity in the Gospel of John* (Grand Rapids: Baker, 1986). Craig Blomberg comments that "particularly in his private teaching to the disciples in the farewell discourse, Jesus comes as close as anywhere in the Gospels to the type of Trinitarian theology that would later issue from early Christian creeds and councils." Craig L. Blomberg, *Jesus and the Gospels: An Introduction and Survey* (Nashville: Broadman & Holman, 1997), p. 164.

[3]This promise probably guarantees apostolic truth beyond that which they are able to take in at this time. It is not speaking of the Spirit leading us beyond the apostolic truth of biblical revelation.

[4]It is worth noting here that *faith*, according to John's Gospel, involves more than espousing correct doctrine or theology. This can be illustrated by attention to the idiom *pisteuō eis* ("believe in"). According to George Ladd, *pisteuō eis* is likely a distinctively Christian construction intended "to express the personal relationship of commitment between the believer and Jesus" (George Eldon Ladd, *A Theology of the New Testament*, ed. Donald A. Hagner, rev. ed. [Grand Rapids: Eerdmans, 1993], pp. 307-8). Of course, faith in Jesus does involve belief in intellectual content. As Leon Morris says, "While it is true that the New Testament looks for a vital faith in a living person, it is also true that this is not a blind credulity. Faith has an intellectual content." See Morris's discussion of Jn 14:11 in *The Gospel According to John*, rev. ed., The New International Commentary on the New Testament (Grand Rapids: Eerdmans, 1995), p. 573.

[5]Here in this use of affective language to speak of the triune God relationally, I am drawing from Augustinian categories. Perhaps the only difference is that I do not consider the Spirit to be the bond of love, but the one through whom the bond of love between the Father and Son is eternally joined and nurtured. In my estimation, this best safeguards a framework for conceiving of the Spirit in truly personal terms.

[6]I have not been able to locate the source, but the statement does resonate with Barth's theological orientation.

Chapter 2: Initial Connections

[1]See Leon Morris's discussion of the historical and theological backdrop to the questions posed to John the Baptist concerning *the Christ, Elijah* and *the Prophet*. Among other things, Morris makes clear that *Christ* was not another personal name for Jesus but was technically a title which over time came to be associated with the Messiah—not a great deliverer or anointed one, but the deliverer and anointed one. The Old Testament back-

drop to speculation around Elijah and the Prophet involved such texts as Mal 4:5 and Deut 18:15-19 respectively. The last item to be noted here is Morris's attention to John the Baptist's emphatic rejection of the suggestion that he himself is the Messiah through the use of the emphatic pronoun in Greek. See Leon Morris, *The Gospel According to John*, rev. ed., The New International Commentary on the New Testament (Grand Rapids: Eerdmans, 1995), pp. 117-20.

[2]Unlike the members of the religious establishment in Jerusalem who will oppose Jesus for his claims about his divine identity, John promotes him. As we will see, the power brokers want to preserve their own position and the nation (Jn 11:48), and so will do anything to remove anyone who stands in their way. They fail to realize that Jesus is the hope for the nation—the Paschal Lamb of God who takes away their sin, and not only their sin but also the sin of the world (Jn 1:29). It is worth noting here that John and Jesus' movement is populist in nature. That is, their followers are mostly from outside the centers of power. This point is reflected in people coming out to John in the Judean wilderness to be baptized by him. This is a new work. We don't find John bearing witness at the temple but in the countryside. People would normally expect God's prophetic presence to be found in Jerusalem, as with prophets of old like Ezra and Nehemiah and Nathan who usually addressed kings in court. It is striking that the writer John tells the readers that the Jews of Jerusalem send priests and Levites out to the wilderness to ask John the Baptist who he is, wondering if he is the Christ, Elijah or the prophet (Jn 1:19). For further discussion of the opposition to Jesus that will ensue in Jerusalem—the center of power—and its relation to John the Baptist's ministry, see my essay on Jn 10, "TV Preachers."

[3]The quotation is taken from Henry Bettenson, ed., *Documents of the Christian Church*, 2nd ed. (Oxford: Oxford University Press, 1963), p. 10.

[4]John M. Perkins, *Let Justice Roll Down*, rev. ed. (Ventura, Calif.: Regal Books, 2006).

[5]As George Ladd points out, the Messiah was conceived in first-century times as a "divinely endowed Son of David who would shatter the hated pagan rule and deliver God's people." Ladd, *A Theology of the New Testament*, ed. Donald A. Hagner, rev. ed. (Grand Rapids: Eerdmans, 1993), p. 279. Ladd also notes that John reveals Jesus not to be a political Messiah who delivers God's people from such pagan rule (ibid.); rather, as we see here in this same chapter, the title *Christ* does not exhaust Jesus' ministry. He is the Lamb of God who takes away the sin of the world (Jn 1:29). In addition to being the Christ and the Son of Man (Jn 1:49 and Jn 9:35-37), he is also the Son of God (Jn 1:49, 3:16, 20:30-31). Ladd also reasons that *the Christ* and *the Son of God* are not synonymous (ibid., p. 280). No matter how one unites or distinguishes them, the terms are related in his person; Jesus is the long-expected deliverer and king of Israel (Jn 1:45, 49) and God's Son (Jn 1:49).

[6]D. A. Carson says of these replacement themes that they fulfill Old Testament types: "again and again the typologies the evangelist develops do not *simply* interpret the OT, or *simply* utilise the categories of the OT to explain Jesus and his gospel, but become as well the vehicles by which Jesus and his gospel effectively *replace* those institutions, events and themes that have anticipated him [. . .] If they anticipate him, they point to

him, prophesy of him; and he fulfils them and thus replaces them. This does not mean, for the evangelist, that they are discarded so much as fulfilled: they find their true significance and real continuity in him who is the true vine, the true light, the true temple, the one of whom Moses wrote." D. A. Carson, "John and the Johannine Epistles," in *It Is Written: Scripture Citing Scripture*, ed. D. A. Carson and H. G. M. Williamson (Cambridge: Cambridge University Press, 1988), pp. 255-56.

[7]Other translations speak of "time" as "hour." We will often refer to it as Jesus' "hour" of glory.

[8]See Raymond E. Brown's discussion of messianic fulfillment and the messianic banquet in Brown, *The Gospel According to John (XIII-XXI): Introduction, Translation, and Notes*, The Anchor Bible 29 (New York: Doubleday, 1970), pp. 104-5. See also Leon Morris for his critical discussion of the view that imperfection is associated with the number six, suggesting that Judaism is somehow imperfect and pointing the way forward to Jesus (Morris, *The Gospel According to John*, pp. 160-61).

[9]Andreas Köstenberger, *John*, Baker Exegetical Commentary on the New Testament (Grand Rapids: Baker Academic, 2004); p. 99. Köstenberger also notes that the revelation of Jesus' glory signifies that the messianic age has dawned in his person. The signs have a twofold purpose in John's Gospel: to reveal Jesus' glory and to lead people to faith in Jesus, as in the case of Jesus' disciples shown here.

[10]Köstenberger notes that "first" here (taken from *arche*) can be translated as "primary" (p. 99). Craig S. Keener says that "by explicitly noting this sign as Jesus' 'first' . . . John makes what he says about it paradigmatic for Jesus' signs in general." Keener, *The Gospel of John* (Peabody, Mass.: Hendrickson, 2003), 1:515.

[11]Ladd makes an interesting comparison between the Synoptics and John regarding miracles. The Synoptics present Jesus' miracles to signify the inbreaking of God's reign in history. They are the means by which Jesus "establishes God's reign and defeats the reign of Satan. In John miracles are mighty works that authenticate the person and mission of Jesus and demonstrate the miracle-working presence of God in his words and deeds." Ladd also says that sign (*sēmeia*) "is a mighty work wrought by Jesus that represents the revelatory and redemptive event happening in him" (p. 309). The Synoptics record far more miracles that John. Those recorded in John are the changing of the water into wine (Jn 2), the healing of the royal official's son (Jn 4), the healing of the lame man (Jn 5), the multiplication of food (Jn 6), the walking on water (Jn 6), the healing of the blind man (Jn 9) and the resurrection of Lazarus (Jn 11). While John refers to Jesus performing other miraculous signs (Jn 20:30), these following are the miracles he focuses on, often using the term "signs" in reference to them: Jn 2:11; 4:54; 6:2, 14, 26; 9:16; 11:47; 12:18. Ladd, *A Theology of the New Testament*, p. 309. John's point is to lead people to faith in Jesus based on consideration of these signs (Jn 20:30-31). Ladd also points out that "works" or *erga* are also used to refer to Jesus' miraculous deeds and are related to believing, but these "works" can also be used to refer to Jesus' non-miraculous activity (ibid., pp. 308-9). Gundry maintains that John views "signs" as the "symbols of salvation" and "works" as "the accomplishing of salvation." See Robert H. Gundry, *A Survey of the New Testament*, 3rd ed. (Grand Rapids: Zondervan, 1994), p. 263.

[12]Carson comments that "Jesus' complaint is not that the merchants are guilty of sharp business practices and should therefore reform their ethical life, but that they should not be in the temple area at all. . . . Instead of solemn dignity and the murmur of prayer, there is the bellowing of cattle and the bleating of sheep. Instead of brokenness and contrition, holy adoration and prolonged petition, there is noisy commerce" (Carson, *Gospel According to John*, p. 179). Richard Bauckham claims that Jesus attacks the entire financial order surrounding the sacrificial system. See Bauckham, "Jesus' Demonstration in the Temple," in *Law and Religion: Essays on the Place of the Law in Israel and Early Christianity*, ed. Barnabas Lindars (London: SPCK, 1988), p. 88. This would make the Galilean Jesus a supreme threat to the priestly authorities in Jerusalem, as Carson also notes (p. 179). Craig A. Evans has repudiated E. P. Sanders's claim that Jesus was not cleansing the temple in any manner but was showing prophetically that the temple would be destroyed. See Sanders, *Jesus and Judaism* (Philadelphia: Fortress, 1985), pp. 61-76. See also Evans, "Jesus' Action in the Temple: Cleansing or Portent of Destruction," *Catholic Biblical Quarterly* 51 (1989): 237-70. The threat to the priestly authorities in this passage is twofold. First, Jesus challenges the financial institution of the sacrificial system (Jn 2:16: "How dare you turn my Father's house into a market!"). Second, his body is the ultimate temple, which he has the authority to destroy and raise again. The sign of the resurrection of his body as the ultimate temple is the basis for his authority to cleanse the temple in Jerusalem (Jn 2:18-21). The political challenge to the priestly authorities is significant and foreshadows the growing opposition that will lead to the death and resurrection of Jesus, just as in Jn 2:4 the hour or time (of glory) which has not yet come foreshadows the cross and resurrection. I appreciate N. T. Wright's point on the eschatological and political symbolism of Jesus' actions such as cleansing the temple; it must have been extremely difficult for the religious authorities that this Galilean is speaking and acting so authoritatively, including his personal offering of forgiveness of sins to people apart from their worship at the temple and sacrifice. See N. T. Wright's chapter "The Challenge of the Symbols," in *The Challenge of Jesus* (Downers Grove, Ill.: InterVarsity Press, 1999), pp. 54-73. In my estimation, in John's Gospel—particularly Jn 2—Jesus is challenging the polluting of the temple system through commerce in the temple area *and* foreshadowing the permanent replacement of the temple with himself as the center of worship for the messianic community.

[13]This is the first instance of the Passover celebration in John's Gospel. There are at least two other Passover celebrations mentioned (Jn 6:4; 13:1). It is worth noting that whereas the cleansing of the temple occurs much later in the Synoptic Gospels (Mt 21:12-13; Mk 11:15-19; Lk 19:45-48), it occurs at the outset of Jesus' ministry in John's Gospel. Traditionally, commentators have often framed John's Gospel chronologically by way of the recurring Passover celebrations during Jesus' public ministry. For a traditional reading, see R. H. Lightfoot, *St. John's Gospel: A Commentary*, ed. C. F. Evans (London: Oxford University Press, 1960), p. 148. Beyond issues of chronology and questions surrounding the possibility of two temple cleansings, we should at least take note of the theological significance of John accounting for the cleansing of the temple so early in his Gospel. Together with the final Passover celebration mentioned in chapter 13, it frames Jesus'

entire ministry in terms of his approaching passion. While his hour of passion to take away the world's sins has not yet come, it is coming. Whereas Keener rejects the chronological approach in favor of a theological framing of Jesus' public ministry (going so far as to say that "Jesus' entire public ministry is the Passion Week"), I believe it is possible to reconcile the two approaches. However, such analysis goes beyond the scope of this present volume. See Keener, *The Gospel of John*, pp. 1:518-19. The Passover celebration and the Feast of Unleavened Bread were combined into one eight-day ceremony in New Testament times. The Passover feast signified God's deliverance of Israel from Egypt whereby God judged Egypt by destroying every firstborn male and preserved Israel through its slaughtering of lambs and putting their blood on the doorposts to cover over and protect the firstborn of each Jewish household. The exodus was the foundational event in the history of Israel and is also associated with the giving of water and manna in the wilderness. Other festivals or feasts mentioned in John's Gospel are the Sabbath (See for example Jn 5:1-47; the Sabbath is listed as a festival in Lev 23:1-3), the Feast of Tabernacles (Jn 7:1-8:59, possibly even up to 10:18), and the Feast of Dedication (Jn 10:22-49). For a detailed discussion of the Jewish religious festivals in John's Gospel, see Gail R. O'Day, "John," in *Luke-John, The New Interpreter's Bible 9*, ed. Leander E. Keck (Nashville: Abingdon, 1995), p. 542.

[14]Brian D. McLaren, *A New Kind of Christian: A Tale of Two Friends on a Spiritual Journey* (San Francisco: Jossey-Bass, 2001), p. 130.

[15]Saint Augustine senses pride in Nicodemus and also recognizes the redemptive nature of the Lord's rebuke when he writes, "Do we think that the Lord meant to taunt scornfully this master of the Jews? The Lord knew what He was doing; He wished the man to be born of the Spirit. No man is born of the Spirit if he be not humble, for humility itself makes us to be born of the Spirit; 'for the Lord is nigh to them that are of broken heart.' The man was puffed up with his mastership, and it appeared of some importance to himself that he was a teacher of the Jews. Jesus pulled down his pride, that he might be born of the Spirit." Augustine, *Homilies on the Gospel of John*, in Nicene and Post-Nicene Fathers, vol. 7, ed. Philip Schaff (Peabody, Mass.: Hendrickson, 1888), p. 83. Later, Augustine considers the Old Testament backdrop to this text, and makes a connection between the serpent in the garden, the serpent lifted up in the wilderness on the pole and the Lord's death: "What is the serpent lifted up? The Lord's death on the cross. For as death came by the serpent, it was figured by the image of a serpent. The serpent's bite was deadly, the Lord's death is life-giving" (Augustine, *Homilies on the Gospel of John*, p. 85). Is there not a connection between the serpent's temptation and the man and woman's prideful and deadly looking to the tree in the garden for life rather than to the Word of God for salvation; the people's rebellion in the wilderness and the outbreak of death at the serpent's bite; the looking to the bronze serpent possibly impaled on the pole and the Lord, the Word of life, impaled on the tree to whom all must look to escape death and find life eternal? While we must be on guard against allegorization, typological frames of reference anchored to the text, as in the case of Jn 3 with Jesus' allusion to the bronze serpent lifted up on the pole, are worthy of consideration.

[16]While I am using Johnny Cash iconically in this essay to speak of the rightful approach

to engaging the Christian faith, Rodney Clapp speaks of Cash's iconic significance for understanding and evaluating America's religious and cultural experience. See especially Clapp's discussion of Cash as a Christian in *Johnny Cash and the Great American Contradiction: Christianity and the Battle for the Soul of a Nation* (Louisville: Westminster John Knox, 2008), pp. xvi-xvii, 17-18, 61-62, 98, 140 n. 1, 148 n. 26.

[17]Maureen Cleave, "How Does a Beatle Live? John Lennon Lives Like This," *London Evening Standard*, March 4, 1966.

[18]Leon Morris writes that "from the standpoint of the orthodox Jew there were three strikes against her: she was a Samaritan, a woman, and a sexual sinner" (Morris, *The Gospel According to John*, p. 225). How noteworthy is it that Jesus reaches out to her. He does not allow the culture wars of his day to keep him from building bridges to people's hearts from across the spectrum.

[19]See the website for Living Water International: www.water.cc. See also the Advent Conspiracy website and the book by that title: www.adventconspiracy.org; Rick McKinley, Chris Seay and Greg Holder, *Advent Conspiracy: Can Christmas Still Change the World?* (Grand Rapids: Zondervan, 2009).

[20]Anne Lamott, *Traveling Mercies: Some Thoughts on Faith* (New York: Pantheon Books, 1999), p. 41.

Chapter 3: Reactions and Rejection

[1]God instituted the Sabbath as a festival that Israel was to celebrate. No work was to be done. There were, however, exemptions noted by the rabbis, including the saving of life. Israel's teachers also claimed that God himself was active on the Sabbath, caring for the universe physically and morally. See Gail R. O'Day, "John," in *Luke-John*, The New Interpreter's Bible 9, ed. Leander E. Keck (Nashville: Abingdon, 1995), p. 542.

[2]See Walter Brueggemann's article on this theme of the fear of scarcity and the abundance of God: "The Liturgy of Abundance, the Myth of Scarcity," *The Christian Century*, March 24-31, 1999, 342-47.

[3]See D. A. Carson's discussion of Jn 6:49-66, including his rationale for why many people take offense at Jesus' words: they are more interested in getting free bread; they want to retain authority in their lives; they reject Jesus' claim to be greater than Moses; and they are disgusted by Jesus' imagery over eating his flesh and drinking his blood. Jesus' offensive language to this point is followed by an even greater offense: his ascension through the cross (Jn 3:13-15). Even his truest followers like Peter struggle over this text, while the majority of his disciples abandon him. See Carson, *The Gospel According to John* (Grand Rapids: Eerdmans, 1991), pp. 294-303, especially pp. 300-301.

[4]The word for grumbling or arguing sharply over Jesus, *emachontō*, is a very strong expression, as Carson notes. See ibid., p. 295.

[5]*Disciple* can simply mean someone who follows as a learner or student. It could even entail someone who is simply following along with the crowd after Jesus. There are different kinds or levels of disciples in the Gospels. Other disciples are those who hold to Jesus' teaching as authoritative. Even such disciples as these may not be those who have experienced saving faith in Jesus and committed their entire being to him. Against this

backdrop of variety of meanings, it should come as no surprise here that many disciples abandon Jesus at this point in the narrative; not all followers have an all-encompassing investment in the life and teachings and ways of Jesus like Peter and the rest of the eleven (excluding the twelfth, Judas, the betrayer). See ibid., p. 300.

[6]Given that the Passover and Unleavened Bread festivals were made one in New Testament times, and that they were originally instituted under Moses, we find Jesus' claims here in Jn 6 to be full of maximum symbolic import. Such claims as these would be especially important to John's church members who are Jewish and those Jews he evangelizes. Nonetheless, while John does seek to show that Jesus is the fulfillment of the Hebrew Scriptures, he does not highlight Jewishness to the extent that Matthew does. While he makes profound use of typology to show Jesus to be the fulfillment of the Hebrew Scriptures, I believe John has Jews and Gentiles in mind, especially those Gentiles who are or were converts to Judaism.

[7]For a careful and sustained engagement of John's Christology through the lens of John 6, see Paul N. Anderson's *The Christology of the Fourth Gospel: Its Unity and Disunity in Light of John 6* (Eugene, Ore.: Cascade Publications, 2010).

[8]In the early church during the times of persecution, the church was wrongly accused of such horrors as cannibalism given its practice of the Lord's Supper. See Cyril C. Richardson, ed., *Early Christian Fathers* (Louisville: Westminster John Knox, 2006), p. 293.

[9]The Feast of Tabernacles or Booths originally celebrated the harvest's completion, but in time came to be associated with God's protection of his people Israel while they were in the wilderness. In the New Testament period, the festival was centered around the temple. Temporary shelters would be constructed in the temple court and on Jerusalem's streets. More information can be found on this festival in O'Day, "John," p. 542.

[10]Jesus may very well be alluding to the priests' practice, during the first seven days of the Feast of Tabernacles, of bringing water from the Pool of Siloam in a golden vessel and taking it into the temple to pour it out in a ceremonial manner. On the last and climactic day of the feast, Jesus claims to be the source of true water—the Spirit of life. I believe this is another instance of Jesus being the fulfillment of Old Testament festivals, types, persons and institutions. See Robert Gundry's discussion of this text and the possible allusion to the festival in *A Survey of the New Testament*, 3rd ed. (Grand Rapids: Zondervan, 1994), p. 276.

[11]The claim that this crowd who believes is blessed and these religious leaders who reject Jesus are cursed is based on John's Gospel's claim that those who believe receive eternal life and those who do not believe are condemned. See Jn 3:16-21, which closes out Jesus' discussion with Nicodemus in Jn 3.

[12]Gundry argues that Jn 8:1-11 does not belong here or elsewhere in the New Testament, for it does not appear in the earliest and most accurate New Testament manuscripts. Nonetheless, he also states that it may be a historically truthful account and part of the church's historical tradition prior to its inclusion in the canon at a later time. See Gundry, *Survey of the New Testament*, 4th ed. (Grand Rapids: Zondervan, 2003), p. 276. While agreeing with Gundry, including his concern with safeguarding assurance over textual accuracy (ibid.), I include here a discussion of the text given its place in the Christian

tradition and its resonance with the disclosure of Jesus throughout the Gospels.

[13]In addition to noting this custom of casting the first stone, Gundry also points out the trap Jesus' accusers try to lay for him: if he says the woman is to be stoned, he breaks the law of the Romans, which forbids the Jews to effect the death penalty; if he instructs the accusers to let her go, he can be accused of not upholding the Mosaic law. See ibid. Jesus masterfully turns the tables on his enemies by redirecting the moral problem and accusing his accusers of not upholding the law themselves, which would include their failure to bring forth the woman's adulterous partner.

[14]Carson maintains that Jn 8:12 follows naturally from Jesus' public utterance in Jn 7:37-39. With this in mind, it is worth noting that Jesus' claim to be the light of the world fits beautifully with his claim to provide the Spirit as life-giving water. Thus, Jesus would still be speaking against the backdrop of the Feast of Tabernacles. Not only did the priests pour out water ceremonially in the temple during the Feast of Tabernacles, but some sources also claim that during every evening of the feast, people danced throughout the night with lit torches, singing music. This celebration took place against the backdrop of the four large lit lamps in the temple's court of women and must have been quite a spectacle, causing all of Jerusalem to glow (see Carson, *Gospel According to John*, p. 337). How spectacular and striking, then, would Jesus' own claim to be the true or ultimate light of the world be against this cityscape of blazing imagery.

[15]Cartoon by J. C. Duffy, *The New Yorker*, November 12, 2001 <www.cartoonbank. com/2001/I-figure-if-I-dont-have-that-third-Martini-then-the-terrorists-win/ invt/121210>.

[16]John uses the terminology of "the Jews" in a variety of ways. See Carson, *Gospel According to John*, 141-42. "Most commonly it refers to the Jewish leaders, especially those of Jerusalem and Judea, . . . and usually they are cast as those who actively oppose Jesus, fail to understand him, and who finally seek his death. Pre-eminently, they constitute the focal point of opposition to Jesus, the concretization of the 'world' " (p. 142). However, there are no grounds for accusing John of anti-Semitism, as Carson and others make clear. The diversity of usage alone makes the charge vacuous. Different uses of the term are found in Jn 2:6 (neutral), 4:22 (positive) and 7:1 (negative). The diverse usage of the phrase alone signifies that John is not opposed to the Jewish people. Moreover, Jesus and John and the rest of the apostles are Jewish. As Jesus himself indicates in Jn 4:22, salvation is from the Jews. I should clarify that not all Jewish leaders stand opposed to Jesus. Here I have in mind Nicodemus and Joseph of Arimathea. In addition to Carson's discussion, see also George Eldon Ladd, *A Theology of the New Testament*, ed. Donald A. Hagner, rev. ed. (Grand Rapids: Eerdmans, 1993), p. 264, and W. F. Howard, *Christianity According to St. John* (Philadelphia: Westminster Press, 1946), p. 89. Ladd makes an important point that all who preach and teach such texts must be very rigorous in guarding against misunderstanding and abuse. As I seek to make clear, I myself must beware of opposing Jesus. If anything, the negative (and ironic) use of "the Jews" in John's Gospel signifies a nationalistic, power-brokering group who oppose Jesus as the Christ. Moreover, I should add that to reject Jesus' people—the Jewish nation—is also to reject Jesus, for salvation is from the Jews. It was their nationalism that was the

problem, not their ethnicity or nationality. Gentiles—especially the Nazis and Aryan supremacists—have been guilty of rejecting Jesus, for they have despised his Jewishness and the Jewish people. In keeping with Karl Barth's critique, the Hitler "enterprise" was that "of an evil spirit" and must be rigorously and vehemently opposed. See Karl Barth, "A Letter to Great Britain from Switzerland," in *This Christian Cause* (New York: Macmillan, 1941), p. 11.

Craig S. Keener points out that John uses "the Jews" in an ironic sense, for John ironically counters the Jewish authorities' claim to be the true Jews. John and his community see themselves as those truly loyal to the Jewish faith; instead of opposing Jesus like many of the rulers of the people who want to centralize (their) Jewish authority and exclude such groups as the Johannine community which they find unorthodox, the Johannine community rightly recognizes Jesus to be the Messiah and the fulfillment of the Hebrew Scriptures and therefore center Jewish authority in him. Thus they see themselves as the true inheritors of the Jewish faith as those truly faithful to it. Following Keener's lead, I have placed the phrase in quotation marks to signify John's use of irony. See Keener, *The Gospel of John: A Commentary* (Peabody, Mass.: Hendrickson, 2003), 1:219-28. It is also worth noting that for Keener, "the Jews" in John's Gospel "are often a flat composite character, representing the evil attitudes of the world." Keener goes on to say that one should not overstate the opposition, claiming that it is usually made up of a small group of influential and vocal people. He maintains (rightly) that the responsibility for the rejection of Jesus in the Gospel of John ultimately rests with the "Judean elite." He adds that, "John appears to believe that his people would have been more open to considering Jesus' claims but were hindered by a small but vocal portion of the Judean elite" (Keener, *Gospel of John*, 1:217). I would add that regardless of the number of individuals bound up with the influential and vocal opposition, and although ultimate responsibility rests with them, those who seek their affirmation rather than the affirmation of God are then and now still culpable for the rejection of Jesus. The question before us here and now is: do we seek to please the influential and vocal opposition in our age, or do we seek to please God?

[17]The "Son of Man" title is Jesus' favorite expression for himself in the Synoptic Gospels. Elsewhere, such as in Jn 8 and 10, Jesus refers to himself as God's Son or says that God is his Father. Here he speaks of being the Son of Man. According to Ladd, "it is obvious that Jesus' sonship [to the Father] is the central Christological idea in John, and that he writes his Gospel to make explicit what was implicit in the Synoptics. The Gospel is written that people may believe that Jesus is the Messiah, but more than Messiah; he is the Son of God (20:31)." See Ladd, *A Theology of the New Testament*, p. 283. The title "Son of Man" is used only by Jesus to refer to himself in the Gospels (p. 280). Jesus as the Son of Man is judge (p. 282), and is explicitly presented as being pre-existent and incarnate in the flesh in John's Gospel (p. 282).

[18]Keener writes that "the dilemma posed to the formerly blind man is equivalent to the dilemma being posed to most of John's audience; Johannine scholarship as a whole is therefore undoubtedly correct to see a challenge to the Johannine Christians through this character." Keener, *Gospel of John*, 1:788.

[19]See Jn 2:23–3:2. John tells us just before Nicodemus (one of the leaders of the people) appears to meet with Jesus that Jesus does not entrust himself to people for he knows what is inside. As in the case with Jn 9 and 10, there is no break in the text between Jn 2 and 3.

[20]There is no break in the text between Jn 9 and 10, and so Jesus has the leaders of Jn 9 in mind when he compares himself as the good shepherd of Ezek 34 with the bad leaders in Jn 10.

[21]"Scientology: 'If you want to make millions, start a religion,'" Religion News Blog, June 28, 2006 <www.religionnewsblog.com/15073/scientology-if-you-want-to-make-mil lions-start-a-religion>.

[22]Some might think, from vv.17-18 quoted above, that Jesus' Father acts this way. But they need to understand that the Father's love for Jesus is bound up with the cultivation and culmination of intimacy involving reciprocity and mutuality in the Father and Son's eternally loving relationship.

[23]I see "the Jews" here as being those Jewish leaders who oppose Jesus. See the discussion of this group in the context of Jn 8 above.

[24]George R. Beasley-Murray and C. K. Barrett also maintain with varying degrees of con-fidence that the leaders do not intend to believe in Jesus if he publicly confesses that he is the Messiah, but rather to discredit him. See their respective commentaries: Murray, *John*, Word Biblical Commentary 36 (Waco, Tex.: Word Books, 1987), p. 173; Barrett, *The Gospel According to St. John* (London: SPCK, 1978), p. 380. In this context, Murray also argues that Jesus has not yet to this point in the Gospel publicly asserted that he is the Messiah. According to Murray, his various claims "were clearly astonishing, but was he prepared to affirm that he was *the Anointed of God*, and so the King of the coming Kingdom of God? That was the crucial matter" (p. 173). I believe that such statements as "I and the Father are one" are clear indications of his being the Messiah, and not simply a human messianic figure, but a divine Messiah, as the leaders themselves claim that Jesus asserts (Jn 10:33; see also Jn 5:16-18; 8:57-59).

[25]John speaks of Jesus' glory as veiled in his creaturely flesh and says that he is revealed in his miraculous signs. Jesus often speaks indirectly about his being the Messiah through his signs and in reference to himself as the fulfillment of Old Testament types. Even so, we cannot believe unless God draws us. So no matter how clear the sign, faith in Jesus always results from God's initiative and determination (Jn 1:11-12).

[26]It is worth noting that the opposition to Jesus here takes place around the Feast of Dedication in Jerusalem (Jn 10:22-24). This feast commemorates the second temple's rededication at the time of the Maccabean Revolt against pagan rule in the second cen-tury before Christ. Much of the opposition in the Gospel of John occurs in Jerusalem around feasts such as this one, the Passover and Tabernacles. The confrontation around the feasts bears witness to the controversy concerning Jesus' identity. I believe John gives prominent attention to the feasts because, like so many other events, persons and institutions in John's Gospel, they point to Jesus' identity as their ultimate fulfillment and replacement. This is one reason why John gives so much more consideration to Je-sus' Judean ministry; the Synoptics give far more prominent consideration to Jesus'

Galilean ministry. It is no coincidence here in Jn 10 that the religious leaders want to hear Jesus confess publicly that he is the Christ. He is getting too close to the centers of power; his appearance and miraculous signs at the feast are disconcerting to them rather than hope-inspiring. If Jesus does confess publicly that he is the Christ, then they can work to destroy him. Jesus' return to the wilderness after their attempt to kill him, followed by the common people's pursuit of Jesus and belief in him in the wilderness (Jn 10:31-42), serve as symbols of condemnation of the leaders. That is, whereas the common people listen to Jesus and follow him into the wilderness and believe in him because of his words, signs and John the Baptist's witness, thereby signifying that they are his sheep, the religious leaders back in Jerusalem cannot hear Jesus' voice and believe in him and so oppose him, signifying that they are not Jesus' sheep. They cannot hear Jesus' voice because they want to be in power rather than submit to Jesus as the Messiah. Among other things, they do not wish to ruffle the feathers of the Romans; if the people go after Jesus as their king, they fear that they will lose their position of power and the nation itself (Jn 11:47-50). This opposition is affective and spiritual and not simply political: these religious leaders love the praise of humans rather than the praise of God (Jn 5:41-44), and they want to carry out the desires of their father the devil and so destroy Jesus (Jn 8:42-47). (I believe "the Jews" who oppose Jesus in Jn 5 and 8 are religious leaders—though not all Jewish religious leaders; two exceptions are Nicodemus and Joseph of Arimathea.) These leaders do not have the love of God in their hearts and so cannot hear Jesus' voice or accept him and his word (Jn 5:41-44; 10:25-30). In addition to consideration of these motives, the religious leaders (who are also political leaders in the theocracy) fail to see that only Jesus can deliver them from bondage.

    With this latter point in mind, see Wright's unique take on the reason for the Pharisees' opposition to Jesus. According to Wright, it is Jesus' different interpretation of the tradition that leads to his rejection. While it appears to the Pharisees, for example, that Jesus' approach will lead to their and the nation's demise, it is actually his interpretation of the tradition that alone will lead them to victory. See Wright, *The Challenge of Jesus: Rediscovering Who Jesus Was and Is* (Downers Grove, Ill.: InterVarsity Press, 1999), pp. 57-58. Craig Keener argues that the festival of Sukkoth or Tabernacles dominates the section from Jn 7:1–10:18 far more than Hanukkah dominates this section (Jn 10:22-42). The two sections are connected in various ways. Paradoxically perhaps, it is as Jesus aligns himself with biblical (Tabernacles) and extra-biblical (Dedication) Jewish festivals and culture, even demonstrating his solidarity with his people in their celebration of their national deliverance, that the nation's leaders' opposition to him increases. Keener also stresses that while Jesus speaks plainly enough from the vantage point of his Jewish and biblical context concerning his identity, he still veils his statements so as to elude his enemies' attempts to seize him; his hour has not yet come (Keener, *Gospel of John*, 1:821-22).

[27]These religious leaders who oppose Jesus in John are like TV prosperity gospel preachers in the sense that they promote *quid pro quo* and the prosperity gospel of nationalism. Were they to believe in Jesus, the power brokers fear that God would remove his blessing from the nation. By following their rituals and practices, they believe God will bless

and preserve them. They live for God in order to receive nationalistic blessings from God, and so cannot come to Jesus for relationship with God through him.

[28]The word translated here as "troubled" may suggest anger. Merrill C. Tenney claims that it literally means "to snort like a horse" and often conveys the sense of anger. He adds that Jesus may be angry with Lazarus's sisters, or that he may be angry or resentful "against the ravages of death that had entered the human world because of sin." Tenney, *John-Acts*, The Expositor's Bible Commentary 9 (Grand Rapids: Zondervan, 1981), p. 119.

[29]See William P. Young, *The Shack* (Newbury Park, Calif.: Windblown Media, 2007).

[30]For a discussion of this topic, see David Hume, "Dialogues Concerning Natural Religion" (1779), in *Dialogues and Natural History of Religion*, ed. J. A. C. Gaskin (Oxford: Oxford University Press, 1993), pp. 100-101.

[31]The problem of suffering and pain and faith has been the subject of unending debate over the centuries, but it is perhaps the most pressing apologetic problem for the Christian faith in the contemporary context. For example, see the post by leading atheist Sam Harris, "There Is No God (And You Know It)," *The Huffington Post*, October 6, 2005 <www.huffingtonpost.com/sam-harris/there-is-no-god-and-you-k_b_8459.html>.

[32]Over against the charge that John's Gospel does not display Jesus as fully human, Ladd rightly points out that this passage clearly discloses Jesus as fully human. See Ladd, *A Theology of the New Testament*, p. 288. For an example of scholarship discounting a truly human portrayal of Jesus in John's Gospel, see G. M. Davis Jr., "The Humanity of Jesus in John," *Journal of Biblical Literature* 70 (1951): 109. In addition to Jn 11, other texts that reflect Jesus' fully human condition include the account of him as tired and thirsty (Jn 4:6-7; 19:28) and as one who dies, from whose pierced side blood and water flow (Jn 19:28-37). For attention to the two extremes of views on Jesus' humanity and deity in John's Gospel, see Rudolf Bultmann, who believed, for example, that Jn 1:14 affirms Jesus' full humanity but not his divinity, and Ernst Käsemann, who did not feel that Jn 1:14 or John's Gospel as a whole gave attention to Jesus' full humanity and who believed that Jesus as God, while taking on human flesh, did not become fully human. See Rudolf Bultmann, *The Gospel of John: A Commentary*, trans. G. R. Beasley-Murray, R. W. N. Hoare and J. K. Riches (Philadelphia: Westminster Press, 1971), pp. 62-63. See also Ernst Käsemann, *The Testament of Jesus: A Study of the Gospel of John in the Light of Chapter 17* (London: SCM Press, 1968), pp. 45, 66, 73; Ernst Käsemann, "The Structure of John's Prologue," in *New Testament Questions of Today* (London: SCM Press, 1969), p. 148. In keeping with historic Christian orthodoxy, I believe John's Gospel and the New Testament as a whole present Jesus as the eternal Word and Son of God, who is equal with the Father and who becomes human, so that he is like us in every way yet without sin.

[33]See Young, *The Shack*, chap. 11, pp. 151-69.

[34]See for example Karl Barth, *Church Dogmatics: The Doctrine of Reconciliation* 4/1, ed. G. W. Bromiley and T. F. Torrance (Edinburgh: T & T Clark, 1956), p. 556.

[35]In Jn 11, the resurrection has both a "now" and a "not yet" emphasis. See, in particular, Jn 11:25-26: "Jesus said to her, 'I am the resurrection and the life. He who believes in me will live, even though he dies; and whoever lives and believes in me will never die. Do

you believe this?'" Eschatology is not realized in full in John's Gospel, contrary to what C. H. Dodd argues. Ladd refers to Dodd's claim that eternal life is a present reality that one can possess, and which no longer entails a last-day eschatological hope (see Ladd, *A Theology of the New Testament*, p. 341). Contrary to Dodd, Jn 6:39, 44 and 54 indicate that eschatology (in John) involves a present and future aspect.

[36]See Michael Spencer, "The Coming Evangelical Collapse," *The Christian Science Monitor*, March 10, 2009 <www.csmonitor.com/Commentary/Opinion/ 2009/0310/p09s01-coop.html>. See also Jon Meacham, "The End of Christian America," *Newsweek*, April 4, 2009 <www.newsweek.com/id/192583>.

Transition

[1]While John mentions the Last Supper, there is no explicit discussion of the institution of the Lord's Supper in his Gospel. See D. A. Carson's discussion of this matter in *The Gospel According to John* (Grand Rapids: Eerdmans, 1991), p. 458. It may very well be that John wants the reader to focus on Jesus as the life, and not lose sight of Jesus by viewing the meal as magical, a view that may have been prominent at the time of John's writing of his Gospel. See C. K. Barrett, *The Gospel According to St. John* (London: SPCK, 1978), p. 85. While some will say that chapter 6 with its talk of eating Jesus' flesh functions as John's Eucharistic text, I maintain that it is not directly referring to the Eucharist but is focusing on Jesus as the new manna from heaven, who is the basis for the Eucharist. The word normally employed in sacramental discourse is *body*, not *flesh*. See Leon Morris's discussion of Jn 6 and the Eucharist in his *The Gospel According to John*, rev. ed., The New International Commentary on the New Testament (Grand Rapids: Eerdmans, 1995), pp. 331-32. See also his extended discussion on the apparent conflict between John and the Synoptics on the Passover, namely, concerning whether or not the Last Supper is a Passover meal. John's Gospel conveys the sense that the Last Supper preceded the Passover, and that Jesus was crucified when the victims of the Passover were killed, whereas the Synoptics seem to convey that the Last Supper was the Passover meal. In the end, Morris concludes that Jesus and the authorities in the temple were following different calendars, and that the Synoptics focus on the former and John the latter. For John, the likely rationale is that he wishes to highlight that Jesus is our Passover (pp. 684-95). Morris's view makes sense in light of John's development of replacement or fulfillment themes throughout his Gospel.

[2]*The Empire Strikes Back*, directed by Irvin Kershner (Los Angeles: Twentieth Century Fox/Lucas Films, 1980).

Chapter 4: Preparations

[1]For a good introduction to this section of John's Gospel, see D. A. Carson, *The Farewell Discourse and Final Prayer of Jesus: An Exposition of John 14-17* (Grand Rapids: Baker Book House, 1980).

[2]The word translated "servant" in the NIV is literally "slave" or "bond servant."

[3]The Hmong are an Asian ethnic group from the mountainous regions of Vietnam, Laos, Thailand and Burma.

[4]I believe "go" and "going" here, as elsewhere in John, signify going to death, resurrection and ascension. This threefold act of going is how Jesus prepares a place for his followers in his Father's house, which already has rooms. Carson writes, "It is not that he arrives on the scene and then begins to prepare the place; rather, in the context of Johannine theology, it is the going itself, via the cross and resurrection, that prepares the place for Jesus' disciples" (Carson, *The Gospel According to John* [Grand Rapids: Eerdmans, 1991], p. 489). It is also worth noting here that John speaks of Jesus' coming in an imminent return in his resurrection (Jn 14:2-3; 16:16), in his coming through the Spirit (Jn 14:18, 23) and in his coming at the end of their lives/the age (Jn 14:2-3; 21:21). See George Eldon Ladd, *A Theology of the New Testament*, ed. Donald A. Hagner, rev. ed. (Grand Rapids: Eerdmans, 1993), pp. 339-40. See also Dodd for a completely realized sense of coming: C. H. Dodd, *The Interpretation of the Fourth Gospel* (Cambridge: Cambridge University Press, 1953), p. 404.

[5]The Spirit is referred to as the "Paraclete"—a comforter or counselor or advocate in John 14:16, 26; 15:26; 16:7. Gundry maintains that as Paraclete (one of the same kind as Jesus), the Spirit *comforts* Jesus' believing followers in his absence, *counsels* them by reminding them of what their Lord has said as well as teaching them of further things he will say to them, and lastly *convicts* the unbelieving world of their rejection of Jesus. See Gundry, *A Survey of the New Testament*, 4th ed. (Grand Rapids: Zondervan, 2003), pp. 283-85.

[6]Of course, they are vitally related. Jesus is the truth (Jn 14:6), and the Spirit is the Spirit of truth (Jn 14:17). And we are like them when we obey Jesus' word in faith. Notice that obedience (Jn 14:15, 21, 23) is bound up with the presence of the Father, Son and Spirit in Jesus' followers' lives; while Jesus will fulfill his word and promises, it is also important that his followers obey his word. That's how the Spirit's presence really comes alive to all of his followers personally. We will deal with the theme of obedience in Jn 14 in "That Dirty Little Four-Letter Word."

[7]George R. Beasley-Murray says of Philip here that "Philip had failed to grasp that in Jesus the glory, grace, and truth of God, whom none has seen or can see, stands unveiled (Jn 1:18)." Beasley-Murray, *John,* Word Biblical Commentary 36 (Waco, Tex.: Word Books, 1987), p. 253.

[8]I appreciate what Lesslie Newbigin says about the relation of love to obedience: "To speak of love apart from obedience would open the way to a purely emotional and sentimental interpretation of the 'abiding' . . . To speak of obedience apart from love would open the way to the slave-mentality against which we shall be warned (15:15; cf. 8:15) and which—in spite of these warnings—has often infected Christian practice. Contemporary Christian thinking tends to avoid the category of obedience and to speak only of love. That is the way to illusion. Obedience is the test of love; love is the content of obedience." Lesslie Newbigin, *The Light Has Come: An Exposition of the Fourth Gospel* (Grand Rapids: Eerdmans, 1982), pp. 186-87.

[9]John Wesley, *The Journal of the Rev. John Wesley*, vol. 1, ed. Nehemiah Curnock (Whitefish, Mont.: Kessinger, 2006), pp. 475-76.

[10]Charles Wesley, "Sinners, Obey the Gospel-Word!" <www.cyberhymnal.org/htm/s/n/snrsobey.htm>.

[11]Leon Morris, *The Gospel According to John*, rev. ed., The New International Commentary on the New Testament (Grand Rapids: Eerdmans, 1995), p. 596. In addition to offering words of comfort and exhortation to the church to abide in Jesus, John is also wanting believer and unbeliever alike to take note of Jesus as the replacement or fulfillment of Israel as the vine: Jesus is the true vine (Is 5:1-7). The extended metaphor is also a warning to John's listeners not to be like Israel, which became like a vine that did not bear fruit and so was thrown into the fire and burned (Ezek 15:1-8). See Carson's discussion of the Old Testament imagery; consider also his claim that John is challenging his Jewish contemporaries to take note that Jesus is the replacement or fulfillment of Israel, and that the warning and promise associated with this extended metaphor of the vine and branches has a direct bearing on them. Carson, *Gospel According to John*, pp. 511, 517.

[12]Merrill C. Tenney, *John-Acts*, The Expositor's Bible Commentary 9 (Grand Rapids: Zondervan, 1981), p. 152.

[13]See Jn 10:28; see also Jesus' preserving prayer for his followers in Jn 17:6-19, including the distinction between them and Judas, who has already departed from their company.

[14]It is worth noting that Jesus' word in which we are to abide is a source of cleansing. John uses forms of *katharos* for both pruning and cleansing. God prunes us and we are cleansed because of his word. See F. F. Bruce's discussion of such word play in Jn 15: Bruce, *The Gospel of John: Introduction, Exposition and Notes* (Grand Rapids: Eerdmans, 1983), pp. 308-9. John's use of abiding in Jesus' word signifies how important our response to Jesus' word is. For Jesus is the word of creation, revelation and salvation, and we are to depend on God's word. See the essay on Jn 1:1-18 ("That Sense of Touch") and the essay on Jn 8:12-59 ("False Redemption") for further discussion on the Word/word.

[15]I am indebted to George Ladd's discussion of "Abiding" on pp. 313-14 of his *Theology of the New Testament*, including his discussion of how mysticism in John does not involve deification as in Hellenism. However, Ladd's claim that Johannine mysticism is one "of personal and ethical fellowship involving the will rather than the emotions" misses the point of union and communion and introduces a stoic understanding of the human person. Apparently Ladd roots union and communion with God in the will rather than rooting the will itself in the affections. The biblical understanding of love from the heart involves the whole person and springs from the affections. This affections-based spirituality was espoused by the Protestant reformer Martin Luther and the early Philip Melanchthon. See my article "Mystical Union with Christ: An Alternative to Blood Transfusions and Legal Fictions," in *Westminster Theological Journal* 65, no. 2 (Fall 2003): 201-13, including the references to Luther and Melanchthon and secondary literature. See also the section "Abiding in Relationship" in W. L. Kynes's article "Abiding," in *Dictionary of Jesus and the Gospels*, ed. Joel B. Green, Scot McKnight and I. Howard Marshall (Downers Grove, Ill.: InterVarsity Press, 1992), pp. 2-3. There Kynes helpfully sets forth how the theme of abiding and mutual indwelling spans John's Gospel and how "abiding in Christ" conveys "the most intimate union possible" (p. 2).

[16]Henry Lyte, "Abide with Me" <www.cyberhymnal.org/htm/a/b/abidewme.htm>.

[17]Morris points out that this wording of a servant or slave not being above his master is

found four times in the Gospels: Mt 10:24; Lk 6:40; Jn 13:16, and here, Jn 15:20. Morris goes on to say that "it was evidently a saying that Jesus loved to repeat." Morris, *Gospel According to John*, p. 552.

[18]The word *world* is used in various ways in John's Gospel, including the sense that the world is the object of God's love and the sense that it is in opposition to God (this is almost always its sense when the world is preceded by "this"). See Ladd, *Theology of the New Testament*, pp. 259-62. It is important to note that John's use of world in the context of Jesus' saving work never signifies universalism, a point George Ladd brings home in his *Theology of the New Testament*, p. 262. Tenney speaks of three senses, possibly four in John's writings: *world* can refer to God's creation (Jn 1:10), the materialistic sphere that leads people away from God (1 Jn 2:15-16) and the world as the object of God's love (Jn 3:16). In Jn 15:18, it refers to unbelievers in their hostility and opposition to God (Tenney, *John-Acts*, p. 154).

[19]In discussing the fundamental difference between John and the Synoptics in terms of its distinctive dualism, Ladd writes that while the dualism in the Synoptics is "primarily horizontal" (whereby this age is contrasted with the age to come) the dualism in John is "primarily vertical"; for John, the contrast and conflict is between the world above and this world order from below, which stands in opposition to God's world order. See Ladd, *Theology of the New Testament*, p. 259. See also pp. 338-39.

[20]Charles Dickens, *A Tale of Two Cities* (Hertfordshire, U.K.: Wadsworth, 1993), p. 422.

[21]Dietrich Bonhoeffer, quoted in the editor's preface in *Letters and Papers from Prison*, rev. ed., ed. Eberhard Bethge (New York: Macmillan, 1967), p. xxiii.

[22]For a classic text on Jn 17, see Marcus Rainsford's volume, *Our Lord Prays for His Own: Thoughts on John 17*, 5th ed. (Grand Rapids: Kregel Classics, 1985).

Transition

[1]For source of title, see George Ladd's discussion of *glory* in John's Gospel: George Eldon Ladd, *A Theology of the New Testament*, ed. Donald A. Hagner, rev. ed. (Grand Rapids: Eerdmans, 1993), pp. 311-12. See "Fifteen Minutes of Fame" <www.phrases.org.uk/meanings/fifteen-minutes-of-fame.html>.

[2]See "Fifteen Minutes of Fame," <http://en.wikipedia.org/wiki/15_minutes_of_fame>.

[3]J. D. Salinger, quoted in Richard Lacayo, "J. D. Salinger: The Hermit Crab of American Letters Lived at Odds with Phonies and Fame," *Time*, February 15, 2010, p. 66.

[4]My use of "in the Spirit" here in this sentence is twofold: the Son is lifted up on the cross as a sacrifice through the Spirit (Heb 9:14) and raised from the dead through the same Spirit (Rom 8:11). Moreover, it is through the Spirit that Jesus and his Father return to be with us now, even while he reigns in his ascension at the right hand of God in heaven. See Jn 14:23, in which Jesus speaks of the Father and he returning to be with his followers; it is set forth in the context of Jesus speaking of the Spirit's ministry in their midst.

[5]Karl Barth, *Church Dogmatics: The Doctrine of Reconciliation* 4/1, ed. G. W. Bromiley and T. F. Torrance (Edinburgh: T & T Clark, 1956), p. 159.

[6]William Shakespeare, "As You Like It," in *The Complete Works of William Shakespeare* (New York: Avenel Books, 1975), Act II, Scene 7, p. 239.

Chapter 5: Humiliation/Glorification

[1]Jann Wenner, "Jagger Remembers," *Rolling Stone,* December 14, 1995 <www.rolling-stone.com/artists/mickjagger/articles/story/5938394/the_rolling_stone_interview>.

[2]*Hero,* directed by Stephen Frears (Hollywood: Columbia/Tri-Star, 1992).

[3]See Merrill C. Tenney's discussion of Pilate and this biblical account in Tenney, *John-Acts,* The Expositor's Bible Commentary 9 (Grand Rapids: Zondervan, 1981), pp. 173-79. See also Craig S. Keener's discussion in *The Gospel of John: A Commentary* (Peabody, Mass.: Hendrickson, 2003), 2:1128. Refer also to Keener's discussion of the historical authenticity of the trial before Pilate and the crucifixion on pp. 1103-4. Keener also provides helpful background information in making known that those who try Jesus are "not the sum total of ethnic Jewry in Jesus' day; there were select members of Jerusalem's municipal aristocracy in league with the high priests and acting to keep peace between Rome and the people. Like most political elites, they gained and held power at the expense of some other people and were resented by various groups they had suppressed or marginalized" (Keener, *Gospel of John,* 2:1084).

[4]For an intriguing analysis of Jesus' kingdom of grace confronting Roman retribution, see Jürgen Moltmann, *The Crucified God: The Cross of Christ as the Foundation and Criticism of Christian Theology* (Minneapolis: Fortress, 1993), pp. 136-45.

[5]See Nine Inch Nails, "Hurt" <www.youtube.com/watch?v=dhh21crSohs&feature =related>; see also Johnny Cash, "Hurt" <www.youtube.comwatch?v=SmVAWKfJ4Go>.

[6]Rowan Williams, *Resurrection: Interpreting the Easter Gospel,* rev. ed. (Cleveland, Ohio: Pilgrim Press, 2002), p. 73.

[7]See Raymond E. Brown's discussion of dominant motifs in John's crucifixion account, and also his comparison of it with the Synoptics, in Brown, *The Gospel According to John (XIII-XXI): Introduction, Translation, and Notes,* The Anchor Bible 29 (New York: Doubleday, 1970), pp. 912-16.

Transition

[1]It is worth noting Stephen Westerholm's discussion of the Pharisees in John's Gospel. He comments that "John paints Judaism with a broad brush." John portrays Jesus' opponents as "Jews" much of the time. When John mentions the Pharisees, he often displays them "as holding positions of power and acting in collaboration with other authorities." While pointing out that the Pharisees speak of their opposition to Jesus being about the Sabbath (Jn 9:16), we find elsewhere in John's Gospel that "it is attributed to spiritual obstinacy (9:39-41)." Stephen Westerholm, "Pharisees," in *Dictionary of Jesus and the Gospels,* ed. Joel B. Green, Scot McKnight and I. Howard Marshall (Downers Grove, Ill.: InterVarsity Press, 1992), p. 614.

Chapter 6: Invitation

[1]Many commentaries look at Jn 20:30-31 as the conclusion to John's Gospel and chap. 21 as an epilogue. I am using Jn 20:30-31 as an overarching thematic text for this section titled "Invitation" and surrounding it with various responses to Jesus in Jn 20:24–21:25.

[2]L. W. Hurtado points out that John views "Jesus' divine sonship as the key christological category. . . . 20:31 reflects the claim that Jesus is the Messiah and that this Messiah is much more exalted than Jewish messianic speculations characteristically allowed." While the Synoptics share this view, John makes this claim with "particular force." L. W. Hurtado, "Christ," in *Dictionary of Jesus and the Gospels*, ed. Joel B. Green, Scot McKnight and I. Howard Marshall (Downers Grove, Ill.: InterVarsity Press, 1992), pp. 114-15.

[3]George Eldon Ladd, *A Theology of the New Testament*, ed. Donald A. Hagner, rev. ed. (Grand Rapids: Eerdmans, 1993), p. 293.

[4]Ladd writes, "The one demand Jesus makes of people to receive his gift of eternal life is faith, belief. This becomes explicit in John in a way that is not evident in the Synoptics." Ladd, *Theology of the New Testament*, p. 306.

[5]Many commentators discuss the different words for love, namely forms of *agapaō* and *phileō*, in this passage and throughout the Gospel. While it may indeed be the case that the words are used interchangeably here as elsewhere, in my discussion above, I am simply suggesting that Peter's grief is bound up with Jesus asking Peter a third time if he loves Jesus. Nonetheless, in contrast to those interpreters who reason that the terms for love here are not interchangeable and who think that the *phileō* form of love is lesser in kind (and as a result argue that Peter is grieved because Jesus is asking him if he even loves him with this lesser form of love), it may actually be the case that the *phileō* form of love may convey greater intimacy at times. In Jn 16:26-27, Jesus says that the Father loves the disciples because they have loved Jesus and have believed that he has come from God. Jesus uses a form of *phileō* here in this third question to Peter in Jn 21, and at that point in the farewell discourse, perhaps seeking to convey in each instance a relational, mutual love, and not simply unconditional love from one to the other. Far from being a lesser form of love, it may convey greater intimacy at points, the kind that is shared by friends. If so, the Lord's third question may further grieve Peter because Jesus asks him if he loves his Lord as a true, faithful, and heart-to-heart friend, causing Peter to recall his Lord's words in his farewell discourse. See Craig S. Keener's and D. A. Carson's discussions of the use of these words in John's Gospel; Keener, *The Gospel of John* (Peabody, Mass.: Hendrickson, 2003), 2:1236; Carson, *The Gospel According to John* (Grand Rapids: Eerdmans, 1991), pp. 676-77.

[6]F. F. Bruce discusses the various views on Peter's martyrdom, noting the accounts of Clement of Rome, Tertullian and Eusebius Pamphilus. Bruce (among others) does not take seriously the claim that Peter is crucified upside down. See F. F. Bruce, *The Gospel of John: Introduction, Exposition and Notes* (Grand Rapids: Eerdmans, 1983), p. 406. See also Keener, *Gospel of John*, 2:1238.

[7]There is much debate as to whether or not Jn 21 is original to the Gospel. I take a traditional stance on this subject and claim that the whole of the text, including verses 24-25, is penned by John the apostle. See Carson's and Morris's treatments of the various views, including their discussions of whether or not verses 24-25 are original to the text, or come from another source or even sources: Carson, *Gospel According to John*, pp. 665-68, 682-86; Morris, *Gospel According to John*, pp. 757-58, 775-77.

[8]As with 1 Jn, which goes back and forth between first-person singular and plural, I believe it is one person (namely John) who is doing the same here.

[9]Against the backdrop of questions concerning this Gospel's trustworthiness, Blomberg provides a very helpful discussion on the trustworthiness and historicity of John's Gospel in relation to the Synoptics. See Craig L. Blomberg, *Jesus and the Gospels: An Introduction and Survey* (Nashville: Broadman & Holman, 1997), pp. 157-59.

[10]John moves from historical and theological depiction of Jesus in Jn 1:1-13 to personal encounter in vv. 14 and 16 of the prologue. He does the same here at the close of his Gospel, moving from objective depiction in Jn 21:1-23 to more direct and personal (while still objectively truthful) engagement in verses 24-25. It is worth noting that Bruce also finds a parallel here in Jn 21 with 1 Jn 1 (Bruce, *Gospel of John*, p. 409). He also draws attention to Dorothy Sayers's observation that "of the four Evangels, St. John's is the only one that claims to be the direct report of an eye witness." Dorothy L. Sayers, *The Man Born to Be King: A Play-Cycle on the Life of Our Lord and Saviour Jesus Christ* (London: Victor Gollancz, 1943), p. 33.

[11]Gary Burge warns of the danger of "doing theology from the outside." Although John is by no means guilty of engaging his subject matter in this way, we as interpreters can fall prey to the sheer "recital of scholarly facts." While championing rigorous scholarly analysis of the text, Burge calls for preachers to experience it personally. Commentaries on John's Gospel that do theology from the inside, so to speak, include the following in Burge's view: Edwin C. Hoskyns and F. N. Davey, *The Fourth Gospel* (London: Faber & Faber, 1947); William Temple, *Readings in St. John's Gospel*, 1st and 2nd series (London: Macmillan, 1945); and Lesslie Newbigin, *The Light Has Come*. See Gary M. Burge's discussion of this point, as well as his entire chapter on "Preaching from John," in *Interpreting the Gospel of John*, Guides to New Testament Exegesis (Grand Rapids: Baker, 1992), pp. 173-80, especially pp. 177-78.

[12]Floyd McClung quoted in Joseph C. Aldrich, *Lifestyle Evangelism* (Sisters, Ore.: Multnomah Books, 1993), p. 35.

LIKEWISE. *Go and do.*

A man comes across an ancient enemy, beaten and left for dead. He lifts the wounded man onto the back of a donkey and takes him to an inn to tend to the man's recovery. Jesus tells this story and instructs those who are listening to "go and do likewise."

Likewise books explore a compassionate, active faith lived out in real time. When we're skeptical about the status quo, Likewise books challenge us to create culture responsibly. When we're confused about who we are and what we're supposed to be doing, Likewise books help us listen for God's voice. When we're discouraged by the troubled world we've inherited, Likewise books encourage us to hold onto hope.

In this life we will face challenges that demand our response. Likewise books face those challenges with us so we can act on faith.

likewisebooks.com

"We have theologians, we have cultural critics, and we have biblical exegetes, but it is difficult to find people who aim to blend the three together in a lively and faithful way. Paul Louis Metzger is such a person, and in this new series he aspires to gather folks who share these passions, aiming to make it ever more clear how the Gospel illumines the world in which we live. This series ably attempts to keep the 'two horizons' always in view: one looking to the ancient text, and the other looking to our day in which we read and apply the text. This is no easy task, and the landmines are many. But Metzger is worth listening to as he carefully yet freshly seeks to chart a path that blends together the story of redemption and cultural engagement, all the while writing in a very accessible manner. May Metzger's book and this whole series help us all to do just that."

KELLY M. KAPIC, professor of theological studies, Covenant College

"The need for practitioners and theologians to come together to engage Scripture and its import in our lives has never been more apparent. What promises to be the first of many exciting volumes, The Gospel of John: When Love Comes to Town offers an exploration of the text that is accessible to the average reader without compromising the depth and complexity in the process. I cannot wait to see more!"

JAMIE ARPIN-RICCI, pastoral and missional leader, Little Flowers Community, Winnipeg, Canada

"The Gospel of John: When Love Comes to Town, Paul Louis Metzger's excellent contribution to the Resonate series, balances historical background of John's Gospel with striking contemporary cultural references that illuminate the intent of the Gospel in vivid, fresh outline. But the true feast in this book is the way Paul unpacks and makes real the impact of Jesus' Word-in-the-flesh incarnation as it unfolds in the narrative and, correspondingly, in the life of the responsive reader. I strongly recommend this book for individual study, personal meditation and for group Bible studies."

BILL GRIFFIN, Ph.D., assistant professor of ministry and Bible, Simpson University, and assistant professor of Old Testament, A. W. Tozer Seminary

"Paul Louis Metzger's exposition of John's Gospel is the ideal resource for students or those who want to take a step deeper into the Gospel beyond reading the Bible itself. Easy to read, filled with popular examples, and accurate on cultural and historical detail, Metzger has offered a practical and beneficial tool for believers in the modern church."

GARY M. BURGE, professor of New Testament, Wheaton College and Graduate School